Creating Economy

Creating Economy

Enterprise, Intellectual Property, and the Valuation of Goods

Barbara Townley, Philip Roscoe,
and Nicola Searle

OXFORD
UNIVERSITY PRESS

OXFORD
UNIVERSITY PRESS

Great Clarendon Street, Oxford, OX2 6DP,
United Kingdom

Oxford University Press is a department of the University of Oxford.
It furthers the University's objective of excellence in research, scholarship,
and education by publishing worldwide. Oxford is a registered trade mark of
Oxford University Press in the UK and in certain other countries

First Edition published in 2019

Impression: 2

Published in the United States of America by Oxford University Press
198 Madison Avenue, New York, NY 10016, United States of America

British Library Cataloguing in Publication Data

Data available

Library of Congress Control Number: 2018950877

ISBN 978–0–19–879528–5

Printed and bound by
CPI Group (UK) Ltd, Croydon, CR0 4YY

To
Dominique Martin
The Roscoe family, two-legged and four
Kenny Sacchini-Searle

Acknowledgements

The acknowledgements accrued in the writing of a book are many. All authors would like to thank all family, friends, and colleagues who offered support and were inevitably discommoded during such a project. In particular, we would like to thank Dr Shiona Chillas and Dr Dave O'Brien. We also thank Liz McFall for her suggestion, 'Creating Economy'.

The book has had a long genesis. The empirical material was collected as one strand in a multi-faceted project supported by the Economic & Social Research Council Capacity Building Cluster, Creative Industries Scotland: Capitalising on Creativity (RES 187-24-0014). The authors would like to thank Eilidh Young for undertaking the interviews. We are also grateful to our interviewees who generously gave of their time to answer our questions.

Preliminary analysis and writing was supported by the Research Councils UK Centre for Copyright and New Business Models in the Creative Economy (CREATe), (AHRC Grant AH/K000179/1). Professor Townley would like to thank Professors Ronan Deazley, Lilian Edwards and Philip Schlesinger for their support on this project. Professor Townley would also like to thank the Leverhulme Emeritus Professor Fellowship for support in the final writing of this manuscript.

Dr Searle would like to thank her co-authors for both their way with words and patience with working with an economist; and colleagues at the Institute for Cultural and Creative Entrepreneurship (ICCE) at Goldsmiths for educating her in the ways of interdisciplinary perspectives of the creative industries and the wider context of cultural policy.

Dr Roscoe would like to thank his co-authors for the opportunity to participate in this fascinating project, and the School of Management at the University of St Andrews for a period of research leave that greatly aided the book's completion.

All the authors are extremely grateful to Mindy Grewar for her help. Mindy closely read several versions of the text, assisted in compiling the references, and assembling the text into its final version. As executive assistant for the Institute for Capitalising on Creativity, Mindy was crucial to the success of the ESRC Capacity Building Cluster. As research assistant she also helped with analysis and writing of projects associated with the RCUK CREATe programme. Throughout, her support, assistance, guidance, and friendship have been immeasurable.

Acknowledgements

Contents

1

Introduction: Creating Economy

Creativity is at the vanguard of contemporary capitalism. The 'new economy' emphasizes the informational, cultural, and technological foundations of economic growth (Osborne 2003), and intangible, knowledge-based assets such as 'investment in ideas, in knowledge, in aesthetic content, in software, in brands, in networks and relationships' are central to competitive advantage (Haskel and Westlake 2018: 15). Global entertainment and media corporations, cultural hardware and software, and an increased influence of cultural intermediary occupations such as marketing, advertising, and design, highlight culture's role in value creation (Lash and Urry 1994, du Gay and Pryke 2002), while policy initiatives constantly remind us that creativity underpins this new economic order: 'creativity contributes to entrepreneurship, fosters innovation, enhances productivity and promotes economic growth' (UNCTAD 2008: 3). Creativity has become a value in itself, 'a form of capital in its own right' (Osborne 2003: 523; Thrift 2002).

Such changes beg many questions. How does this creative economy come about? What is economic about creativity? By what processes can creative labour, often characterized as profoundly uneconomic, unalienated, and inseparable from its maker, become the basis for a distinctive global economy? And how has the solitary artist, a figment of Romantic thought, become the creative entrepreneur of twenty-first century economic imagining?

These questions matter, not least because the creative economy has changed the nature of work. Immaterial labour—labour that produces services, cultural products, or knowledge—is the foundation for much of the new economy's capitalization (Lazzarato 1996, Hardt and Negri 2000, Scholtz 2013). The artist, characterized by 'passionate attachment' to her work (Gill and Pratt 2008, Hesmondhalgh and Baker 2011) and previously positioned at the social margins, has now come into her own 'as the ideal definition of the post-industrial knowledge worker' (Ross 2000: 11). Displaying the self-direction, commitment, and sacrifice in demand across a range of knowledge and service sectors, the artist has become an archetype (Menger 1999, Ross

2003, McRobbie 2016). Cultural workers, artists, writers, film makers, designers, and new media workers are the new 'creative class' of model entrepreneurs (Florida 2002, Gill and Pratt 2008, Ross 2008) and the cultural entrepreneur stands between capital and labour, 'doing the job of both at the same time' (McRobbie 2016: 188). As boundaries erode, the creative economy has been linked with casualized, insecure employment, and a derogation of responsibility on the part of government and capital.

Intellectual property and associated intellectual property rights (IP and IPR) have been identified as central in creating the creative economy (Haskel and Westlake 2018). And for economists and policymakers, firm in their beliefs that economic incentives drive agents towards a particular course of action, the creative industries are no different. Intellectual property is understood as a crucial mechanism for incentivizing creative producers and rewarding them for their work. Intellectual property offers a foundation for both the legal and economic regulation of the creative industries; it is the fuel that turns the engine of creative production. Original artistic works, protected by copyright and design IP rights, are recorded as investments in national accounts (Haskel and Westlake 2018) and 'copyright is now supposed to be playing the same role in the "creative economy" as patents did in the heyday of the manufacturing industries' (Towse 2006b: 84). But incentives do more than simply encourage certain courses of action. We argue that they bring into being the very social structures that they assume: they are 'performative' (Austin 1978, Callon 1998). Intellectual property and associated intellectual property rights do more than encourage creative production. They organize the creative economy, creating the social structures of a market in creative goods and configuring economic agency on the part of creative producers. Intellectual property is the fountainhead of the creative economy.

This book invokes the growing sociological literature of markets—with a particular focus on the literature of economization and 'marketisation' (Çalışkan and Callon 2010)—to examine the world of creative production. We set out to analyse the many interactions, whether social, cultural, or material, that constitute the 'creative industries'.[1] We show that IP is the 'creative capital' with which cultural entrepreneurs engage in the new economy; it forms a link between symbolic and economic value, and between the

[1] 'Creative industry' is a discursive construction of the UK government's Department for Digital, Culture, Media and Sport (DCMS), as a 'coherent and actionable field of activity' (Banks 2007: 49; see also DCMS 1998, Leadbeater and Oakley 1999, Hesmondhalgh and Pratt 2005, Schlesinger 2009, O'Connor 2010). The DCMS definition emphasizes the importance and potential economic value of IP to its owners: the creative industries are 'those activities that have their origin in individual creativity, skill and talent, and which have the potential for wealth and job creation through the generation and exploitation of intellectual property' (DCMS 1998: 3). This definition notwithstanding, IP has been neglected in studies of the independents and microbusinesses, the 'Me & Co' (Beck 2000) within which much creative production takes place (Hargreaves 2011).

individual creative producers and the collective structure of the field that gives creative products worth. IP provides the book's analytical framework as well: we follow its thread (Latour 1988) through the market to see how it constructs products and economic agents, how it helps creative producers manage risk and qualify value, and how it forms the basis of realizing and protecting economic worth. In tracing creative texts as they make the transition from idea to saleable product, we outline some of the experiences of these new 'cultural entrepreneurs'. We focus on a construct we label IP/IPR, a material and market object that links two spheres of value—the symbolic and the economic. This IP/IPR—explained in more detail shortly—allows not only an understanding of how cultural producers adapt to and adopt a calculative persona, but also offers a re-examination of the theorizing of the art-commerce relationship that permeates discussions on the creative industries.

Throughout the rest of this chapter, we outline our argument in more detail. We examine the nature of the creative industries and the identification of the new entrepreneurial role. We then turn to the understanding of IP and its functioning within a market economy, and the specific aspects of IP that make it a distinct form of property. We then outline our object, IP/IPR, based on an understanding of its functioning as a material, market object. We illustrate the advantages of examining IP from this perspective before outlining our discussion of its functioning in the chapters that follow.

The 'Creative Industries'?

'Creative industries' is a political rebranding of the term cultural industries (Gill and Pratt 2008: 1), an active shift from treating the arts as a subsidized sector toward asserting the importance of these activities to the creative economy (Schlesinger 2016). The creative industries combine an established concern for classic cultural production (performing arts and literature) with a new interest in culture's commercial elements (such as advertising and video game software), reinforcing the Department for Digital, Culture, Media and Sport's (DCMS) 'economic edge' (O'Brien 2014, 2015).[2] The traditional policy focus on heritage management and humanist ideals of cultural opportunities, community involvement, and access gave way to forging a systemic role for the sector in increasing value in the economy (Hutter 2011). Culture and creative subsectors became ranked according to revenue, employment, and exports (Banks 2007). This new delineation had administrative and economic

[2] The inclusion of software in general did much to enhance this, with 44 per cent of the value of creative industries coming from the IT, software, and computer services sector (DCMS 2017). Before July 2017, DCMS was known as the Department for Culture, Media and Sport.

consequences: governments, local authorities, and development agencies generated 'creative industry' city and regional policies as harbingers of urban regeneration, economic development, and wealth creation (Leadbeater and Oakley 1999, Murdock 2003, Garnham 2005, Bakhshi et al. 2015).

Despite this policy endeavour, the coherence of the creative industries as a sector is questionable (Matthews and Smith Maguire 2014). Denotative definitions 'with severely limited analytical power' amount to no more than 'what's in' and 'what's out' (O'Connor 2004: 38). Comparisons internationally are hindered by a lack of standard definitions (European Commission 2001, OECD 2006, KEA 2007; see Jones et al. 2015). The DCMS *Creative Industries Mapping Document* (1998) identified advertising, architecture, art and antiques, crafts, design, designer fashion, film and video, interactive leisure software, music, the performing arts, publishing, software and computer services, television, and radio. Writing from an American perspective, Caves (2000) includes the visual arts, painting, and sculpture, 'even' fashion, and toys and games. Further refinements produce concentric circles of artistic authenticity in the attempt to distinguish 'pure art forms' based on the creator as the source of 'ideas' (music, dance, theatre literature, the visual arts and crafts, and performance art) from those with more commercial concerns (Throsby 2001, NESTA 2006, Work Foundation 2007).

More analytic definitions focus on symbol-making and production (Hesmondhalgh 2002), a focus, however, that is not restricted to the creative industries. Banking, accounting, law, computing (Allen 2002), and religious organizations also play across symbolic registers. Creative industries, however, may be distinguished as being *primarily* concerned with symbolic or aesthetic production, associated with cultural, artistic, or simply entertainment value (Caves 2000). They serve an aesthetic and expressive rather than utilitarian function, the two poles, for Hirsch (1972: 642) being 'intuitively distinct'. They produce 'commodities whose core value is derived from their functions as carriers of meaning in the form of images, symbols, sign and sounds.... The production of meaning is seen to be deliberate and self-conscious, designed to appeal to aesthetic preferences, or related to existing or emergent economies of taste, style and distinction' (Banks 2007: 2).

The term 'creative industries' also belies a history of conflicts over the boundaries of 'culture' and 'economics', and the deep normative division between art understood as something of intrinsic, even sacred, worth and art seen as a commodity (Ryan 1992, Jeffcutt et al. 2000, du Gay and Pryke 2002, Banks and O'Connor 2009, O'Connor 2010). This divide reflects grander philosophical debates over human activity as intrinsically meaningful or calculatedly rational, articulated since the ancient Greeks, through Max Weber (1978) and Alasdair MacIntyre (1981), to more recent popular-academic contributions from authors such as Sandel (2012), Skidelsky and

Skidelsky (2012), and Roscoe (2014). The Frankfurt School reflected on the relationship between culture and commerce, and the transformation of culture into mass commercial and marketable goods, or 'mass culture' (O'Connor 2010). Adorno and Horkheimer's (1972) critique of the commodification of culture and industrial cultural production—the 'culture industry'—saw artistic freedom (their conception of which was heavily influenced by the nineteenth-century Romantic myth) undermined, and the 'authentic' qualities of unique, auratic art debased (O'Connor 2010). The continued preference for the term 'the cultural industries' signals a lineage to this critique (Murdock 2003, McRobbie 2016). Commerce is held as corrupting the cultural impulse of creativity, with the market, rather than aesthetics, dictating the range and quality of cultural products, limiting genres and expressive styles, and responsible for the 'banality' of cultural products that results (Peterson and Berger 1975, McRobbie 2002, Negus 2002, Murdock 2003, Banks 2007).

This 'art-commerce relation' is fundamental to academic commentary on the creative industries (Ryan 1992). Opposing binaries appear throughout its literature, variously identified as art-capital, art-commerce, culture-commerce, creativity-commerce, culture-commodity, culture-economy, or aesthetic-utility (Hesmondhalgh and Baker 2011: 81). Likewise, the dynamism of these relations is captured in varying terms, such as 'value spheres, regimes of value, institutional spheres, spheres of justice, regimes of justification or institutional logics, each having its own conventions and routines, rituals and symbols, and shared understandings of what is appropriate or legitimate' (Velthuis 2005: 24). Debate is impeded by the fact that 'culture' and 'art' do not have precise, unambiguous meanings (Ryan 1992). Warde (2002: 185) refers to their 'profligate' use, variously synonymous with 'non-material, social, aesthetic, informational, intellectual, normative, communicative, meaningful, human and civilising'.

Their contradiction is further informed by the nature of the labour process (Banks and O'Connor 2009, McKinlay and Smith 2009). Cultural work is complex (Banks 2007). The artistic desire is for autonomy; the creative process is non-standardized and unpredictable, economically irrational. The commercial imperative is for predictability in profit generation. As symbol creator, the artist represents 'a valorisation problem' (Ryan 1992: 25), her autonomy resistant to external 'rationalisation' of reliable cultural production, positioning authenticity and autonomy against 'management' control and routine (Ryan 1992, Boltanski and Chiapello 2005, Banks 2007, Lazzarato 2007, Hesmondhalgh and Baker 2011). For these reasons, creative production often takes place in a workshop system more associated with craft activity, with its discrete working methods and distinct knowledge, or among small networks of creative specialists (Ryan 1992, Banks 2010).

The disputed genealogy of the terms cultural and creative industries is reflected in the extreme heterogeneity in the sector, not least between not-for-profit, community sectors, and the commercial (Oakley 2009, 2013), the latter varying considerably in its extent of capitalization of production and degree of industrialization: '[i]t does not take much research to discover that every type of capital from small family capital to large-scale multinational capital is present in the culture industries' (Miège 1979: 306 quoted in Banks 2007: 21). Miège (1989) distinguishes between 'publishing' (artefacts sold directly, such as books and films), and 'flow' (the provision of continuous sequence, e.g. broadcasting), although these categories are blurred by the Internet. Economic distinctions relate to 'private' (recordings, books, magazines, and publications), 'quasi-private' (film, plays, concerts, festivals, tours, live performances), and 'quasi-public' goods (e.g. media, radio, and TV, although pay-for-view channels transform quasi-public goods into private goods) (Ryan 1992); again, the Internet renders these increasingly problematic. There are, nonetheless, different types of cultural commodities, each with different production and circulation systems, and different realization challenges.[3]

Perhaps of greatest significance, most subsectors are bifurcated, even 'bi-polar' (Coe 2015, Fitzgerald 2015, McRobbie 2016). An increasingly concentrated, globalized, oligopolistic, largely distribution sector coexists with production carried out by independents, micro- and small businesses, and self-employed freelancers (Pratt 2007, Oakley 2009). Small, independent production predominates (Banks 2007), with the norm as 'self-organized entrepreneurial activity' (McRobbie 2004: 133–4). As Hesmondhalgh and Baker (2011: 14) note, 'the vast majority of cultural production we share in modern societies [is] still produced by people who are trying to make a living out of that activity.' While independents engage in cultural production, larger firms, previously gatekeepers such as record labels in music, distributors in film, and publishers in games, but now increasingly information and communications technologies (ICTs), dominate in finance and distribution (Oakley 2009), creating an 'uneven structure' that necessarily has implications for symbolic products available (Deuze and Lewis 2013). Indeed, cultural distribution based on the control of IP rights, not cultural production, is 'the key locus of power and profit' (Garnham 1987: 37). Hence some definitions of the creative industries emphasize mass-produced goods and services and industrial-scale production (Towse 2003).

[3] Hence Miège's (1989) 'culture industr*ies*', which recognizes that the balance varies greatly according to 'subsector', each with different systems of financing and organizing cultural production, different commercial–symbolic balance, and different organizational mechanisms and procedures 'to relate these two worlds to one another' (Swedberg 2006: 260, Hesmondhalgh and Baker 2011).

Cultural Entrepreneurship?

The creative economy presages dramatic changes in the labour market, with increased insecurity and casualization (McRobbie 2016). Casualization has always been a feature of the cultural labour market, with self-employment 'three times as likely as [for] the working population in general' (Baines and Robson 2001: 349). Employment traverses contingent, flexible, casual, temporary, and freelance, and, reflecting a well-recognized dual labour market of a well-placed minority and the rest, encompasses low-paid part-time workers as well as independent, highly skilled, well-paid, and high-status contractors (Gill and Pratt 2008, Oakley 2009, Menger 2015). The divestment and outsourcing of specialist functions, especially in film and TV, has resulted in many small, specialist service providers, freelancers, and owner-managed enterprises (Barnatt and Starkey 1994, Beck 2003, Christopherson 2008, Oakley 2009, McRobbie 2016). There is, as a consequence, an increasing number of individuals in the cultural and creative sector 'who have to make a living from micro-entrepreneurialism' (Ellmeier 2003: 3), their numbers swollen by recent graduates, driven by the expansion of higher education (McRobbie 2016). With fewer permanent jobs and secure employment, 'many consider the idea of self-employment or setting up some sort of small creative business as a realistic option, not because young people . . . are natural-born entrepreneurs, but because, when weighing up their options, this emerges as a hope for a more productive and perhaps exciting future. . . . A risk-taking stance becomes a necessity rather than a choice' (McRobbie 2016: 11). In the context of economic insecurity and the growth of non-standard, casual, unstable forms of employment, self-employment is a means to an end, a form of 'making do', 'creating a space', 'earning a living' without feeling unduly compromised (McRobbie 2016: 22–3). These are the 'new' microbusinesses in the cultural industries, 'the independents' (Leadbeater and Oakley 1999), the 'Me & Co' (Beck 2000).

We have already seen how the shift in nomenclature to creative industries has been identified as a 'performative shift or a new habitus' (O'Connor 2004: 51), a transformation in the way that artistic work should be understood (Ross 2008). This echoes a reframing of work within the 'new economy' where a 'heroic vocabulary of enterprise' (McRobbie 2016: 5)—note, not 'small business'—becomes part 'of a wider assemblage of romanticism and subjectivism allied with economic performance' (Osborne 2003: 523). Entrepreneurship becomes the key trope; individuals are cast as entrepreneurs, small firms as high growth (O'Connor 2004, Banks 2007, Oakley 2009, 2013, McRobbie 2016). In an exercise in governmentality, the economic agent becomes the embodiment of human capital and an 'entrepreneurial self' (Lemke 2001, Foucault 2008, Bröckling 2016).

Investing in their creative capital, creative producers become 'entrepreneurs of their own human capital' (Ellmeier 2003: 11), the individual 'his or her own enterprise' (McRobbie 2002: 519). From its origins as investment in education or training, human capital now encompasses innate, parental, and social influences, and even lifestyle. And, as the heuristic ambitions of economic theory seek to model an increasing range of phenomena for rational individuals maximizing returns on their personal endowments (Becker 1964), human capital becomes synonymous with embodied capital: 'my human capital is me' (Feher 2009: 25). It is 'a version of personhood which assumes that subjects may own property in the person and may abstract or disentangle that property and trade it as a resource for exchange' (Adkins 2005: 112). The development of human capital is both an individual responsibility and a risk (Ekinsmyth 2002). The entrepreneurial individual must constantly calculate 'the best way to enhance, preserve, maintain and exploit those capacities constituting the basis of his or her own treasure trove of value', while saying little of the 'manner or mode of acquisition of such capital' (McRobbie 2016: 75). Individuals become 'personally responsible for the education and development, growth, accumulation, improvement and valorization of the "self" in its capacity as "capital"' (Lazzarato 2007: 7, Gill 2010), a move that conveniently absolves the owners of capital from responsibility for the precarity increasingly prevalent among knowledge workers (Gershon 2017).

The lived experiences of those who are subject to the 'Me & Co' realities of contemporary creative enterprise have not received as much focus as studies of creative labour (McKinlay and Smith 2009, Oakley 2009, Hesmondhalgh and Baker 2011; see Ursell 2006, Banks 2007, Neff 2012, McRobbie 2016). The tendency to 'see creative workers' careers as self-expressive entrepreneurship' (Christopherson 2008: 74) neglects the 'humdrum' (Caves 2000) work driven by the economic necessity of engaging with the market economy. The freelancer or microbusiness incorporates aesthetic and expressive autonomy with the need for saleable commodities and, through this, profit: not only successful completion of production but also of circulation. The issue is not just how to be more creative, but how to make a living. The cultural producer must be conscious of the full trajectory of production, exchange, distribution, and consumption; must understand how value is created, distributed, and captured. Microbusinesses and small- to medium-sized enterprises (SMEs) need to understand both artistic and commercial/business imperatives, and blend creative and managerial roles. Owning the materials and equipment used, they are 'small capitalists' who may employ others to work on production. From this perspective, the ideal of 'disinterestedness' (Bourdieu 1993) implicit in stereotypical presentations of 'art for art's sake' seems increasingly problematic. As Ross (2000: 3) notes, we run the risk of depicting art as 'so quarantined from the world of "wont and use" as to render its devotees ineffectual as economic or social actors outside of their professional sphere'. As a consequence, McRobbie (2016: 4) argues, we must 're-think the sociology of employment to engage more fully with the entrepreneurial culture and the self-employment ethos now a necessity for survival'. She calls for a 'vocabulary and methodology for tracing freelance pathways in the cultural sector' with the aim of understanding 'at the level of experience how this terrain is negotiated' (McRobbie 2002: 523–4). We need to question whether the term 'creative industries' is the 'industrialisation of bohemia' (McRobbie 2002, Ellmeier 2003, Dyer-Witheford and de Peuter 2009), whether the business of creative work is 'actively incorporated into the artistic identity' and whether there is a 'new relation between art and economics' (McRobbie 2002: 520–1).

Throughout this book we argue that the analytical lens provided by IP/IPR can offer new insights into this problem. The entrepreneur of the self is not simply a trope of governmental discourse, but a performatively enacted, socially constructed entity (Ellmeier 2003, Foucault 2008, Read 2009, Bröckling 2016); as economized thinking has diffused into administrative and organizational settings, so those settings have evolved—or been consciously redesigned—to enact just that kind of economic agency (Ferraro et al. 2005, Roscoe and Chillas 2014). We will show that IP/IPR plays a crucial role in configuring the economic agency of individuals, facilitating the calculation necessary to participate in the market. IP/IPR constitutes the capital that is traded and valorized in the marketplace; when creative producers generate an income from their work it is not through labour alone, but labour transformed into intellectual property and exploited through intellectual property rights. Although we have much sympathy with the critiques of labour relations in the creative economy, we argue that a focus on the entrepreneurial self and human capital fails to distinguish the 'entrepreneurial self' from an 'authorial self'—the 'autonomous self-directing creator' of creative endeavour (Cohen 1992: 179). The authorial self creates or contributes to the creation of texts: 'symbolic, aesthetic and informational artefacts, intended to inform, edify and/or please audiences' (Hesmondhalgh and Baker 2011: 59). This authorial self highlights a distinctive feature of cultural work, most notably, that in creating cultural goods, creative workers also create IP (Ryan 1992, Stahl 2013). Rather than Ellmeier's (2003: 3) characterization of the cultural worker as being a cultural entrepreneur without capital, we assert that cultural workers do have capital, or the potential for capital. This comes in the form of IP. As producers of IP, Me & Co (Beck 2000) necessarily engage in the production of a tradable commodity, and in doing so become caught in the network of market relations that forms the basis of the creative economy.

Doing 'Cultural Economy'

We have so far highlighted the contested associations in the term 'creative industry' and the strained relation between art and commerce, culture and the economic: binary, 'hostile worlds' (Zelizer 1994) forced to interact with one another. From the mid-twentieth century, social sciences reflected this divide, with economics taking matters of value and sociology 'values', an arrangement that Stark (2011) calls 'Parsons' Pact'. More recently, across the social sciences the distinction between the economic and the social has increasingly eroded. Following Granovetter's (1973, 1985) then ground-breaking work on social ties, the 'New Economic Sociology' sought to demonstrate that rational economic action is embedded in, and shaped by, networks of sociality (Uzzi 1997, Krippner 2001, Fourcade-Gourinchas 2005). Since Polanyi (2001) first suggested that the separation between economy and society is a historically situated and politically charged event, anthropologists have investigated the social and cultural structures that give rise to particular understandings of the economic (e.g. Slater and Tonkiss 2001, Miller 2002). Zelizer (1994, 2005) has been particularly influential in demonstrating the overlapping of domestic arrangements and economic transactions, and her approach has matured into a relational sociology that examines how economic relations are implicated in the construction and maintenance of social relations (Zelizer 2012, Chen and Roscoe 2018). Economic-sociological investigations of creative industries have elaborated, for example, on the meaning and practice of pricing in art markets (Velthuis 2005, Coslor 2016), or social relationships and cultural norms in fashion and garment manufacture (Uzzi 1997, Entwistle 2009, Aspers 2010).

As the analytic distinction between culture and economy has been problematized, research has sought to elaborate how actors might, in practice, do 'cultural economy' (Entwistle and Slater 2014, McFall 2015). Most recently, the glibly termed 'new, new economic sociology' (McFall and Ossandón 2014) has shifted analytic attention to the material architectures, social practices, and shared understandings through which the economic is constituted, and the role of calculation in the construction of economic agency. For example, Coslor and Spaenjers (2016) consider the financialization of the art market as an epistemic community depending on shared knowledge production, strategies of valuation, and practices of legitimacy in calculation, all necessary to develop art as an 'asset class'. In other words, researchers have begun to ask how a market comes to function like a market, and what it is about market situations that make them specifically market-like: to understand the market as a complex instance of social organization rather than a taken-for-granted backdrop for economic transactions.

Central to this move is the work of Michel Callon (1998), who suggested two related but separate research programmes. The first concerns the role of economics (broadly understood as ways of economic thinking and doing, academic, lay, or professional) in shaping the economy. The economy, Callon punned, is embedded in economics and not vice versa. Following the contributions of the philosopher of language J. L. Austin, this became known as the 'performativity thesis' and has been elaborated in a growing array of empirical studies, most famously MacKenzie's (2006) account of how options pricing theory shaped the market in financial derivatives. The second programme proposes an 'anthropology of calculation' (Callon and Muniesa 2005, Çalışkan and Callon 2009). It understands markets as collective calculative arrangements where the work of calculation is shared across networks of individuals and material devices known as socio-material assemblies. Callon's work follows the broader Latourian injunction to describe networks of association and in doing so to 'reassemble the social' itself (Latour 2007); the challenge for researchers is to present an ethnography of these socio-technical agencies (Hardie and MacKenzie 2007). We pay particular attention to the concept of 'market device', which we understand as a socio-material arrangement capable of holding market agencies together (Callon et al. 2007). Market devices may be as simple a mechanism as an equation (MacKenzie 2006). We will argue that IP/IPR—the text and its associated rights—is a market device capable of coordinating and formatting market action as it travels through the creative economy.

Callon's programme allows us to question the opposing positions that have already surfaced in our discussion of creative industries. On the one hand, economics has employed the instrumentally maximizing rational economic agent as an explanatory device to be deployed across an ever-increasing disciplinary remit—including mechanisms for incentivizing and protecting creative production. On the other, anthropologists, critically inclined scholars of organization, and others have lambasted this *homo oeconomicus* as a fictional construct to be unpicked by detailed fieldwork. They seek to show within the social and cultural constitution of economic action, the power relations, governmental projects, and humdrum necessities underpinning market situations. Callon offers a synthesis, proposing that economic man *is made*.[4] The calculative competency that is *homo oeconomicus* comes into being in specific circumstances as a result of a prolonged socio-material process of configuration, 'consisting of material elements and discourses, competencies and embodied skills, routines and so on' (Callon 2007: 142). Callon's innovation is to ask what kinds of social interaction make up the economy (McFall and Ossandón 2014), and to suggest that studies of economization consider the social construction of the economy via an analysis of the construction

[4] It should be noted that this position is also adopted, though from different theoretical foundations, by Bourdieu (2005) and Foucault (2008).

of economic agency. In doing so, he revives a stale debate and suggests a methodological programme:

> a means of sidestepping the endless dispute between economics and sociology about how natural or realistic the character of economic rationality may or may not be, in order, rather, to acknowledge the social existence of calculative practices...to explain the mystery of the pervasiveness of calculative practices in unveiling the thousands of skills, actors, and tools that render calculation possible.
> (Cochoy 2014: 113)

Economic agents calculate; their calculation constitutes markets; a market becomes a collective calculative device for the evaluation of goods (Callon et al. 2002). Çalışkan and Callon (2010: 3) map out a programme for the study of markets as 'institutions that favour the creation and the production of values by organizing competition between autonomous and independent agents'. They suggest that markets work to construct two kinds of entities. Calling on the insight of science and technology studies that natural objects must be 'pacified' in the laboratory before they yield stable facts, Çalışkan and Callon (2010) suggest that markets create 'pacified entities' that can be transferred as property and that have sufficiently stable attributes to be the subject of calculation. Property rights and specific legal devices are thus an essential part of this pacification. Then there are entities that engage in calculation, settling disputes through the mechanism of price; power differentials within the market stem from calculative disparities, where 'the most powerful agencies are able to impose their valuations on others and consequently to impact strongly on the distribution of value...by affirming the autonomy of calculating agencies, markets are able to conceal and to legitimately impose the asymmetries that develop out of the achievement of calculative capacities' (Çalışkan and Callon 2010: 13). Already, these questions focus attention on the work of IP/IPR in the creative economy, both in terms of creating goods and enacting power relations.

Our approach also allows us to return to the vexed question of value within creative production. Creative industries, as we have seen, are concerned extensively with symbolic production. In these commodity markets, valuation is highly problematic. For Callon, calculating agents are at work in the qualification and the singularization of goods through the elaboration of associations. The roles of producer and consumer overlap. Products gain networks of associations not only in their manufacture but also in their consumption, in what Callon et al. (2002) term 'an economy of qualities'. In the creative industries, for example, the symbolic meaning and value of goods is bestowed by knowledgeable consumers as they are purchased, as much as it is when they are manufactured by creative producers. Callon's approach here differs starkly from other accounts of creative consumption—or the consumption of 'singularities'—that posit judgement devices and intermediaries as mechanisms separating active producers and passive consumers (see, for example, the treatment offered by Karpik 2010).

Institutional Facts and Scholastic Fallacies

We start our analysis here by returning to intellectual property. Our focus on IP provides some of those methodological pathways demanded by McRobbie (2016) for understanding self-employment and freelance terrains because it provides a particular entrée into understanding the aesthetic-commerce relation identified as characterizing the creative industries. As 'content' industries, the creative industries' *sine qua non*, as has been recognized, is the exploitation of IP (Christopherson 2006). Indeed, one of their unifying features is that 'producers rely upon copyright law to establish property rights and protect revenues' (Towse 2002: 7). The creative industries are sometimes referred to as copyright industries (e.g. Gantchev 2004, Siwek 2016). Before commenting on our approach, we explicate some aspects of how IP functions institutionally (see Searle and Brassell 2016).

IP is described by the World Intellectual Property Organization (2004: 3) as 'legal rights that result from intellectual activity in industrial, scientific, literary and artistic fields'. These are rights to *property*. Property associated with ideas is problematic: 'with property disputed—not least as it may refer to an object, a system, a series of rights, and a conceptual abstraction—adding "intellectual" to the equation does little to clarify definition' (George 2012: 16). As a form of property, IP carries connotations of a tangible product or entity, ownership, and scarcity, but these are misleading. As non-rival (it can be used multiple times and by many people) and non-excludable (it is difficult to exclude others from using it), IP is distinguished by the ease with which it may be appropriated (Towse 2006b).

In economic terms, IP is more a public than a private good (Garnham 1990), and the economic justification of copyright law stems from the difficulties of restricting access to such a public good, and its attendant 'free-rider' and market failure arguments (Landes and Posner 1989, Towse 1999). Indeed, it is the need to establish boundaries around, and claims to, products that offers cultural work the defence of copyright (Toynbee 2001, 2013). Copyright law functions to provide incentives to both create and disseminate the expression of ideas (not the ideas themselves). Given the discrepancy between fixed and marginal costs of production (the costs of creation as opposed to copying) there is a 'general welfare' in ensuring the latter do not undermine the former (Landes and Posner 1989, Towse 1999), especially as the Internet and digital reproduction substantially reduce marginal costs. The legal framework of IP therefore affords the holder of IP rights (who may not be the creator) a legally enforceable (temporary) monopoly of ownership and exploitation of the expression of ideas: 'Copyright finances the creation of works of art by charging users for the use they make of those works' (Towse 2006b: 85). This is the 'incentive-to-innovate' theory, whereby statutory property rights 'overcome the free-riding problems of information goods and therefore provide an incentive mechanism for rewarding creators and for the disclosure of their work' (Towse 2002: 5).

Monopoly rights, however, may present a cost to society both in reducing use and raising prices. Thus, under social contract theory (where IP is framed as a social contract between society and creators), society, interested in benefiting from creativity and innovation in the long run, offers creators short-term rights over the fruits of their labour. During the monopoly period, creators are able to appropriate the returns to their investment. As these time-limited rights expire, creative or innovative works become part of the public domain where they can be freely used. Society continues to benefit from innovation and creativity; creators reap the rewards of their innovation and continue to create.

It is important to note that IP rights do not protect ideas themselves, but the manifestation or expression of ideas: the idea of a book about a boy wizard who goes to a special school is not protected, but a Harry Potter book is. The incentive scheme is designed not to hinder creative and intellectual progress. Because protection attaches only to creative expression, 'properly tailored copyright protection can avoid frustrating the needs of future authors. And because ideas and other noncopyrightable subject matter exist in the public domain, they are freely accessible to everyone' (Cohen 2012: 62). Protection of the expression of an idea, rather than the idea itself, also facilitates practical issues of determining ownership and the limits of protection.

The IP legal framework is largely constructed of IP rights (IPR). In the creative industries, the most relevant rights are copyright (arising automatically with the documented expression), trademarks (a graphical representation, a sign capable of distinguishing goods, requiring registration), design rights (propertizing the appearance of a product), and sometimes patents (which propertize novel invention). In addition, there are related rights concerning, for example, secondary uses and adaptations of copyrighted content (Cohen 2012). There are also trade secrets. Each of these IPR is designed to protect a different expression or product of creativity and innovation, and each provides protection with various levels of strength, duration, and breadth. A second important tenet of IP is the right to exclude. In copyright, the clue is the name, granting the rights holder the right to control who has the right to make copies. In practice, this means that the rights holder has the ability to license the copyright, prevent others from making copies, and pursue damages in the event that copying occurs without permission. IP's 'theft' thus comes from the loss of being able to exploit monopoly rights attached to it.

It is important to note that IP comprises property carved out of what is otherwise the public domain (MacMillan 2015). The public domain often refers to works covered by expired rights (e.g. Shakespeare's works) and works that have never held protection either because of their collective nature, such as cultural heritage and folklore, or because they did not qualify for protection to begin with (e.g. they fail to meet originality requirements). The public domain has an important role in the creative and cultural industries as a valuable source for the creation of new works (Buccafusco and Heald 2013). Colloquially, works that are protected by copyright but have been made available to the public through licensing, such as Creative Commons, are also often referred to as public domain. Copyright-protected works in the creative industries also can be inappropriately treated as public domain, particularly in more informal environments including the fanfiction and computer game modding scenes.

Discussions about copyright have traditionally revolved around the balance between private and public domains and themes of freedom (access) and control (property rights) (Lovink and Rossiter 2007, Smiers 2007, Kretschmer 2015). Contestants of copyright reflect a political spectrum from those who believe claims to property amount to theft from the public domain, thus they reject IP outright, to those who celebrate an open, innovative sharing of IP. Information-as-freedom approaches celebrate a 'digital commons' where work is licensed for public use (Lessig 2002), for 'unimpeded, end-to-end communication' facilitating 'vibrant, broadly participatory popular culture' (Banks 2007). Information-as-control advocates, content owners, and online intermediaries, on the other hand, propose enhanced copyright control, 'digital rights management', and strategies to protect commercial interests (Cohen 2012). Within the creative industries, the discussion of IP has been heavily influenced by the author–publisher distinction, their presumed congruence of interests concealing a process whereby 'autonomous creativity is captured and converted into "intellectual property"' (Dyer-Witheford and de Peuter 2009).[5] Toynbee (2013) identifies an 'ideological mobilization' by corporate copyright holders seeking to maintain control over a diminishing revenue base. He writes:

> It is true that in many cases copyright does in the first instance belong to the creator, rather than the cultural and media corporations, but even in these cases, labour market conditions, whereby supply greatly exceeds demand, mean that the

[5] The Statute of Anne (the UK's Copyright Act of 1710), introduced at the behest of London booksellers, allied authors' rights with property rights with the assumption in IP that publisher and author interests are convergent (Towse 1999). 'The first English copyright law produced a commodity form tailored for organized business' (Toynbee 2001: 5).

> cultural industries are able to insist on the signing over of rights from the creator to the cultural industries via a publishing contract... Thus the argument that copyright, and the industrial system based upon it, protects creators per se—rather than the corporations—is especially disingenuous. (Toynbee 2013: 92)

Within mainstream copyright scholarship the parameters of theoretical debate are shaped by the fault lines either of economic analysis or theories of rights (Cohen 2012: 16). As we have seen, non-rights-based justifications of IP refer to its economic function, and often form the foundation of policy positions. Economic theorists are concerned with the 'overall efficiency in the production and distribution of social resources, and with factors that might produce distortions from optimum production and distribution' (Cohen 2012: 17). Here, IP is an incentive to create and to counter free-riding, on the basis that, without recompense, 'people are unlikely to invest labour, effort or money and other resources into producing' cultural and creative goods (George 2012: 345).

Other approaches to IP are shaped by a theory of rights. One, informed by the work of Locke (specifically his *Second Treatise on Government,* 1966) and known as the labour-desert theory, is akin to a labour theory of value. Here, IPR is an intrinsic right stemming from ownership of one's own labour and therefore its fruits: write the song, own the score. Such property rights derive from the expenditure of labour, effort, or capital. Another rights perspective, informed by Hegel (1991) and sometimes termed the 'personality theory' of rights, derives from the person of the creator herself. Created work represents an expression of self, the denial of which would be a form of alienation. This perspective informs the moral rights doctrine that grants the right of attribution, and to object to the derogatory use of one's work even after sale.

Although apparently distinct, both economic and rights approaches are premised on a subject–object distinction. Each creates its own individual subject: rights theory, *homo juridicus*; economic analysis, *homo oeconomicus*. *Homo juridicus* is, as Cohen (2012: 17) notes, a 'definitionally autonomous being possessed of abstract liberty rights that are presumed capable of exercise regardless of context'. Equally, economic analysis regards the atomized rational economic agent as axiomatic to any theory. From both economic and rights perspectives, the legal framework assigns individuals an autonomy that exists outside of culture (Cohen 2012: 24). Both are situated within a tradition of enlightenment rationalism: 'the liberal subject has a body but is not understood as being a body' (Cohen 2012: 16). *Homo oeconomicus* parallels *homo juridicus*; they are abstract and disembodied visions of the self. Both are 'fictions', scholastic fallacies[6] that 'supply the economic and legal systems

[6] '*Homo oeconomicus* as conceived (tacitly or explicitly) by economic orthodoxy, is a kind of anthropological monster; this theoretically minded man of practice is the most extreme personification of the scholastic fallacy, an intellectualist or intellectualocentric error very

with the agents they need in order to operate' (Bröckling 2016: 11, Bourdieu 2005). Equally, both economic and rights approaches see IP as a 'pre-legal object': for lawyers and economists it acquires an imagined existence, an existence akin to being a physical object 'out there in the world' (George 2012: 8).

IP law is, therefore, predicated upon simplified models of individual agency and economic motivation. It holds a set of presumptions about the interaction between property rights and culture, but 'is relatively incurious about users and their behaviour' (Cohen 2012: 66). The presumption that copyright supplies incentives for authors to produce creative work implies that creativity is a 'pre-existing preference that matters only to the extent that it is presumptively enhanced by the possibility of an economic reward' (Cohen 2012: 65). There is also an assumption of a linear process: 'Authors produce knowledge and the public receives it' (Cohen 2012: 62). Copyright scholars have not been particularly interested in creative practice: 'Although users of copyrighted works play important roles both as audiences and as future authors, copyright theory and jurisprudence have evinced little interest in understanding how users assimilate culture and whether that process is as passive as copyright's incentive story presupposes' (Cohen 2012: 62). Creativity is constantly invoked, but never really explored.

We argue that the economization research programme discussed in the previous section can offer new ways of tackling these problems. It helps us to see that markets are constructed as exchanges of property rights: 'The conception, production and circulation of goods depend on the voluntary transfer of property rights attached to them, invoking monetary compensation' (Çalışkan and Callon 2010: 3). Property rights ensure objects are alienated, with transfers of ownership ending all claims of the previous owner (Slater 2002b). Such rights necessarily involve 'specific technical, material, textual and legal devices' identifying owner(s), defining the 'nature of the rights attached', and the 'terms of their enforcement' (Çalışkan and Callon 2010: 7). Property rights may be predicated upon scholastic fallacies but they have performative consequences, constructing both the objects that are subject to exchange, and the subject that holds such rights. While legal scholarship—and the law—presumes a pre-legal object, we explore how the law becomes part of the network of associations that constitute objects, texts, or works as market commodities, capable of travelling between owners, of being exchanged and being the subject of calculation. If property is integral to the functioning of a commodity market, we need to document how that

common in the social sciences . . . by which the scholar puts into the heads of the agents he is studying . . . the theoretical considerations and constructions he has had to develop in order to account for their practices' (Bourdieu 2005: 209).

property comes into being and the forms of calculation imposed upon it. We will show that IP/IPR is a central device in the constitution of the market objects on which the creative economy depends and the economic agency capable of dealing with this.

The IP/IPR Nexus

We must now elaborate our central concept: IP/IPR. We draw here on the distinctions George (2012: 32) makes between ideational objects, their documented forms, and the IP object constructed through IP law. These distinctions recognize important aspects of the legal structure of IP. As stated, IP does not confer rights over ideas—'the ideational object'—but protects their material expression in documented forms (George 2012). Authorial ownership is based on the *expression* of ideas; the 'intellectual propertyness' of the ideational object is evidenced in its documented form (George 2012: 18).[7] The copyright system assigns rights thanks to 'the doctrinal emphasis on *works* of authorship that emerged in late-nineteenth century copyright law[,] accorded with the nineteenth-century liberal ideology of propertisation' (Cohen 2012: 63, emphasis added). This emphasis on works enshrines an ideas–expression distinction, and the assumption that the two can be distinguished. There is an intuitive appeal to the distinction, for 'the intangible character of creativity implies that it has to be observed in some material support which contains and reveals it' (Santagata 2004: 83). Indeed, it might be seen that the legal framework with its ideas–expression distinction undermines the claims of 'immaterial' labour (Lazzarato 1996, Hardt and Negri 2000): 'the major problem with symbolic labour... is quite simply that it is not immaterial' (Toynbee 2013: 90). As we shall see, in practice this idea–expression dichotomy corresponds poorly to the cultural reality that authors and users must negotiate (Cohen 2012: 62); their understanding of this nuance is less clear in creative practice than the law presumes.

The 'IP object' is 'expressed in [written form], original, created by the author and *specified in connection to the jurisdiction* in which the legal right is claimed' (George 2012: 96, emphasis added). Although the terminology suggests that IP has existence prior to, and independent of, the law, the IP object exists because it is 'constructed, defined, created and sustained' by IP law. IP law is, in Callon's terminology, performative; the 'IP object' is the 'legal delineation of the part of the ideational object over which IP law provides a monopoly'

[7] The 1886 Berne Convention establishes that property inheres in the 'entity of the intellectual work expressed in written form by an author', and by allowing for the reciprocal recognition of national copyright law establishes copyright on an international basis (Toynbee 2001: 5).

(George 2012: 97). A trademark, for example, is the expression of the ideational object but the IP object is established through registering the trademark in the territories desired. The IP object is thus distinct from the ideational object and the physical object, being instead a legally constructed entity. By this account, IP law is 'fundamentally an institution that provides for the conversion of ideational objects into private property through the application of a series of conceptual requirements' (George 2012: 236).

It is thus possible to distinguish between IP and IP which is 'propertized', the latter the performative production of the law. This important distinction is also found in the economic bible of IP law: for Landes and Posner (2003: 1), 'IP denotes ideas, symbols, images, expressive works (verbal, visual, musical, theatrical) that [have] an existence separable from a unique physical embodiment, whether or not the product has actually been 'propertized', that is brought under a regime of legally enforceable property rights'. We therefore have three entities, 'the ideational object', 'the documented form', and the 'IP object' (George 2012); or, in economic terminology, 'IP' and 'propertized IP' (Landes and Posner 2003).

We pose IP/IPR as the object of our focus. In our usage, IP/IPR represents IP both as 'ideational object' and its documented form; and IPR, as the IP object, or propertized IP. For the creative industries, the text (IP) is central to production. Texts are their creators' expressive, tangible form, be this film, music, TV programmes, plays, books, dance, fashion, or computer codes (Hesmondhalgh and Baker 2011); we will use the terms text, creative work, and IP interchangeably throughout this book. IPR links or ties the idea and its expression to property. It is a point of engagement with the economic. While IP denotes the artistic idea and its expression in material form; IPR denotes its propertized, economic, and potentially commercial analogue. The concept of IP/IPR thus expresses both the manifestation of intellectual labour and intangible property.

IP/IPR serves as a nexus for the proliferating associations that cling to creative works as they circulate in the market (see Figure 1.1). As such it offers a promising analytic tool to approach some of the dualities we have identified in the earlier parts of this introduction, in particular, the culture-commerce relationship that has been taken to characterize the creative industries. In texts 'whose primary economic value is derived from their cultural value' (O'Connor 2000: 27), the concept of IP/IPR formulates that relationship. Culture cannot be devoid of issues of ownership and property: they are intricately related and mutually informed. Translated through the networks of the marketplace, the associations grow stronger or weaken in different phases: IP as creative text may be more prominent in one phase, while in another IPR as property may be. As Appadurai (1986: 17) notes, the meanings of an 'object' are inscribed in 'forms, uses and trajectories'.

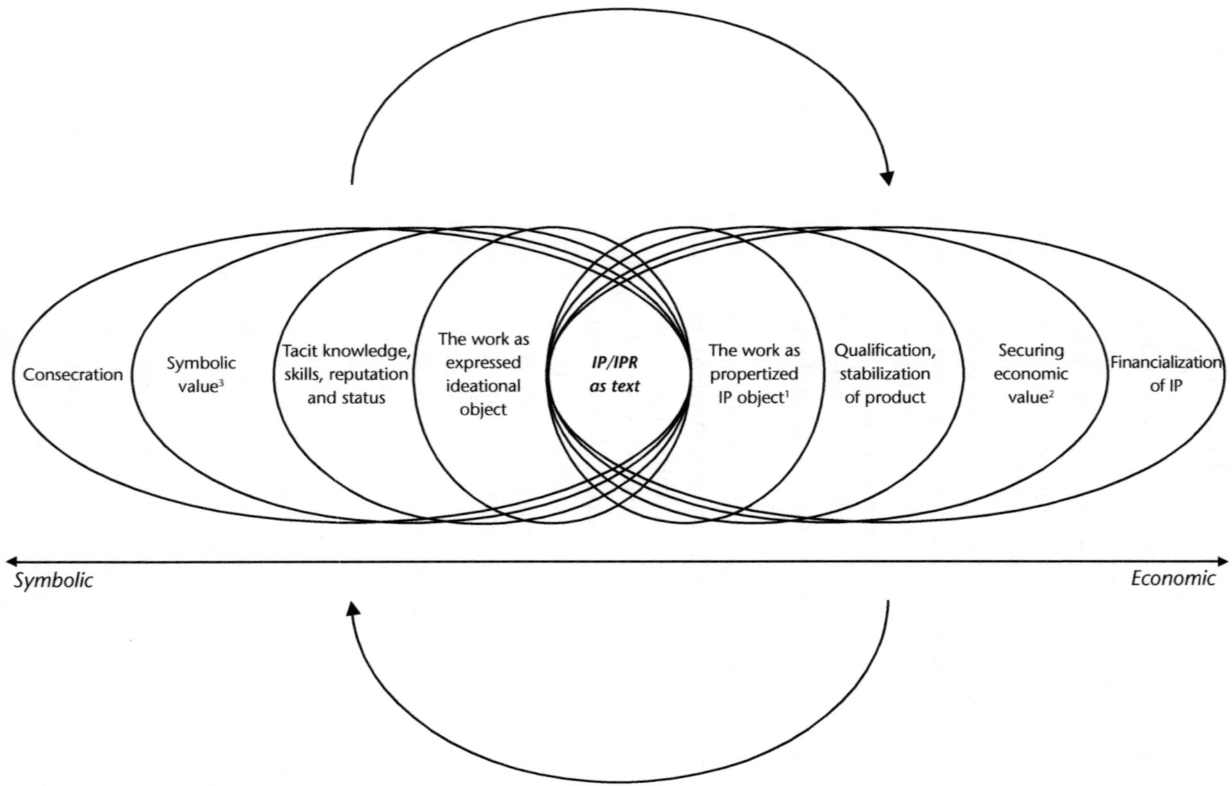

[1] Copyright, design rights, trade mark
[2] Through licensing or exchange
[3] Mediated partially by cultural intermediaries and judgement devices

Figure 1.1. The liminality of IP/IPR

An analogy might be useful here, so we will take one from the world with which we are most familiar. The book you are holding, or reading on your screen, is a 'creative work'. In the spring of 2018 it existed as a clutch of texts, digitally processed documents that could be printed out and annotated. This was the authors' IP, to which certain legal rights immediately and automatically accrued: notably copyright, a right of exclusion, and a right not to be copied. This IP, embodied in our texts, has an overspill in a more colloquial conception of IP as the intellectual careers, experience, knowledge, and projects of the authors, inseparable from the intellectual context of the community in which we work. All judgements of merit and worth stem from and make sense within that community. A library's decision to purchase the book will be dependent upon such judgements of esteem, some of which we signal from the dust jacket of the finished product. Other judgements, good or bad, may be signalled by the quality of the imprint or the institutional position and reputation of the authors: metrological devices such as citations can play a role here as a means of signalling worth to outsiders. These can be recognized as judgement devices (Karpik 2010) or mechanisms of qualification (Callon et al. 2002). Our text is a material figuration of all of these associations.

At some point, however, the IP changes to more specific IPR, which, through assigning copyright, renders it separable, detached, and ready for sale. Rather than recognizing pre-existing rights to a pre-existing artefact, IPR performatively disentangles and alienates our work as an item of our property.[8] Rights proliferate: the right we passed to the publisher to turn our documents into a book that can then be sold to fellow scholars and libraries; the rights for the Hollywood blockbuster and *Sunday Times* serialization that will inevitably follow; rights for translations, future editions, merchandising commodities, and so forth. We are not convinced, however, that IPR provides any real protection against infringement. While legal theorists might suggest this is the case, we know our work is primarily safeguarded by social norms within our community of practice. IP/IPR also may be exploited in other ways: we may promote its circulation in the academic labour market as we bid for new jobs or promotions. In other words, the creative work becomes the centre of ever-denser networks of association that perform value, protect it, and offer means of generating commercial returns.

Our working lives tell us how closely academic creativity and economic concerns mesh. Rather than present culture and economy as antonyms, IP/IPR recognizes the necessary interdependence of economic and cultural practices within cultural production: film editing, for example, is key to a film's aesthetics and commercial viability (Caves 2000, du Gay and Pryke

[8] A Marxist critique might describe the constitution of our work as property as an act of enclosure and expropriation from the community (Beverungen et al. 2012, Harvie et al. 2012).

2002, Banks 2007, Pratt 2007, Hesmondhalgh and Baker 2011). The value of the cultural industries lies in the aesthetic and expressive, but as a business, its aim is also to make profit (Hesmondhalgh and Baker 2011). The IP/IPR focus provides a particular slant on the materiality of entities, namely that 'ideas' are rendered material both through the requirement that they are expressed, but also rendered material by the necessity of financial recompense, playing a role in 'the accumulation imperative' (Banks 2007: 7). Production, distribution, and consumption are market exchanges (Garnham 2000).[9] We therefore take the IP/IPR nexus as a market device (Callon et al. 2007), holding together the networks of association that give creative products meaning and worth, and at the same time pacifying them, rendering them stable, disentangled, and able to circulate in the market for creative goods. IP/IPR encompasses the art-commerce-legal relation of the creative industries.

Our Study: The Journey of IP/IPR

Our task throughout the rest of this book is to follow the associations and to describe the proliferating networks that constitute the IP/IPR object. We seek to focus on the core aspect of activity in the creative industries: the making of creative product (IP) and the attempts to secure money from its production through the sale of IP rights (IPR). We 'follow the thing' (Kuipers 2014: 56) that is IP/IPR, starting with ideas and their expression, following their careers and metamorphoses (Appadurai 1986, McFall 2014). By examining the journey in the productive cycle from idea to valued entity, we can locate IP/IPR in the valorization process. IP/IPR has a career. Its qualities are in flux, depending on its positioning in social space (Appadurai 1986). As it moves from one setting to another, its specific characteristics and attributed meanings change, as it gradually establishes a connection between itself and the various market actors and intermediaries (Beckert and Musselin 2013).

For most putative (economic) agents, both IP as text and IPR as ownership/rights are concepts that encompass a variety of forms and functions. Creatives stumble into their practical knowledge of this arena through their ongoing attempts to negotiate their practices. We explore this array of knowledges and know-how, or lay knowledge: the 'material realities of everyday practice' (Cohen 2012: 24) help us understand the functioning of IP/IPR, and we stress the embodied perception and everyday practice appearing within an existing narrative of institutional forms of the law and the economy.

[9] Indeed, it might be argued that 'art', previously the province of the church, the court, and aristocratic or private patronage, emerged from or was created by market relations.

IP/IPR are lived realities rather than formal categories; both the economic and legal become constructed through practice and engagement. We are concerned with what happens when those working within cultural production engage in a business context, how they read the symbolic material of law and economics without necessarily being in 'possession of the relevant code of competence' (Toynbee 2001: 15). What we aim to do is replace the 'autonomous, rational, disembodied self' (Cohen 2012: 26) of *homo oeconomicus* or *homo juridicus* with the subject who exists in and is constituted by the field of cultural production understood in terms of practices, materialities, and calculative strategies. In doing so, we approach IP/IPR 'with a set of more mundane and far more important questions in mind: how do processes of creativity play out in places inhabited by real, embodied individuals and communities, and how does copyright affect the scope for the play of everyday practice?' (Cohen 2012: 57). The IP/IPR framework allows us to interrogate the processes through which 'lay' agents construct their understandings or perceptions of, and relationships to, IP; the extent to which they view their creative products as property or as having economic salience; and where they do so, how they exploit this. In this sense, we also respond to calls for more empirical studies of the effect of copyright on the production of cultural goods, but more significantly we hope to contribute to an understanding of law 'at the ground level in order to understand its loftier principles' (Towse 1999: 369).

Our focus is those self-employed, micro- and SME organizations, the 'small-scale... independent micro-economies of culture' (McRobbie 2016: 18) that make up the bulk of the creative industries outside of the major international conglomerations. Our aim is to illuminate 'the practical ways in which "economically relevant activity" is performed and enacted' (du Gay and Pryke 2002: 5). In trying to understand the patterns of everyday practice, of making a living, we draw upon interviews with small and medium enterprises, microbusinesses, freelancers, and sole traders. As Banks (2007: 10) notes, 'in most firms cultural workers are not "stars", nor are they rich or even partially successful'. Many reflect the classic small-firm model of low-growth companies in sectors that have low barriers to entry, often dependent on large enterprises for distribution and sales.

Of the total 122 interviews, twenty-six are in design (including interior, product, service, jewellery, craft); fourteen in fashion and textiles (including specialist textiles, e.g. hand-knits); twelve in computer games; twelve in TV; eight in film; twelve in publishing, including two authors; twelve in music; eighteen in theatre; eight in dance.[10] In terms of legal form, 56 per cent of the

[10] Our respondents do not coincide with those of McRobbie's (2002) study, which primarily focuses on graphic designers, website designers, event organizers, media officer managers. She writes: 'granted there are still fashion designers, architects, writers and musicians and other creative occupations, but being a specialist rather than a multi-skilled "creative" is becoming a thing of the past and a mark of being over 35' (McRobbie 2002: 525). We would argue that McRobbie illustrates

total interviewed had limited status, 21 per cent were sole traders, sixteen (13 per cent) had both limited and registered charity status. Others were partnerships, limited liability partnerships, limited not-for-profit, and one was a not-for-profit registered charity. In the main they were microcompanies: ninety-nine (81 per cent) had nine employees or fewer, with forty-eight (39 per cent) having one employee, and sixteen (13 per cent) having two. While nineteen of the 122 (16 per cent) interviewees represent organizations that were founded more than thirty years ago, 103 (84 per cent) had less experience: forty-one (34 per cent) organizations had less than ten years' experience and forty-two (34 per cent) had between ten and twenty years of experience; the average across the cohort was 18.6 years (see Appendix).

The initial interview list comprised a small cohort of those who had received an instance of funding from a central creative industries funding body; this was then greatly enlarged by snowball sampling. Some in the sample had overview roles in their sectors, e.g. trade associations, who were interviewed in order to gain their broad perspectives and insights into sector-specific challenges. The primary interest lay in understanding the organizations' comprehension and management of IP. Questions related to the nature of their business, its brief history, their main products, projects, audiences, markets, and challenges; and how they understood IP, what IP issues they faced and how these were managed. All interviews were recorded and transcribed.

The interviews were read to identify the main themes. Initially, sectoral overviews, e.g. for games, theatre etc., outlining principal issues were identified (see Grewar et al. 2015). Although the interviews were approached from the perspective of IP being an extant object, the nature of the 'research object' became less clear as the interviews were interrogated. Not only this, we observed that the centrality of IP to micro- and SME functioning failed to conform to legal or economic expectations. This prompted a re-examination of the material, both empirically and amongst academic literature, and our identification of the IP/IPR composite as our focus: a happy juncture of the theoretical and the empirical, a market device capable of holding together our case material and our theoretical framing. The IP/IPR nexus therefore provides the structure of the book: we trace the journey of this composite in its many manifestations as it travelled from idea to marketable object, examining its interplay with agents, networks, and other market concepts along the way.

Our narrative begins in Chapter 2, where we explore how IP/IPR functions to constitute creative work as a market object that can be disentangled and sold: it is a liminal place of social attachment, a source of symbolic and economic value

some of the problems in defining the sector, i.e. the creative industries, as well as reflecting the geographical location of the creative scene in London. Other areas' creative populations do not necessarily match this.

as creative producers trade in the symbols of existing fields and their works are deemed as valuable within such settings. Chapter 2 deals first of all with the performative role of law in constructing market objects. We examine how, through originality, the law embodies a particular conception of solitary artistic creation, inherited from nineteenth-century Romantic aesthetics; at the same time, the law also mandates property rights as a means of constituting a market object, and these property rights necessitate a creator to whom they can attach, producing 'authorship'. Both creation and authorship seem highly artificial in view of the collaborative and collective processes that produce creative work, which we examine in more detail. As the latter, unsurprisingly, is crucial to the production of IP, it becomes clear that creative producers have to manage this multifaceted, liminal object in the shape of the IP/IPR nexus.

The third chapter considers the construction of economic agency among creative producers. We illustrate how agents are configured as market agents in the spaces of the creative industries, and how they come to understand what makes a market situation. We argue that a form of economic agency comes through and is facilitated by engagement with IP/IPR; as its journey continues, IP/IPR functions performatively to encourage dissonant yet productive varieties of calculation (Stark 2011). IP/IPR introduces a temporal dimension to their productive activities and helps agents to distinguish tradable assets while disentangling themselves from these creative works. In doing so, we show how IP/IPR becomes a vital market device in the assembly of an economic market for creative products. Chapter 3 also picks up the ambivalences of business and creativity. It deals with creatives' experiences of coming to entrepreneurship and shows a profound uncertainty towards the term, with some rejecting notions of business entirely, while others embrace commercial astuteness as a way of building and developing the sector. For this latter group, there is a moral responsibility to be financially literate, perhaps exemplifying a particular, productive creative subjectivity.

Creative industries have been characterized as pervasively uncertain, beset by what Caves (2000), following Goldman (1983), calls the 'nobody knows' problem. In classical theories of entrepreneurship, however, uncertainty is the source of profits, and the entrepreneur is the market agent willing to organize uncertainty in pursuit of return. Chapter 4 examines how creative producers do just that. We show that risk and uncertainty are managed through the same processes of symbolic production as those that give rise to creative goods and creative agency, mediated by the IP/IPR nexus; as creative products solidify into market goods so the uncertainties are transformed—at least in part—into risks, and uncertainty management through the social relations of the field develops into the legalistic protection of IP rights.

Chapter 5 invokes recent advances in the sociology of valuation (Muniesa 2011, Helgesson and Kjellberg 2013) to contend that the IP/IPR nexus is the mechanism through which creative products are constructed as valuable: that it orders and settles the multiple evaluative principles at play in creative production, that it bounds and singularizes goods. IP/IPR is constituted by valuations as diverse as knowledge, networks, or legal stratagems and game playing. Such settlements are only temporary, but they are vital in the operation of markets for creative products. The chapter shows that the business of creative work is the construction and exploitation of value through IP/IPR; its core is symbolic production and this symbolic worth is traded in markets for cultural goods. The symbolic valuation of worth, meanwhile, is contingent upon the slicing of IP/IPR facets into works of all kinds that can circulate in the market and be valued. Subsequent chapters explore how this market object can then be exploited as a source of revenue.

Chapter 6 turns to the issue of the realization of value for economic benefit, illustrating how economic value becomes identified and registered. Strategies include work-for-hire, sale, and licensing, and market intermediaries and collecting societies play an important role. We illustrate how arriving at prices for singular products in an exchange can be difficult, either because of a lack of 'equivalence' or because what should be taken into consideration has to be learnt. We also examine practices as producers try to maintain control of IPR through licensing agreements. We draw links between the structural forces identified earlier in the book, especially debates over creative labour and entrepreneurship—casualization, precarious labour, the oligopoly of corporations—and the day-to-day activities of creative producers as they seek to realize substantial enough returns to allow them to continue in the business of creative work.

Our final empirical chapter, Chapter 7, examines the strategies that are available for creative producers to protect their expressed ideas. We illustrate the ambiguity associated with copying, its being a highly nuanced activity in the eyes of producers, sometimes reflective of the zeitgeist, pedagogical practices as people become established in the field, or simply business practice. The community of producers informs the interpretation of experiences of copying or piracy. Although having had experience of work being appropriated, enforcing IPR through the legal process is not a usual practice, rather producers rely on the development of their IP and practices of the field to protect their claims to property.

The concluding chapter summarizes our arguments and our contributions to broader debates. We offer some policy recommendations. We argue that any evidence-based policy should be built on an understanding of the role of IP/IPR within the valorization process as a whole, and suggest that education policy should focus on developing the craft skills that underpin the process. We finally stress the importance of cultural policy for the future of creative production.

2

IP/IPR as a Market Object

Our journey through the creative economy begins with the production of goods for sale. The making of creative products (IP), and through this, the creation of IP rights (IPR) with the intention of securing money from their production, are core aspects of the creative producer's activity. We show that IP/IPR functions as a market device (Callon et al. 2007) capable of mediating between the individual maker and the collective field, disentangling creative products and domesticating them for exchange while at the same time maintaining the rich symbolic links to the field that give such products worth. We explore how IP/IPR functions as a liminal object, a source of both symbolic and economic value as creative producers trade in their particular fields.

At the same time, we can begin to deconstruct the legal fictions that underlie IP/IPR, showing the social construction of these market devices. Our chapter deals first of all with the performative role of law in constructing a market object. Influenced by nineteenth-century Romantic aesthetics, the law embodies a particular conception of solitary artistic creation as the source of original work. It is also informed by a nineteenth-century liberal ideology of propertization, whereby property rights become part of the apparatus of constituting a market object. Property rights demand a creator to whom they can attach, a placeholder who may briefly possess the rights to an object before transferring it on. The law thus makes use of notions of originality and creatorship, personified by an instrumental conception of the solitary artist, as means of attributing ownership. These concepts appear highly artificial given the collaborative and collective process that produces creative work, yet are crucial to the production of IP. We explore how such fictions of the solitary creative work underpin the legal conceptions of IP, performing certain understandings of creative objects. Yet the law is quite different from the practices that we uncover: the creative process is a profoundly social one, and artists' conceptions of property rights are enmeshed in chains of social relations.

'Perhaps the greatest flaw of creatorship and originality is . . . that *they are so difficult to understand*', writes George (2012: 236, emphasis added). She discusses the legal aspects of creatorship, authorship,[1] and originality which scarcely coincide with 'ordinary' understandings of these terms. For those working as creative producers, the situation is even more complicated: they have to manage a multifaceted, liminal object in the shape of the IP/IPR nexus. On one hand, they recognize the legal constitution of particular rights and are able to operate within these, at least in a limited form. On the other, they understand that much IP is embedded in the social organization of teams and the knowledge of participants. Interviewees are able to manage a simultaneous, dual vocabulary, moving between legal and social structures as a means of creating IP in the form of valuable market objects with property rights attached, objects that can be transferred through sale to generate income for their maker. Property is central to this endeavour. Ownership is understood in various ways and is a theme that runs through all conversations as creative producers seek to maintain their status and value, and thus their future revenues, in the marketplace. This ownership may be understood in terms of moral rights—another legal form—as well as copyright. The construction of a market object is a complicated affair.

Originality and Creatorship

The Romanticism of the late-eighteenth and nineteenth centuries positioned individual artists at the centre of the world of art, glorifying them as the source of uniqueness and creative genius, free from discipline and boundaries and dependent only on the 'muse' (Ryan 1992). As the source of cultural value, they countered emergent capitalism's control of nature, opposing a utilitarian, rationalist industrial world (Ryan 1992: 38, Williams 1958, Ross 2000, Luckman 2013). The myth of the solitary artist is an enduring fiction, and we have inherited from the Romantic Movement 'a theory of imagination which endowed the author with god-like powers of creation' (Toynbee 2001: 5). Those who have special gifts and talents 'cannot be subjected to the constraints imposed on other members of society' and in return society receives work of 'unique character and invaluable quality' (Becker 2008: 14–15). This historical provenance informs a number of assumptions in creative production: artists represent a distinctive category of unalienated labour, preserving the integrity of conception and execution (although this is open to debate: see Beck 2003, Banks 2010, Hesmondhalgh and Baker 2011, Stahl 2013, Toynbee 2013); the role of vocation, or 'priestly calling' (Caves 2000: 24), invoked as motivation for entering a creative sector (Taylor and Littleton 2008, Oakley

[1] Creatorship is the general legal term for creators of works; 'authorship' refers to copyright.

2009); the privileging of self-realization or self-actualization over security and income (Hesmondhalgh and Baker 2011); and the aesthetic and artistic as distinct from the 'laws of the market' (Hesmondhalgh and Baker 2011).

The Romantic imagination has influenced the legal framing of creative work. Toynbee (2001: 3–4) argues that it is the 'romantic discourses of authorship' that have 'legitimated the most important commodity form in the symbol world: copyright.... Copyright is derived precisely from the notion of a singular, expressive author, proprietor of their own creative faculties and fully responsible for their own creative work' (Toynbee 2001: 4). Furthermore, the legal framework conflates authorship and economic incentive, coupling 'romantic appeal and apparent efficiency' (Boyle 1996: xii quoted in Toynbee 2001: 4). Copyright, therefore, enshrines a certain conception of economic action and motivation in law, while the Romantic myth of originality and imagination, and 'the sole and privileged originator of the cultural work' (Hesmondhalgh and Baker 2011: 62), underlie IP law's conceptual constructs of 'creatorship' and 'originality' in judging legal rights. The artist is understood as a creative producer within a social vacuum, a poor representation of the social process of creativity. From this conception of the solitary genius, however, the legal constructs of originality and creatorship provide means of attributing the ownership of rights as they transfer within the market.

We begin with originality, the threshold requirement for copyright. Legal protection of copyright requires creative works be 'expressed in (written form), original, and created by the author' (George 2012: 211). If there is the communication of the same 'ideational object', this must not be in a form that copies earlier work[2] and must comply with the requisite legal understandings of creatorship and originality. In order to claim monopoly rights there must be the 'requisite degree' of 'original documented form' to qualify as such. This refers to the expression of ideas, not with the originality of the ideas or thought; an original work (copyright), novel invention (patents) or novel design (registered or unregistered design rights), or a dissimilar sign (trademark), refers to the documented form. Nor is originality the same as artistic merit; work is protected however bad it may be (Towse 2006a).

Originality is one of the tests of legal protection, varying dependent on jurisdiction, doctrine, and historical context; without it, an object remains in the public domain. Originality separates 'new' IP from existing IP, thereby establishing 'private' ownership. As George (2012: 217) notes, the 'difficulty for IP doctrines is determining the point at which a creation passes the

[2] This is to be contrasted with earlier traditions where replication and copying were previously essential parts of a trade; fifteenth-century commissioners of paintings, for example, specified the character, quality of colours, and methods of payment, resembling 'the contract one might make with a builder' (Becker 2008: 15).

originality threshold and qualifies for IP protection, thus transforming in status from an article in the public domain to an item of private property'. These thresholds prevent copies and, in general, mechanically produced works from inappropriately receiving protection. They also mean that the reuse of works, common in the creative industries (e.g. new editions, new formats, mash-ups) do not receive protection unless the originality requirement is met.

If the legal framing of IP invokes particular ideas of individual creativity and solitary motivation, it is unsurprising that the legal tests on which property rights are predicated invoke those same individualistic and de-socialized notions. Yet it is evident that the articulation of originality by those working in the creative industries is a social process, where expressions of IP are valorized in the course of numerous conversations and interactions.

Ideas themselves are ubiquitous, heavily dependent on socio-cultural influences and prior expressive thought. They are in the zeitgeist: 'I think very often things are in the ether' [TV 68], or 'Trends [in fashions] come around and whether you are absorbing them consciously or unconsciously, stuff can appear at the same time' [Design 25]. References to zeitgeist and trends reflect the nature of creative production that takes place within a social and professional milieu of conversations and interactions with others. There is an inevitable circulation of similar ideas, as this TV producer mixes metaphors to explain: 'Because we all work in the same cultural manure. We are all swimming around in the same stuff and everybody comes up with the same idea at the same time' [TV 63]. For creatives, there is no such thing as an original idea:

> All ideas are borrowed. Everyone borrows from everyone, right? [In] the music industry, is there any real true originality? There is, but it tends to be an amalgamation of other things and to say that we came up with this and it is truly original, well, that is absolute nonsense. [Games 48]

The originality of creativity is thus 'centrally dependent on the freedom to appropriate and experiment with artefacts and techniques encountered within the cultural landscape' (Cohen 2012: 31). The identification of originality within trends paradoxically confirms the artist or producer in her work, as she struggles to be in vogue and at the same time to display distinction; as ever, there is the issue of fitting in and 'standing out' (de Clercq and Voronov 2009). Creative workers must wrestle with the practical necessities of demonstrating originality at every stage of the social process, whilst also fitting in, demonstrating the ability to draw upon the existing cultural resources of the genre in new, exciting—and ideally, profitable—ways. Zoellner (2009: 520) tells us that the first questions asked of a production pitch tend to be 'Has it been done before?' and 'What's new about it?'. 'New' and 'original' however, have to be qualified, with the conceit of originality understood more as 'novelty', a new take or aspect of some topic that has been covered before. 'Originality... lies less in the idea... but in the way it is addressed or presented... a new "angle" on the familiar' (Zoellner 2009: 523):

> We have got to be grown up about this. There is no such thing as original ideas. The chances are that whatever it is that has stimulated us into thinking something, somehow, somewhere else, someone else will have had the same stimulus. But what we try to be is original in our take and that is what they will generally ask us. It is in the take and how you are going to spin it. 'What is the conceit?' they say. What the hell does that mean? It means, what is your take on it? What is your interpretation? What is your angle? For instance, you might describe in one paragraph a long-running television series based on a fairly crappy regional English hotel with some fairly eccentric and useless people in it. Is that *Crossroads,* or is it *Fawlty Towers*? [TV 56]

Even this limited requirement for a new angle may be testing:

> [With] history [programmes], there are no new ideas because they are all in the past. They have all probably been done before, so how do you put a new twist on to it? The 100-year anniversary of the Great War. A programme on ideas about that. They cannot all be wildly different, can they? They must be quite similar. [TV 53]

The central paradox of creativity is 'the need to produce difference in and through recognition' (Toynbee 2001), to generate novelty within the established conventions of the field, the historically accumulated fund of symbolic resources of the domain in question—those 'things that the people who [make] art and the people who read or look at it, share' (Becker 2008: xv). Social conventions shape what is possible and what is not. They are particularly important in constructing creative goods. Literary genres, or styles of using field conventions and resources, heavily circumscribe the form 'originality' might take; similarity is thus an inevitable consequence of this restriction. Although often unable to articulate these conventions, successful creative producers have an implicit understanding of 'what works', what the text or piece 'demands'. They understand their audience, and the symbolic experts—the critics, reviewers etc., whose task it will be to validate the originality and quality of new works.

'Creatorship', meanwhile, denotes an identifiable 'author', inventor, or creator. Creatorship is the legal understanding of how an individual might be identified as the originator, and therefore owner, of a piece of work. There is a dyadic relationship here: the IP object with attendant rights of ownership requires an owner, and 'without the creator such rights cannot exist' (George 2012: 14). Who might this creator be? It seems natural to assume—thanks, once again, to the enduring Romantic-era conceptions—that labour is the source of ownership, and that the individual whose work constituted the documented form of the creative object would be the creator, except when employment relationships determine the proprietor. This assumption obscures the legal foundations of property itself. From the legal perspective, creatorship creates attribution and from this, proprietorship and legally enforceable property rights. The performative role of law is indicated by Bently (1994: 980 quoted in George 2012: 173), who writes that:

> in law, authorship is a point of origination of a property right which . . . will circulate in the market, ending up in the control of the person who can exploit it most profitably. . . . Since copyright serves to vest authors with property only to enable them to divest that property, the author is a notion which needs only to be sustainable for an instant. This means that copyright law is able to imply and invent authors where there is no corresponding (cultural or other) 'reality'.

It is, in other words, 'the requirement of property that creates creatorship' (McGuigan 2010: 326). The author is an instrumental fiction constructed by property law to enable the circulation of creative goods within the marketplace.

Such an artificial concept, based on an understanding of creative action that is scarcely reflective of most creative labour, naturally struggles to deal with the collaborative and incremental nature of creative work. Creatorship *can* belong to a group, if members of the group and their contributions can be individually identified (George 2012: 162): their creations are known as 'works of joint authorship' and are the result of collaborations with two or more 'authors'. Yet this can be problematic. Where ownership is unclear to the collaborators, disputes may arise over rights to revenues and the ability to use the work, and one party may be able to obstruct the others. The clear lines of law obfuscate the collaborative, motley-crew (Caves 2000) nature of creative production.

Art as Collective, Collaborative Work

As we are beginning to see, the legal notions of creatorship and associated terms are at odds with the practice of creative work. The law shifts attention to the creative product rather than the creative process. It also singles out the 'author'. In law, the figure of author is an instrumental mechanism that makes it possible to attach property rights to an expressed ideational object and then transact in those rights. The author's brief possession of this object serves to crystallize the rights that surround it and make a market in creative work possible.

The tension between law and practice has not been unnoticed. First of all, the notion of creation ex nihilo, with the individual as the 'source' of creative production, is heavily critiqued (Becker 1974, Becker 2008, Pang 2015). Creative producers serve a long apprenticeship in their trade, learning the material and symbolic resources available to them, all of which pre-exist their creative activities. Creative production is a conversation within a community, with many art forms involving a dialogue between the past and present:

> Artists may not be able to tell us why they create, but they can tell us a lot about the where, what, who, and how of [a] particular creative process—where they were in space and time, what they were looking at, reading and listening to; who they were talking to; what insights or experiences sprang from those interactions.... This requires us to consider authors as *users of cultural works first* and creators only second. (Cohen 2012: 65–6)

Indeed, it is 'natural' for the artist to draw upon the creative resources available within the community:

> I think in whatever work you are doing in terms of being an artist or working in the arts, it is natural for people to reference your work and see who you are influenced by, so that is normal. [F&T 29]

Social authorship recognizes a dependency on other works (Toynbee 2001, 2003). The process of creating 'new' products involves existing cultural products being reused and reworked: 'social authors work by recombining symbolic materials from a historically deposited common stock' (Toynbee 2001: 2, Toynbee 2013). For Toynbee (2001: 8), the social author is 'an agent who produces symbolic difference or difference which matters in a particular taste community', while recognizing that difference is usually reflected in a 'small creative act', or a 'slight change' to a performative code. Change is thus largely incremental, 'in which small differences accumulate'. Difference does not emanate from 'internal resources of the creative subject', as assumed by the Romantics, but comes through 'the selection, combination and revoicing of what is already there' (Toynbee 2001: 8). Social authorship is defined by expertise, rather than genius, for it is knowledge, skills, and intimate awareness of a specific canon, that allow innovators to be able to identify 'unlikely possibilities' or new combinations (Toynbee 2001).

Only through working with, and through, ideas in a collective context—through working directly with others, conversing with them, or being in an artistic milieu—can creative producers develop the beginnings of an identifiable creative product. This example from TV production recognizes the importance of sharing ideas in order to develop them:

> Through my career, people who, in a meeting, are worried about expressing their ideas and thinking that they are really precious to them, don't get very far. Because actually an idea should be a group thing: I say to you that it would be fantastic to make a programme about stuffed rabbits, and you would say, 'No I don't think that

it would'—but that would spark a better idea and suddenly [the programme] is the history of the teddy bear. [TV 68]

To recognize art as a collective process is to do more than broaden the Romantic image of artistic creator by locating her in conversations within the artistic world—it is to recognize an essential part of creative production, as the entanglement of choreographer and dancer illustrates:

Dance is very much about the process. There is a lot of improvising initially and creative tasks from the choreographer, and then more choreographed work. Dancers are part of the creative process. It is just understood that is the process. There are a couple of solos that came from me asking a specific question and asking the dancers to answer it, and then through seeing how they were answering it, I choreographed and shaped these solos that are very much coming from the essence of them. But they wouldn't have made those without me asking the question. [Dance 120]

Different types of collaboration reflect both the different stages of production and the different skills partners bring to the ventures, as this producer explains:

I don't write. I think writers particularly are a very unique creature because they have this huge world in one head and are very creative. I have absolute respect for the way that they work. But frankly I don't have the patience. I am much better at working with a writer and inspiring them and trying to fix problems than I would be from making it from the first instance. Part of what I do is to protect them from too many people telling them what to do—the crap, really. [TV 72]

Although the producer appears to embrace the idea of the solitary writer with a 'huge world in one head' the quotation then elaborates on the collaborative aspects of creating a written work: inspiring and fixing. It epitomizes creative production as negotiation, with the role of the producer being to balance the different interests and concerns voiced by stakeholders involved in the production, 'as well as coping with all the emergencies that come his/her way' (Berkeley 2003: 117).

For most involved in creative production, the creative process is precisely that: a process, involving many stages and many types of collaborative input as ideas are translated into creative product. Scholars such as Becker (2008) and Bourdieu (1993) have emphasized the collective activity of creative labour. In publishing, for example, the process involves commissioning or acquisitions editors, manuscript editors, proof readers, designers, rights negotiators, and sales teams. Dance relies upon choreographers, composers, set, lighting, and costume makers, as well as dancers—who might come last in terms of organizing budgets. In other sectors, such as games, the cultivation of a customer base is integrated in the process as consumer 'testers' support the product development. Creative production is effectively the result of 'elaborate cooperation among specialised personnel' (Becker 2008: 28).

Social authorship recognizes not only 'the common stock of latent possibilities in the field of works', but also that 'each maker is obliged to enter the field of production with its rules, hierarchies, and clusters of positions' (Toynbee 2001: 12). Art worlds are organized by conventions—mutually accepted rules for collected action (Caves 2000, Becker 2008). Conventions facilitate efficient coordination of agents with different creative input, whether artists or support personnel (Banks 2010). Though standardized, they are not rigid and unchanging, but rely on 'customary modes of interpretation . . . and negotiation' (Becker 2008: 31). As people repeatedly, even routinely, cooperate in similar ways to produce similar works, the art world becomes 'an established network of cooperative links among participants' (Becker 2008: 34).

Learning conventions involves accumulating the symbolic and social resources necessary to function in a creative field, and is a crucial part of learning to be a creative producer. Even where creative processes appear similar, there may be substantial distinctions between the conventions and resources of different sectors. Working on music production for film, said one interviewee,

> has educated us in the way that a lot of people think about music. They have been spending two years making their film. They have finished, or are getting to the very end of the film, the last dubbing and editing, the tweaking stage. They have got a very tight-knit team who are usually getting annoyed with each other because they have been working together for so long. If they find that their film isn't quite working there are very few things which they can, at that time, change. The one thing that they can change is their music. We find a lot of the time, when film pitches come our way, [they say,] 'We have got a guy on this and it is not working out. Could you take a look at it for us?' And, 'What would you do?'
>
> [Music 88]

The same speaker goes on to explain the conventions of the game sector, which are quite different. Although the output is the same—a soundtrack—working with games producers involves interactions at a much earlier stage in the production, a 'proper creative collaboration' that requires an entirely different 'mindset':

> TV and film is very linear. But games are not linear. [They are] all over the place. Having to get yourself in the mindset of how a game universe is divided up: what may happen in these places, how long you might be in an area for, what barriers you might face, what might be the transition that will come after that? You might be in a space for 40 minutes, so and so might arrive and then you have to chase, then you are speeding up the music. The games people are so into what they are doing. They have got so much love for it and the creation and passion. It is a proper creative collaboration. It wasn't just a 'Just fill in something there. That

> sounds all right'. It is so integral, compared to being secondary in TV, and 'We have got no time left and we are going to run out of budget, just fix the problem and that will do'. It was a collaboration. [Music 88]

Whether by a last-minute patch to a film that 'isn't quite working' or ongoing creative collaboration with games designers, both examples circle around a crucial point: the production of IP as a commercially viable product. In order to reach this goal there are other necessary roles and contributions within the collaborative creative process, as acknowledged in Hirsch's (1972) 'cultural industries production system'. This portrays creative production from inception to consumption: development of new ideas and valuable IP rights, manufacturing, reproduction, and exchange in a market; and has since been expanded by Pratt (1997, 2005) to include education, critique, and archiving. Crucially these recognize consumption as well as production, and are not restricted to positions within a value chain, but all the networks these positions rely on (French et al. 2004). An orchestra concert, for example, requires instruments to have been invented, designed, manufactured, and maintained; people to learn to play them and to read a common system of music notation; there must be rehearsals, advertisements and publicity, and tickets sold.

There must also be sufficient distribution of the symbolic resources necessary to appreciate the output; 'an audience capable of listening to and in some way understanding and responding to the performance must have been recruited' (Becker 2008: 2). An audience and its reception of work is significant in influencing what gets produced, a notion that brings us back to a more philosophical deconstruction of authorship as 'the privileged moment of individualisation' (Foucault 1984: 101), or the intertextuality and multiplicity of text and its readers (Barthes 1977). The reception of symbolic materials needs careful curating, the activity of 'creating and maintaining the rationale according to which all these activities make sense and are worth doing' (Becker 2008: 4). Aesthetic argument, philosophical justification, critical review, and specific evaluation of individual works determine whether they meet a field's standards. Indeed, as Becker (2008: 36) reminds us, art worlds typically devote considerable attention to trying to decide 'what is' and 'what is not' art, and 'who is' and 'is not' an artist. Art worlds not only produce works but also give them aesthetic, and thus economic, value.

If creative work takes place within a densely knitted field of symbolic and social resources, it also takes place within a project-based, creative, and administrative community tied to particular spatial and temporal locations (Becker 2008). Boltanski and Chiapello (2005) have argued that 'the project' is one of the organizational forms most closely associated with high capitalism, and, indeed the creative stage of production often has the organizational logic of a project (Ryan 1992, DeFillippi 2015, Vinodrai and Keddy 2015). As in the factory, there is a division of labour, often with significant hierarchies and distinctions (Banks 2010). Specialized professional groups take over the performance of production activities, often with 'specialised aesthetic, financial, and career interests which differ substantially from the artists' (Becker 2008: 25). 'Primary' creative personnel,[3] craft and technical workers,[4] creative managers, executives, and directors, as well as 'humdrum' or 'mundane' labour provided by accountants, lawyers, and administrators, ensure that creative product is finalized (Caves 2000, Hesmondhalgh and Baker 2011).[5]

Cultural production reflects not only elaborate divisions of labour but also spatial distributions of functions: 'the city as studio, the world as backlot' (Christopherson and Storpor 1986, quoted in McGuigan 2010: 327). Certainly, the reliance on a functioning ecosystem means different roles and specialities frequently agglomerate, providing services and dense networks of social and informational contacts for each other (Grabher 2002a, 2002b, Power and Scott 2004, Currid 2007). Production is focused on 'specialised but complementary firms' (Power and Scott 2004: 12), dependent on 'clustering' and 'rich webs of traded and un-traded relationships' (Pratt 2005: 32). Once again, trends in contemporary employment relations permeate the organization of art worlds; Murdock (2003: 23) argues that 'as cultural production moves toward more project-based alliances and as freelance work becomes the norm, so command of social capital becomes an even more important resource'.[6] Individual creative talent on its own is insufficient, but requires a suitable geographic context for its dissemination and the networks to access this (Wittel 2001). The London-centric nature of British broadcasting is one such example: 'If you are not in London listening to the gossip then you don't know about it and you don't pitch your idea' [TV 53].

Although the creative process, as we have shown, is a collaborative affair, embedded in dense webs of symbolic, social, geographical, and material

[3] Hesmondhalgh (2002) identifies 'those directly involved in the composing, designing, imagining, interpreting and manipulating of symbols to create music, TV programmes, films, art, clothing, graphic designs, images and other forms of text' (in Banks 2007: 189).

[4] As Banks (2010: 305) notes, creative labour tends to focus on 'creatives' as opposed to craft labourers, thus denying the importance of 'craftsmen who help make art works [who] are as important as the people who conceive them' (Becker 2008: xxiii). Given technological change, the production and post-production of design, music, film and television is in danger of the workshop being replaced 'by the workstation' (Banks 2010: 315), creative work therefore forming a microcosm of ongoing debates about the degradation of labour under capitalism (Braverman 1974). The division of labour spills over into the division of rewards: the artist is valorized as the source of creativity, while the craft worker is 'usually debarred from royalties and denied the pleasure of consecration and fame' (Banks 2010: 312).

[5] Maxwell and Miller (2013) raise the important critique of the emphasis on a small 'cognitive cognitariat' at the expense of those, often in developing economies, essential for the material products that allow this cadre to function and be 'creative'.

[6] The influence of social capital has important impacts on diversity (see Grugulis and Stoyanova 2012).

resources, it all centres on the production of creative works. The creative process itself collaborates with a performative structure of property law to constitute original, authored IP. Only then can it begin to circulate in the market.

The Liminality of IP/IPR

For creative producers, the object of IP/IPR occupies a liminal position between a bundle of rights allowing ownership of a certain property and an object of value embedded in the symbolic orders of the field. It is simultaneously the result of collaborative production and a manifestation of the individual creative agency of its maker. This liminality becomes the source of IP's economic value, allowing it to draw on multiple, ontologically separate, and potentially contradictory reservoirs of worth.

We have seen that IP law, derived from a Romantic aesthetic of lone authorship, places the locus of production in the person of the solitary individual. This individualism is further reinforced by concepts of property; property rights attached to creative work demand, and therefore construct, a proprietor of some form. Creative work takes place within a market, and IP law offers creative producers a means of generating rewards for their labour. But the law does not necessarily match the experience and practice of creative producers. Creators have a sense of inherent authorship and consequently ownership of their creations, regardless of the context of their production. The law draws lines across such intuitions, and these lines may be further complicated by the industrial and project-based organization of production within their industries. In the case of work-for-hire, where one party produces copyrighted works for another, the legal default is that the creator of the work owns the copyright; an employer, however, owns works created in the course of employment.[7] At the same time, creative producers understand that creativity is a collective and collaborative act not well-suited to classification of a legally owned entity produced by a single individual.

First of all, let us deal with practitioner understandings of rights attached to intellectual property (IP) as opposed to the legal rights attached to specific property objects (IPR). There is what might be termed an 'intuitive definition' of IP, an 'I know it when I see it' (George 2012: 71), that characterizes creative labour's understanding of the term. Perhaps reflecting the legal difficulties of defining IP, creatives use a combination of allusions to the self and intuition.

[7] This varies with jurisdiction. France, for example, takes the default approach that ownership lies with the creator.

Implicit within these terms is some concept of authorship, particularly related to notions of artistic signature and the self. Cohen (1992: 182) identifies an authorial identity as a 'right to selfhood': the 'authorial self' is a 'self-directing' individual (Cohen 1992: 179). 'Authorship' is the institutional link between the creative labour process and the creative work. It locates a particular kind of property in the person (Adkins 2005): where the law sees authorship as linked to originality and the first instances of documentation of a particular ideational form, the understanding of authorship among creative producers hinges on self-direction and artistic authority. Authorship establishes cultural work as a maker's property because it defines 'the distinctiveness and value of cultural work in terms of what the creator of cultural works already owned—his creative will or personality' (Adkins 2005: 118).

Authorship is inherently related to naming. A reflection of the legal attribution of ownership, naming encompasses the symbolic orders of the field and the artist's position therein, and the creative will embedded in the work. Because the distinctive aspect of cultural creation relies on, or reflects, the work of 'expressive, individual artists... artistic objects must appear as the product of recognizable persons' (Ryan 1992: 42). If not the named labour of the artist, an individual signature is paramount. Developing the creative voice is the essence of creative practice, as is recognized by the interviewee who asked: 'Where is the joy unless you are creating something that is... idiosyncratically yours?' [Dance 116]. Artistic content represents voice. Creative work retains the auratic element identified by Benjamin (1968). Voice is the product of authorship and through this represents 'truth' and 'authenticity'. A designer explained why she hand-moulds her pieces, despite the physical toll this labour takes:

> My boyfriend is always saying to me, 'You should cast things and make things quicker for yourself', because I am always getting sore bits, sore hands, sore shoulders. He says it would just make sense. It would cut costs I would guess, the amount of time I spend making the pieces. *But it would not be the same.* [Design 22]

The physical process of making the work is intimately related to her understanding of the work. Autonomous craft labour leaves space for signature, as this designer reflects: 'As a craftsperson your hand, your voice through your hand, is what makes the work yours and unique and interesting' [Design 12]. The focus is not commodification of an 'object' which may be made more quickly and with less labour through a manufacturing process, but the autonomy and authenticity of handcrafted production. This is a sentiment echoed by a jewellery designer who rejects using external manufacturers:

> I have real control issues. It is my design and I want to make it and I want to make the customer happy. People, I think, are buying into you as an artist. They want a

> piece of your jewellery, not a piece that [X] can mass-produce for you. It is not just about the design, it is about who has made it. When you register with the Assay Office you register as a jeweller and you get an individual mark which is related to you. This is not a registration of a design, it is a *registration of its authenticity*, in terms of the materials used and who made it. [Design 14]

Here, legal attributions in the form of the maker's mark become entangled with symbolic attributions of authenticity and quality. The intimate relationship between creator and creation is part of the signature of the piece, the aspect that gives it a unique identity, authenticity, and value. Ownership, this embodied artistic will, is handled through mutual respect among those in the particular community, in that creative producers 'accept or pretend that intellectual property is akin to something with a physical or "real" existence' (George 2012: 8). Creative goods are often ascribed with an existence independent of the creator, but one that remains symbolically linked to them. The 'work' has a concomitant expectation to be treated properly and respectfully, as seen in this description of a dance work devised by one dance company but toured by another: 'They were very happy for us to continue touring the dance. They knew that we would look after the work' [Dance 122].

As these quotations indicate, artists are also aware of the *economic* value of their work as market objects. It is authenticity and signature that make work valuable. The sentiment might be expressed obliquely with the claim that work is unique and interesting—but of course, uniqueness and interest are attributes of commercial value within a particular art world (Ryan 1992). The point is more strongly made by the designer quoted who claims to be making the customer happy, and points out that the customer is 'buying into you as an artist'.

Within the market for creative goods, actors simultaneously manage IP, embedded in social and symbolic relations, and the more formal prescriptions of legal IPR, as artworks begin to circulate in the market. We can consider the IP/IPR nexus as a further moment of liminality, with the economic value of formal rights constituted by the symbolic worth folded into the work. The following quotation shows the work under discussion occupying a liminal position between these two regimes, as two choreographers discuss the rights accruing to a jointly produced piece. The existence of the 'work' as an independent entity provides a means of moderating the discussion:

> The idea for the piece came from being involved in a workshop—being put with another choreographer, working away for 10 days, people being interested in the work. We kept working on it together and so right from the beginning we were equal co-authors. Then there was a point where we talked about it growing and going further. We are down as co-creators, co-choreographers. But the other choreographer was becoming more interested in setting up his own company,

> which he did. The two companies, and the two co-authors, needed rights. If we are doing it in our separate companies we have to try to agree to do it as close to the original as possible. The other choreographer said at one point, 'We have to uphold the design and as co-creator we have to uphold each other's creation'. But also, he was saying, 'What if I want to change it? I want creative freedom'. Eventually I said, 'Okay, but you cannot call it [X]'. Because you cannot. Eventually the penny dropped. It wasn't just about me and him and what we had done. It is about the whole thing. [Dance 120]

The liminality of IP/IPR is reflected here, as creative ideas (IP) finally result in a piece of work that generates IPR. Legal issues over ownership of the collaborative product of the two dance companies involve trying to specify exactly what is being protected, bringing the realization that the dance is a production process as well as an object in final form. Ownership is informed by, and related to, such notions of the integrity of the product, the 'IP', rather than solely being informed by an interest in 'property', 'IPR'.

Ownership inevitably becomes a problematic and contested term: linked to signature and self-direction, imposed over work the creation of which is likely to be collaborative and take place over a period of time. The ascription of ownership references property, and with this the connotation of private property, material goods, land, or capital. Concepts of property also map more directly onto the perceived boundaries of things (Cohen 2012: 18), conceptions which are alien from the 'everyday ways in which situated, embodied subjects experience their culture' (Cohen 2012: 6), as expressed here:

> IP is always a grey area in dance because dancers put so much creation into the work and they are left out of the loop. Dancers are quite often writing the work as much as choreographers, because they are the ones who are then performing it. Without them... steps are like nothing. You don't go in with a script. You go in with an idea, where the dancers contribute a lot. Some choreographers have everything worked out and they go, 'This is it'. But when you work a lot with dancers and see what they bring, I think the [dance] is a shared thing and the idea of owning these steps does not really make sense. But they don't own any of that property. Because copyright is really all about ownership isn't it? It is maybe a generalization, and maybe I am just in my own world, but it feels as though it is quite alien [to] the community of performance and the way that people work in dance. It feels like something [where you would say,] 'Do you know that is "mine"?' It is not a way of working that I am used to. It is not that I don't accept that it isn't—of course it is your [dance]—but the fact that it is brought up. I think that is maybe not a failing on our side, but we are not used to it. We are not used to speaking like that. [Dance 117]

In this example, the process of seeing something as belonging to an individual is not a common way of speaking in the sector; it is not part of the process through which creative output becomes understood or known. The concept of ownership has no place within a community. At the same time, however, conversations over IP are *always* about ownership, precisely because of the inalienable nature of attachment to one's own work. Creative producers therefore see claims of IP/IPR in terms of their own individual knowledge and expertise. They understand IP/IPR as embodied knowledge, as in a simple statement of self and authorship: 'I would say that it is me, because I am at the hub of everything' [F&T 27]. IP rights are here described in terms of the self—where the ideas or creations come from—and style, meaning uniqueness and identity. By this account, IP is intrinsic to the person. Responses are in terms of the intimate relationship between self and product. Interviewees strain to articulate IP beyond their own personal attributes—their 'ideas' and 'style'.

> I still struggle to know what it is. Partly because I think it is my character and my passion about what I do. I think it is my work, my ideas, and my recognizable style that people know. I would call that intellectual property. I suppose it is what makes us unique, it is what makes our business stand out, so yes, it is everything really. I find it quite hard to say, 'It is me. My USP is me', but that is what it is, I think. [Design 20]

Understanding IP in terms of knowledge, style, and identity suggests that creative producers might draw back from casting it as a market object (IPR). After all, style and identity are inalienable aspects of a person, not easily transacted in a market setting. The often-repeated remark that '[i]ntellectual property is an artist's knowledge' [Dance 121] would seem to signify the intangibility of such IP. Yet the liminality of IP/IPR is once again demonstrated by the following respondent, a knitwear designer who talks about ownership of this IP:

> We are working with traditional stitches a lot of the time, although we do invent stuff. We do it all the time, actually inventing new ways of doing things. But that is the IP within the business... we own that intellectual property, that ability to do that. Some of it is tangible and some of it is intangible. [F&T 34]

Some IP is tangible and some intangible—stitches and new forms of invention—yet the designer recognizes the property rights inherent in this knowledge, and thus its latent ability to be alienated and traded. IP is understood as the knowledge, largely embodied, that renders products possible. It is acquired through training and resides in the skills and knowledge of people; there is concern when it is lost to competitor organizations, if for example, the business loses graduate placements to poaching. The economic significance of the IP, its potential to generate value and be enmeshed in more formal, tradable IPR, is not lost on these individuals. It is the building blocks for future products, 'the things that we could reuse... the techniques we learned or some of the things we can do again' [Games 44]. It lies in the knowledge of personnel, integrated into a functioning process of collaborative production. The following quotation, from the video games industry, suggests that the real value in IP/IPR—as opposed to the superficial worth of a product that can be easily duplicated—is both embodied in the skills of individuals and embedded into the collective design team:

> I take a long-term view, so I think it is about building a team, building the expertise inside that team so that if someone does clone a game of ours, we could come up with something better and constantly improve. Someone can clone your idea but no one can clone the thinking and expertise behind that. [Games 46]

At the same time, those working in the games industry have a detailed knowledge and understanding of the law, learnt as the 'accepted' conventions of the field:

> Usually it is accepted that if the developer does not maintain some kind of ownership over the code they will at least get the right to use it in perpetuity. They will have access to it if not ownership, which is just as good really, because you can use it in any future products as long as it does not directly compete with the original customer's product. [Games 43]

And:

> You have to secure it, especially if you are doing something unique, you have to secure that as best you possibly can. Intellectual property is simple things such as your copyright, your trademarks, design patents, your normal patents. [Games 41]

These games designers are clearly aware of the multifarious, liminal nature of IP/IPR. On the one hand it exists as the skill of individuals and the organizational processes within the development team. These are the fount of originality, the true source of worth and competitive advantage in a fast-changing industry. On the other, IP is embedded in a nexus of social conventions and legal rights that allow developers to derive economic benefit from their innovations. Games designers manage a simultaneous dual vocabulary that matches the complexity of the IP/IPR nexus, zooming from social organization to legal tests in order to produce and protect economic objects.

Ironically, knowledge of the complexities of IP/IPR is embedded in the same social networks as those attaching property rights to ideational objects. Understandings may be 'vague' and workaday:

> I think I have a vague working knowledge of it, but I am not sure if I know how to define it. I suppose it is just who owns the copyright and moral rights to the work that we produce and having a working understanding and abiding by the laws of that. [Theatre 103]

There is some understanding of the formal elements of law, in that to be protected IP/IPR must be recorded: 'It is protecting your ideas and your designs, through trademarking or through design registration, the design protection of both drawings and three-dimensional pieces' [Design 1]. For many, industry associations (for example, the Theatre Managers Association for theatre or dance or Equity in the performing arts) are important sources of information about IP/IPR, often offering standard contracts to follow. For others, knowledge about IP/IPR comes from experience and 'learning on the job', accumulating the conventions of the field:

> We were one of the first people to commission him. I felt we were educating him as to how the whole thing worked. [We said,] 'We will pay you a fee and then we will have the rights of this for a number of years'. Obviously you don't want to take advantage of people just because they don't have that knowledge. [Dance 122]

Moral versus Legal 'Rights'

As we have shown, ownership—while clearly central to the production of creative objects—tends to be understood in terms of artistic signature, self-direction, and labour. Such conceptions of ownership point towards the morally significant issue of 'rights'. Although legally 'Moral Rights' is a concept created by a legal framework (Towse 2003, 2006a), non-legally enforceable 'moral rights' are experienced as deriving from the effort of having worked on an idea for a period of time. They are experienced through the act of authorship. The issue arises, however, as to the relationship between the experience of 'ownership' and 'property' as a moral right, and the legal framework of formal rights. Once again, these complexities are bound up in the IP/IPR nexus.

Moral Rights include the right to attribution, the right to object to derogatory treatment of a work, and the right to object to false attribution, and generally they coincide with the period of the work's copyright protection. They are influenced by the Hegelian view that 'a person should not be alienated from the products of his or her creative labour' (George 2012: 240). Some legal codes, such as that of France, explicitly recognize moral rights, including those of 'first publication, attribution, integrity, withdrawal, and the protection of the honour and reputation of the author' (George 2012: 153). These rights give the author protection against distortion, mutilation, modification, or derogatory action, even though there may be no claims to ownership. In the UK, moral rights cannot be sold or transferred, but they can be waived. In other jurisdictions, such as France, moral rights do not expire and cannot be waived.

Although legally defined Moral Rights arise from copyright law, as a sense of moral entitlement informed by the mores of a particular field, they are keenly felt independent of this, protected by social practices and understood as a social responsibility:

> An American choreographer created a work for us and our ex-artistic director wanted to teach that piece to his students, so he phoned up the choreographer and said, 'Can I have permission to do this?' But if he had done it without asking, *that would have been morally wrong*, I think. [Dance 122, emphasis added]

Crediting, permission, and appropriate use are important moral issues, even where there is no claim to formal rights, particularly where there has been commissioning. Crediting is the currency of 'releasing' products into the field, as is shown in this comment from a contemporary musician:

> One of the pieces we commissioned was recorded by somebody else, and they had not let us know. [As commissioners,] you feel a slight ownership even although obviously the composer retains the rights and we had put on a performance. We often feel quite a lot of investment in those works. We like to be credited, but we don't ask for any remuneration. Because you want the music to have a life—you don't want to hold that back. We just want to be credited. [Music 95]

This highlights an important aspect of 'felt' moral rights being recognized or 'credited'. Failure to credit is a sign of disrespect, taking advantage of goodwill: 'I have done choreography within theatre, a small aspect of the work, but then [I was] not credited' [Dance 119]. Credits act as a complementary compensation where monetary return may be limited: 'I can see that there is no money being made but actually I want people to know that is my work' [Design 12]; 'Dance and theatre are just about having the credit, the acknowledgement when there is not a lot of profit' [Dance 120]. As 'professional capital' (Caves 2000), formal recognition of authorship becomes the 'reward' (Towse 2010).

Acknowledgements of an identifiable artist or creative professional are 'the bricks from which the structure of a career and reputation are built' (Caves 2000: 107); moral rights thus reflect status and professionalism, as well as the preservation of 'image':

> I worked with a national theatre on a play as movement director. A New York production company bought the play. But when it went on Broadway, I did not get to work on the production. I was credited, so that was good. But [what I want] is control over artistic work as well... It is controlling your work and your image. They should be under pressure to get you back in and make sure that it looks like it should. [Dance 120]

However, the collective nature of creative production, of, for example, a script that has gone through many writers, or choreography, presents difficulties:

> I choreographed a piece and it had a further life. It went on tour. But I wasn't employed to continue the rehearsals for that and they re-cast and essentially

> changed loads of the material. But my name would still have been listed there somewhere in association with it. That made me really concerned because when people went to see the other version they were saying how it had changed so much. Then you feel that is really problematic. [Dance 119]

As we see, authorship is related to the integrity of the product. A name has 'sign' value; it is an indicator of quality (Ryan 1992, Mears 2011). As a symbolic currency, it translates reputational value into financial value (Becker 2008). Not wishing to be credited is not wanting to be misrepresented, to be devalued. This is difficult within some conventions. Within film, for example, co-productions name all co-producers regardless of whether they endorse the artistic interpretation taken: 'Creative co-productions are more difficult. Because if you are not agreeing with the direction of the material and how things are going then . . . it becomes an issue of reputation' [Film 67].

Someone reproducing a particular work is responsible for upholding standards because these are linked to the future economic value of the creator's ongoing work, as is reflected in the ongoing audit of productions where earlier pieces are restaged:

> I know with ballets—for example, the daughter of a very famous ballet choreographer, because he is no longer here, basically she goes and checks, when they allow other companies to perform his ballets—they have that time to go in and have a look and make sure that it is actually of the standard and it is all appropriate. [Dance 119]

Those with copyrights, and hence an economic interest in the production, also ensure the Moral Rights of the creator, i.e. that the work is not defamed or damaged in its reproduction.

Once again, the rights of creators to their own work occupy a liminal position. The value attached to an artist's work stems, as we have seen, from the creative signature of an individual. Authorship of IP is experienced as a 'moral right', even though these do not have the legal effect of Moral Rights. They are secured through the conventions of the field. Equally, moral rights ensured through ownership and in the first instance constructed by word of law are largely protected by social responsibilities. This emphasizes the importance of conventions of the field, which vary enormously in relation to formal rights.

This chapter began our journey through the creative economy with an examination of the construction of creative works (IP), from which flow associated rights of economic exploitation (IPR). The creation of goods for sale is a central activity of the creative industries. We have shown how IP/IPR acts as market device capable of mediating between several separate, ontologically distinct, and practically incompatible value structures. First of all, there is the notion of individual ownership, as performed by the law, itself influenced by Romantic notions of artistic creation and nineteenth-century ideals of property. We then discussed the reality of creative production as a collaborative, socially and materially embedded endeavour. Moreover, the value of artistic work depends on the symbolic structures of the field from which it can never be properly separated. At the same time, the act of creation itself—the artistic will of the creator—is understood to confer ownership, and this ownership is respected according to the social norms of the field. The act of creation gives rise to certain moral rights that organize collective behaviour still further. Finally, intellectual property is negotiated into formal intellectual property rights. These also exist in a liminal state, drawing on the symbolic and artistic notions folded into intellectual property as a source of economic worth. We argue throughout this book that the business of creative industry is the development and exchange of intellectual property: this chapter has explored some of the many mechanisms by which the IP/IPR nexus facilitates and performs creative products as market objects, and we will now move to consider how IP/IPR constructs creative producers as market agents.

Notes on Rights Conventions by Creative Field

For the **fashion** industry, copyright is often not the first point of call, as the utility aspects of fashion and design goods make them generally ineligible for copyright protection. However, aesthetic elements such as patterns on fabric, decoration of cookware, and other purely artistic elements do qualify for copyright protection. In the absence of copyright, the fashion and design industries rely on a combination of social norms, branding, design rights, and even a culture of copying to protect their works (see Chapter 7).

Copyright in the **performing arts** is typically associated with the right to perform or record a particular work.

In **theatre**, the scripts produced by playwrights have a number of copyrights, but key are the rights to reproduce (copy) the scripts themselves and to perform the works. Theatrical agents often negotiate these licensing agreements. The agreement will dictate the right to record, video, or live-stream a performance, or, rarely, the right to make changes to the script, or to perform it in certain geographical locations. Producers may seek agreements to 'license in' copyrights from other sectors, such as music. There are design rights attached to costume design. Copyrights applied to elements such as stage direction, lighting, and sound design are more ambiguous but these elements can attract copyright protection (Freemal 1995). There is also ambiguity around the creative input of performers into a work, which the legal structure generally does not recognize (Pavis 2016). Copyright in **dance**, namely choreography, functions largely the same. However, choreography often is an evolving IPR and is rarely presented in a manner easily recognized by copyright. Waelde and Schlesinger (2011: 260) note that, while copyright can be applicable, '[i]t is immensely difficult to institutionalise experimental, experiential forms of music and dance, that is, to establish stable, predictable relations of production and circulation easily susceptible to fixation or policy intervention'. In addition, the collaborative nature of dance and choreography, combined with the precarity of careers in the sector relying on a recognized name, mean that financial incentives associated with copyright ownership are not always at the forefront of artists' minds.

Computer games is a 'born digital' sector, in that it has only ever existed in the context of digital technologies. It is largely still developing its own IP practices, but is probably most similar to film in that games also rely on the input of other sectors including music and images, which are often licensed in. Copyright is important for the sector as it protects the images, artwork, and dialogues of games. Trade secrecy also is important, as it may serve to protect source code. In computing, 'ideas' may be incorporated in processes and procedures, and methods of operation. As Cohen (2012: 75) notes, '[p]rocedures and methods of operation expressed in computer micro-code are very difficult to separate from their concrete instantiations'. While code is generally copyrightable, copyright protection has limited effect as the copyright covers only the expression, and not the system or process—which is where the value in code lies. Likewise, trademarks can be very important as game franchises may enjoy significant profits from merchandising and the licensing of characters, etc.

The **publishing** sector, which includes book, newspaper, and magazine[8] publishing, largely uses IPR as a means to license in and out content; indeed, it is axiomatic to the operation of the industry:

> To understand the publishing industry is to understand copyright, without which we cannot operate. It is fundamental to our business because the intellectual property that is concerned with a book, or a book-like product, usually is the actual written text, which is the copyright of the author and which, as the publisher, we are there to exploit. We are basically there to promote it on behalf of the author who owns the copyright. [Publishing 84]

Unless self-published, copyright is usually assigned to the publisher, but other associated rights might not be (see Chapter 5).

Television production and broadcasting, like games and performance, also licenses in content in addition to generating its own copyrights. There are copyrights associated with scripts, filming, film stills, recordings, music,

[8] Some definitions of publishing include the music publishing and digital content sectors, but for the purposes of this discussion music publishing will come under the music sector.

and images. It is a generally sophisticated system and heavily influenced in the UK by the Communications Act 2003, which ensures that independent television producers retain their copyrights when working with broadcasters.

> The Communications Act was a massive step change. It kick-started this whole Indie Revolution that has happened, and very successfully I think for Britain as a creative economy. What that means is that we are the authors of our work and as authors we would always be the first owner of that work. Previously when we entered into a contract with a broadcaster they would have acquired that ownership and we would have had no real interest, say, for some income backwash from the rights exploitation. Now we retain ownership and we license that to them on a limited basis. It depends on the broadcaster how limited that is. Public service broadcasters—unfortunately there are only four, you are talking about BBC, ITV, Channel 4, and Channel 5—their licensing arrangements define them as broadcasters and their terms of trade are governed by OFCOM and they are required to take a licence rather than an acquisition. Sky and every other broadcaster in the world take an acquisition of rights. The terms of trade only apply to terrestrial broadcasters and as a result, other broadcasters such as Sky can still demand ownership. Independent producers must negotiate these deals. [TV 55]

The practice of IP in **film** is similar to that of television. However, the importance of using windowing strategies heavily influences licensing agreements. Different 'windows' are strategically used to target different audiences at different times. For example, a film may have a box office release, and then be made available via DVD or electronic downloads, before being put on the market for renting. Copyrights underlie these licensing agreements, as the reproduction, performance, and rental rights are restricted by copyright.

Music has the most sophisticated and well-established IP practices. Collective Management Organizations (CMOs) dictate the flows of licensing revenues across a large portion of the sector (see Chapter 6). Copyright practice in music takes advantage of the basic right to copy, reproduce, rent, import, or distribute, in addition to the host of related rights in performance, broadcast, translation, broadcast, and moral rights. Different contributors to music produce different types of rights. Songwriters and composers, for example, generate copyright in the lyrics and the sheet music, which translates into a right to print copies of the lyrics/sheet music, the right to distribute copies, the right to perform the music publicly, and the right to make a derivative work. This is in addition to the moral rights associated with the music. There are also rights associated with recorded music.

3

IP/IPR and Economic Agency

The previous chapter explored how IP/IPR assembles a market object that occupies a liminal state between legal constructions of individual ownership of creative activity and the everyday work of creative producers within dense networks of social and symbolic capital. As creative producers consume and rework symbolic objects, IP/IPR mediates between the individual and the collective, allowing legally tradable market objects to surface, detached from the circumstances of their creation. It serves to disentangle the creative product from its social context, allowing it to travel through the market, while at the same time, that very same social context provides the content and value of the creative work.

The present chapter considers the other side of this dyad, the construction of economic agency among creative producers. We come to understand that the creative product is a process, reflexively coordinated between buyers and sellers (Callon et al. 2002). We show how IP/IPR becomes a vital device in the assembly of an economic market for creative products. Economic theory suggests that IP law provides incentives to create, yet it offers limited empirical evidence to demonstrate the efficacy of IP rights and more than a little conceptual difficulty. Our data, however, suggest that IP/IPR does have effects. While it does not offer simple incentives to produce, IP/IPR configures calculative economic agency. It introduces a temporal dimension to the productive activities of creatives—central to economic calculation—and helps agents to distinguish tradable assets and disentangle themselves from them. IP/IPR is a central mechanism through which such translations are made, as goods are categorized and stabilized in the marketplace.

The coming to economic agency on the part of creative producers must be understood in its broader political-economic context. As market actors become economic agents, so they enter—perhaps unwillingly—the domain of the 'entrepreneur' and the 'entrepreneurial', a process exemplified by the policy engagements cited in our introductory chapter. Yet entrepreneurship and associated theories of human capital have been understood as disciplining mechanisms under high modernity (Foucault 2008); the reality of autonomous, creative self-employment is often one of precarity, long hours, and low wages. The central part of the chapter deals with creatives' experiences of coming to entrepreneurship and shows a profound ambivalence towards the term, with some rejecting notions of business entirely, while others embrace commercial astuteness as a way of building and developing the sector. For this latter group, there is a moral responsibility to being financially literate—perhaps exemplifying a particularly productive creative subjectivity.

Economizing Actors

We have already seen that two competing theories provide economic and legalistic justifications for IP rights. In both cases we noted that the law demands an individual as the holder of those rights and therefore constructs the solitary creator of artistic work. The economic argument is that IPR provides an incentive to create. Here we briefly turn to economics of IPR in practice and the limited evidence of their efficacy. We will discover that IP/IPR is unexpectedly performative (Callon 1998): it is a crucial mechanism for configuring economic agency among creative producers.

Nuanced economic approaches to an incentive-based theory of IP point to the mechanisms by which it incentivizes creation and stimulates innovation (not all of which apply to the creative industries). Granstrand (2006), for example, identifies six key schools of economic thought: incentive-to-invent (focusing on encouraging investment in R&D), incentive-to-disclose (encouraging innovators to make their works public for both use and building of knowledge), incentive-to-innovate (focusing on innovation and competition), prospect theory (encouraging the efficient exploitation of resources), joint incentive-to-innovate and diffuse (encouraging continued innovation), and IP as a governance mechanism (incentivizing and organizing for governance and management).

Economic theories recognize a number of unintended consequences of IPR. One is the propensity for it to encourage over-investment in innovation and lead to innovation races, where competitors may invest in developing the same innovation as they both chase after protected IP—with only one winner. While the notion of 'infinite variety' (Caves 2000) suggests that competitors are unlikely to develop the same work, this may not be the case with works such as translations of public domain literary works, digitization of images (e.g. multiple museums may invest in digitizing the same Andy Warhol print), or standardized sounds (e.g. the works of Foley artists). While some fields have negotiated common practices to avoid such duplication of efforts,[1] the re-duplication of effort is an inefficient and wasteful consequence of markets that increasingly resemble winner-take-all, or 'tournament' markets (Frank and Cook 1995). Ironically, the social nature of creative production, with ideas embedded in discussions and current trends, is likely to exacerbate the duplication of efforts.

A second challenge, particular to the creative industries, is the limited evidence that IP rights incentivize the creation of creative works (Towse 2013b). If creative producers are motivated by the intrinsic satisfactions of making art for its own sake (Caves 2000), then further, pecuniary motivation is not needed, thereby fundamentally undermining the incentive-to-innovate theory; creators would create in the absence of the incentives granted by copyright. Scholars have long worried that extrinsic, economic motivations will 'crowd out' intrinsic motivations (see, for example, Titmuss' (1970) spirited defence of altruism as a mechanism for procuring blood donors). In this context, support for incentive schemes hinges upon the appropriate design of those policies (Towse 2006b). Frey (2000), for example, argues appropriately designed arts policies incorporating extrinsic motivators can 'crowd in' and serve as complements to intrinsic motivation. Copyright and moral rights, and the associated licensing and contracts, may formalize recognition of creativity and thus satisfy the intrinsic motivations of creators. We have, claims Towse (2003), insufficient empirical understanding of the interaction between copyright and the motivations for creativity, and she notes the relatively inelastic supply of creative labour. And it remains difficult to see how creators are motivated by specifics of copyright policy: how, for example, can the marginal incentive effect of the last ten years of copyright protection (which apply after the creator's death) be accurately measured?

Yet copyright is undoubtedly important to the creative industries. It is, in particular, important to successful creators, as the A-list/B-list nature of the creative industries lends itself to an unequal distribution of financial rewards (Frank and Cook 1995, Caves 2000). Empirical evidence suggests successful creators earn disproportionately more than their less successful colleagues, with the top 10 per cent of literary authors earning about 60–70 per cent of total income; while the top 10 per cent of composers/songwriters earn about 80 per cent (Kretschmer et al. 2010). In addition, successful content is more likely to result in cross-media (e.g. book to film) and merchandising deals—both reliant on copyright to underpin licensing. The interested few benefit disproportionately from expansion of copyright as incomes increase, whereas the diffused many may not benefit at all, for expanding copyright means

[1] For example, the Marrakesh Treaty to Facilitate Access to Published Works for Persons Who Are Blind, Visually Impaired or Otherwise Print Disabled.

higher costs. Overall, incentive aspects of copyright are murky when faced with the unique motivations of creators.

Seeing in Time

The lack of clarity around the efficacy of incentives in terms of their intended outcomes should not, however, be taken as indicating that these incentives are without consequence. Throughout the chapter we argue that incentives attached to IP/IPR are an essential part of the construction of economic agency in the creative industries. They are unexpectedly performative, giving rise to the economic behaviours upon which they are predicated (Ferraro et al. 2005, Roscoe and Chillas 2014).

The ability to calculate with regard to time is central to economic agency: much creation of value within a capitalist economy is linked to processes of forecasting, and their corollary, of discounting (Muniesa et al. 2017). Technical devices bring new calculative dimensions into markets through the feature of temporality. IP/IPR is one such device. For Bourdieu (1998: 28), also, 'the acquisition of new temporal habits' is an essential aspect of acquiring an 'economic habitus', allied to calculation and anticipation. Orientation to time involves having a sense of being able to project into the future and plan accordingly. Bourdieu (1998) leverages this claim into a critical argument about temporary work. Casualization—common in creative industries—has negative consequences for potential economic agents. 'Casualization profoundly affects the person who suffers it: by making the whole future uncertain it prevents all rational anticipation'; casualized workers, he writes, suffer 'a blow to their capacity to project themselves into the future, which is the precondition for all so-called rational conduct, starting with economic calculation' (Bourdieu 1998: 82). To be able to project into the future, there needs to be a minimum of security in the present.

Indeed, creative producers are often reluctant or unable to project themselves temporally: 'The speaker positions herself entirely in the present and does not project her life narrative into the future' (Taylor and Littleton 2008: 278). Gill remarks: 'One striking feature from my research has been the inability of workers to imagine—realistically—their futures' (Gill 2010: 259). Her interviewees either portray a life of extreme success (champagne on a yacht) or complete failure. Radical uncertainty induces an inability to project ahead 'in a realistic or meaningful way', and is one of the 'hidden injuries of precarious work' (Gill 2010: 262).

Bourdieu's astute critique of insecure labour suggests problems for the functioning of the creative economy as agents are unable to deal with the necessary temporal dimensions of calculation and planning. Our data suggest that the IP/IPR nexus has a compensatory effect. IPR forces a degree of 'long-termism' into a situation where patterns of working life constantly reinforce short-termism. It contrasts with the dimensions of temporality that experience of the new entrepreneurial economy instils. For example, one aspect of anticipating the future is trying to pre-empt issues that might arise in collaborative projects. This is especially the case if there are no formal agreements on understanding ownership of input, or contribution to joint projects. An example contrasts those working with content and 'in the moment' against lawyers thinking of the range of possible future permutations:

> We were working with another company. We negotiated all the terms then we went to the lawyers and said, 'How do you draw this up?' We got three quotes. They were all about £2,500–£3,000. We were [thinking], 'Wow, that is quite a chunk of the contract, and this is fairly standard stuff'. But they kind of got freaked out about things like, 'Oh so they get all the IP to the characters in the story line' (so that they could exploit that in animation), and we get all the tech and the IP for the code. But the IP lawyers got freaked out. They were like, 'Well hold on, so what happens if you build something on top of that, who owns the IP, because the project is finished and who will get the revenue for that?' I suppose as lawyers, they have to. They were covering every possible eventuality, to cover their own backs basically. But it is important to consider the possibilities of what could be done with the original IP beyond that project. [Games 46]

In this example, lawyers, strategically focused on IP rights, strive to compensate for the games company's inability to see its contribution as a potential asset in the future. IP/IPR forces agents to extend their calculations into the future via a process of reflection on possible outcomes, known as 'future proofing'. While a rational economic agent would seek to transact as cheaply as possible, it may in fact be worthwhile spending more in the present to manage future uncertainty, whether in trademarking across multiple categories, or buying rights for future use of creative products across a range of media. Future proofing is the awareness of the need to cover any possible bases of product lines and third-party licences even where they may not be immediately needed:

> The [X] name is trademarked across five or six categories, publishing, software, games and play things etc. We can do games but we can also control merchandising, how the toys are made, how the t-shirts are made, how the hats are made or whatever. [Games 50]

Part of this process is forecasting the different media that might require a creative product. Music for film, for example, might be needed for a soundtrack, or for a trailer for another film by the same trailer house or studio, so all things must be anticipated: 'Thinking ahead we buy everything out as much as we possibly can, so that we don't have to ask again' [Film 66].

Learning to anticipate future outcomes as technological media change comes to be seen as a central skill of the economic agent, developed over a career. In publishing, actors try to capture rights for a variety of different platforms as they (potentially) evolve: 'It is attempting to put in some wording that would say, "all electronic or digital platforms in the future"—that kind of thing, so-called "future proofing"' [Publishing 76]. More experienced producers practise anticipating and securing issues as they arise: 'What I am understanding more of as I progress in my career, is that what might not seem very big four years ago, and probably wasn't, will start affecting you as you get bigger four years down the line' [Design 11].

Creative outputs may bring their own timelines, for the commoditized product must fit into the timescales of others and the sector:

> This film is going to be finished by the end of March and it will start to go out into the marketplace in May in Cannes and we will do some London screenings probably in April. It is beginning to have a, if not public, an industry life at that point. So I would guess by next September/October it will be starting to get distributed. [Film 69]

There is an intuitive understanding of time as a resource, as is illustrated by this identification of 'unnecessary' labour:

> I mean, from a technology point of view, my approach is always, 'Don't reinvent the wheel'. If there is tech out there, or platforms out there, that are good enough for us to use, then we will use them. We won't rebuild our own. Inevitably there are always holes. You think, 'If only it did this', and you can see how easy it is to get caught up in, 'Oh we will just build another tool to do it'. But actually that does not help you get what matters, which is product. [Games 50]

Managing time becomes more complicated with the need to combine several jobs and to regulate their flow (Gill 2010). Start-ups need to balance the time spent on paid-for work, developing products for others, and efforts poured into their own creative output. There is constant pressure to pitch for work, and 'a marked tendency to underestimate how long an assignment would take' Gill (2010: 254).

> The only way we can actually build a business which is scalable, is by creating our own IP. Doing stuff for other people is fine up to a point. But it is not what I want to do. It is not secure. It is not stable. You can use it to generate funds for your own thing but if you get on to that treadmill then you can get stuck pretty quickly. It is really about balancing two sides. The work-for-hire is the bread and butter. The self-publishing is the fun bit. Well, it is the part that most people want to do. It's how you break out of that circle. I have never yet found the right balance between trying to juggle those two sides. You have to do one or the other, and it is a tough decision to make. [Games 50]

As 'contract work just keeps the cash on the table' [Games 43], it also raises difficult issues of cash flow, project management and timing. Time budgeting is important as are other business and self-management skills. With this, as Lazzarato (2007) notes, the clear-cut distinction between wage-earner and entrepreneur is increasingly irrelevant, with cultural workers adapting to the demands of cultural production as well as bringing their own projects to fruition: 'They are neither wage-earners, nor entrepreneurs, nor freelancers. They combine their different functions without necessarily being confined to any single one of these categories' (Lazzarato 2007: 9).

Recognizing the need for balance introduces the concept of opportunity cost, i.e. the time spent on one activity entails neglect of another, and with this the need to set criteria and justify choices. This is especially an issue for games companies:

> We try to steer away from contract work, simply because any investment into another person's project means all that investment we have spent goes somewhere else. We will probably end up doing some contract work in the not-too-distant future for cash reasons. A licensor we are talking to wants us to do something within one of their brands. We want to know what happens when you do another game inside a brand . . . so we will be getting the knowledge. It would be a mobile game, so we would be doing that because they are not a mobile game studio and that is the different type of value exchange. But I would quite like it if I could keep us away from contract work. Contract work is the slow death for us game companies. [Games 49]

Time is an investment. Choosing one activity means forgoing another. Choice introduces calculation. Action thus has its price. Although interviewees may not deploy the vocabulary of opportunity cost, they are aware not only that time spent on other projects means less time for company products, but also that this should only be compromised when there is a learning opportunity. The individuals are learning to be 'the entrepreneur of their own labour' (Bröckling 2016: xi).

Distinguishing and Securing Assets

Creative producers learn to appreciate the temporal dimension of their work through IP/IPR. The same calculative nexus also allows them to understand how assets are individually distinguished and constituted as valuable through a legal process. Students, for example, who 'have just been making films in their garage and putting them up on YouTube and not considering any [ownership] stuff because making money or paying for anything was never a consideration to them,' have 'to think about the work in terms of future possibilities of commercial return' [TV 63].

A teacher describes a process of helping students to see how

> their film and their own profile, how that is tied up with IP and clearance—by being able to show their work to other people at shows or at festivals, where there may be restrictions because of a failure to get permission to use a music track. It is also about them shifting from consumers to producers because for so long, and probably still, they are finding the site where they can download something if not illegally, perhaps slightly unethically, and watch it. Now they are producers they have to find a way to make money out of their creative work. Sometimes they exist in two planes at the same time, thinking they should be paid for their work but not paying for anyone else's work. [TV 63]

Awareness of IP/IPR is used to prompt a shift in persona, part of the development of a professional persona and identifying oneself as a member of a community.

In establishing property rights, IPR creates a durable asset (Towse 2002), with benefits accruing to copyright holders—in Caves' (2000) terms, *ars longa*. Assets, necessarily in the form of IP/IPR, secure future viability yet at the same time become the site for complex calculations of probability and return:

> IP management is going to become more of an issue when we start working with publishers. We have just come to accept that we are going to need assistance in launching our games properly. So, whenever we start dealing with publishers and they start talking about, do they want a revenue split or do they want IP ownership, do they want partial IP ownership? That is when it is going to become a bigger issue. Because, obviously, we want to retain the IP ownership so if it does well then we can use it again in the future. A lot of the time publishers will give you a better deal initially, if you hand over IP ownership. They will give you a greater revenue share. It is balancing the short-term and long-term. Sometimes it is just better to sign it over completely to get the bulk payment, so you can get to work on something else, and sometimes it is not. We are much more receptive to doing a revenue share partly because my business skills have improved. [Games 43]

The need to register and protect IP as an asset demands the exercise of foresight and becomes the site of calculative activity.

Securing IP is an essential element of ongoing business viability, especially with increasing collaboration across media, e.g. between theatre, film, animation, games, and digital in general, where collaborative IP issues are more salient. For some, however, the immaterial nature of IP/IPR, as well as the baroque complexity of the formal process, produces a reluctance to become involved in the legal aspect of ownership:

> Especially when you are starting out, I think you could call it overly complex, a pointlessly complex legal framework that has to surround IP for the obvious reason. You cannot touch it. You cannot smell it. You cannot feel it and therefore its ownership is more intangible and a little bit more opaque than it perhaps would

> be if it was a pen. You know: 'I own this pen. It is my pen. You have stolen my pen and I want my pen back'. Protecting yourself with lawyers, with contracts, with agreements that are very specific as to the nature of what you are doing with the material, are very important from the beginning. If I were to give advice to my younger self, or my emerging or coming-into-the-business self, it would be to start at a very early point in protecting the material that I want to develop, especially material that may be generated by someone else. [Film 67]

As Bröckling (2016: 88) notes, '[f]riction-reduced exchange requires above all, clearly defined property rights—if people want to buy and sell things they must know to whom they belong, what belongs to whom.' Ownership of IP must be settled clearly, even within a working relationship, as in this example:

> There are some things that you do need to protect, and you have to know clearly what is yours and what isn't yours. Particularly where we work, in areas where we are given a brief by a designer, then we do not have the IP right in that work—that is purely technical development; that is development and production. But if we are asked to collaborate and design then the IP is different, and that we own. [F&T 34]

Protection of ownership involves future proofing for any and every eventuality, as this film example demonstrates:

> I would say out of a bit of experience, be careful about your co-production, because companies go down. People die. I actually make provision for dead co-producers, because I have seen it happening. I have seen companies going down that you would never expect. The only way to be absolutely certain, is that if the company goes down the rights revert to you. [Film 66]

The literature offers limited evidence that IP incentives have a direct effect on creative producers, especially as they are motivated at least in part by intrinsic, art for art's sake motivations. Our study shows, however, that IP/IPR is unexpectedly performative: it produces aspects of economic agency. Creative producers develop a temporal aspect in their thinking, and learn to distinguish and secure assets, once again planning into the future. These are traits not much associated with the artistic vision; they are the traits of the creative entrepreneur.

Disciplining the Creative Self

We have suggested that IP/IPR is a market device capable of coordinating the economic agency of creative producers, through such mechanisms as attention to temporality and the singularization and valorization of assets. Such calculation requires a competent, well-calibrated market agent, as well as a ready supply of market goods that are alienable and ready for exchange. IP/IPR supplies both the actor and the goods. We must be aware, however, that IP/IPR also coordinates, at least in part, the disciplinary mechanisms of the enterprising self within the creative industries.

Within economics, entrepreneurs play a distinct role in the operation of markets (Bröckling 2016: 66), as 'discoverers of speculative profit opportunities', 'innovative creative destroyers', and 'risk takers'. They are transgressors. The entrepreneur also stands as a function in economic theorizing to explain 'imperfections' in the market (Görling and Rehn 2008). There is a tendency to fuse concept and practice (Lindgren and Packendorff 2003), and in the literature the entrepreneur often becomes an embodied, often embellished, characterization of an identified role. Gill (2010: 253), for example, identifies entrepreneurialism with economic organization of microbusinesses and independents, but also with the 'habits, dispositions and mentalities' of 'aspirations to innovate, create and be pioneers'. The entrepreneur stands in the shadow of Schumpeter. Being entrepreneurial is associated with the 'enterprising qualities' of, *inter alia*, autonomy, self-reliance, flexibility, and being risk-taking rather than risk-averse (Bröckling 2016, McRobbie 2016). Indeed, '[i]t is precisely the capacity to seize on what is novel and also to carry it through to its completion that is the characteristic of the entrepreneur' (Swedberg 2006: 246). Entrepreneurial activity, in other words, is defined by market success (Bröckling 2016).

Following Foucault (2008, Read 2009), another strand of debate has informed discussions on the experiences of 'Me & Co'. It identifies *homo oeconomicus* as the particular 'subject' of neoliberalism, a particular production of subjectivity, constituting individuals as human capital. Transformations in capitalism result in transformations in subjectification (Bröckling 2016), capitalization helping to 'turn the worker into a kind of multi-purpose business' (Lazzarato 2007: 7). As a source of capital and revenue, the worker is a producer and entrepreneur of themselves. Indeed, Bröckling (2016: xvi) identifies human capital theory as reconstructing *homo oeconomicus* as an entrepreneurial self, *homo oeconomicus'* offspring (Bröckling 2016: xiv). For those emphasizing the subjectification or governmental role of interest in entrepreneurialism, discussions of the 'enterprising self' and a 'talent-led economy', 'populated by youthful individuals who demonstrate a perpetual capacity for energy, creativity, resourcefulness, resilience and enterprise' (du Gay and Pryke 2002: 14), must be placed within the context of 'delayered' organizations and the growth of non-standard, casual, unstable forms of employment (McRobbie 2016).

As we noted in Chapter 1, 'creatives' are identified as individual producers, 'paradigms of entrepreneurial selfhood' (Ross 2008: 32). It is a perspective that has engendered the term 'cultural entrepreneurship', understood by Swedberg (2006: 260) as 'the carrying out of a novel combination that results in something new and appreciated in the cultural sphere'. Some have identified the 'cultural entrepreneur' as providing an antidote to any association of entrepreneur with the calculating, cost-benefit maximizer allocating scarce resources, i.e. with *homo oeconomicus*. Bröckling (2016: 67) suggests that 'entrepreneurial activity begins precisely where cost-benefit calculation stops'. The creative role ensures that entrepreneurs identify 'new possibilities', opportunities for 'profit' in their cultural offerings and the 'pitch' or 'slant' they cast on them. They are entrepreneurial in terms of pushing back limits of what went before artistically. They are *homo agens,* offering 'creative innovation'. In a twenty-first-century reinvention of the Romantic myth of the lone artist, these aspects 'distinguish the entrepreneurial function from the calculating, instrumentalist, rationalist.... Entrepreneurship finds its model rather in the artist genius' (Bröckling 2016: 75).

The Ambivalence of Creative Enterprise

The adoption of the enterprising self—of Me & Co—is an undertaking rich in ambivalence. Notions of 'good work'—of autonomy, creativity, and the rejection of purely economic concern—circulate alongside other concerns that demonstrate the responsibility for staff and to the sector, and the ability to manage business activities. Business itself is a contested territory. The specialist knowledge and vocabulary of business discourse presents 'a form of representational and technological... practice that constitutes the spaces within which... action is formatted and framed' (du Gay and Pryke 2002: 2). Creative producers think of 'business' as a discrete field, and have some familiarity with 'business terms' but these are used vaguely, even apologetically. The 'business model' is acknowledged as something one 'should probably have'—'the business model, well, "model" might be gracing it with too sophisticated a term' [Film 69]—and becomes pragmatically retranslated into 'doing what one does'. 'Most people who I know that do this sort of thing are self-employed and they start to actually find their own way. There is no real business model at all' [Design 8]. There is also resistance to their use: 'I definitely do not have a business model for what I do, which is probably a problem. But it is the truth of it. I am an artist and I pursue projects because I am interested in them and also to generate an income' [Design 12]. Rather there is a tendency for 'DIY learning' on the job and through trial and error (Raffo et al. 2000a, Gill 2010), particularly where entry costs for start-ups are lowest and expertise in the creative abilities provides the basic investment: 'We were a new start-up. We had no clue what we were doing for the first 18 months. It was fantastic. The best education ever. Sink or swim. It is pretty much all about learning as we go through' [Games 49]. As Banks (2007: 60) identifies, the 'rhetoric of enterprise culture places great emphasis on entrepreneurial "war stories" particularly regarding rites of passage and "hard knocks" to be endured while building a business'.

Justified for artistic purposes, self-employment is also a means to an end in terms of securing an income. Creative producers are acutely aware of a 'logic of capital', namely, the need to turn a profit (Ryan 1992). The need to make money is just the recognition of 'basic facts' or the 'real world':

> Unfortunately, a lot of musicians, artists and writers still have this idea that it is somehow distasteful to create music and money. It is not about greed. It is about survival, and it is about making a basic, average wage from music. I just think that you have to respond to the world that is around you, and you have to be able to see where you really are. I mean I am not a Tory capitalist, not by any means, but I think you do, these days, have to have an entrepreneurial spirit and if you don't, as a musician, you are just not going to survive. You might as well start signing on now. [Music 93]

The entrepreneurial tag is ambiguous, reflecting both the compulsion of life in a capitalist society, and the possibilities it offers—survival and a basic wage set against the optimism of the 'entrepreneurial spirit'. Although an economic necessity, self-employment offers the prospect of 'good work', namely work that offers some freedom in what and how work is done (Hesmondhalgh and Baker 2011). In this, it is to be distinguished, as Keat (2009) notes, from 'decent' work, which refers to working conditions, remuneration and security. This sense of freedom has many facets, representing the 'desire on the part of the self-employed and the small business owner to be in control and maintain personal independence' (Baines and Robson 2001: 350). The autonomy of 'being in control' has attraction, regardless of the vagaries of precarious or poor rewards. One games developer places autonomy and creative freedom above the more entrepreneurial activity of growing a company:

> If I wanted to build a company quickly then I could go out and write a business plan and raise the money and so on. But that is not what I want to build. It is about picking the right products and picking the right partners and picking the right moments to go on your own, and when to do something with somebody else. [Games 50]

Creative labour offers another kind of 'good work' (Gill 2010, Hesmondhalgh 2010). It is a privilege to be a creative producer. For many, the primary motivating factor lies in the creative act, the belief in the intrinsic value of the possibility 'to be a creative individual, to be a director, to be a screen writer, to be a producer, to be a creative producer and to tell stories about the world in which we live and believe that they have validity, value and interest' [Film 67]. Many 'entrepreneurs' aspire to a form of 'craftwork', where they maintain control over the conception, design and creation of the cultural goods. Creative labour holds out the prospect of 'realizing [one's] purpose in the materials of nature' (Marx 1976: 283). 'Retaining ownership and retaining control of your work comes through choosing to run your own business. That is the purpose of having your company. That is the conscious choice. It is the only real way that you can have control over what you are doing' [TV 59].

The worth of the project, for the creative craftsperson, lies in seeing a project through all its stages. This might mean being involved, for example, in the film production process from the early script development stages, so that there is a deep understanding of the artistic purpose of the project, rather than coming to a defined project at a later stage and engaging in the process of trying to raise money:

> Some producers have been lawyers. Others have been accountants, coming at it from a financial engineering point of view. But I want to work with the writers, so we get to a stage where when I am being asked to actually raise money and produce the film, by that time it is in my DNA. [Film 69]

A business thus becomes a vehicle for the production of a creative project or product. It is the means to an end, a necessary construction to ensure that creative work can be engaged in to ensure control and autonomy. The aspiration for realizing a creative product becomes the justification for setting up a business, here a film production company: 'To own the means of production. To work on projects that I was interested in. To develop ideas myself. To have things that came from our gestation and development so that we basically owned the ideas' [Film 67]. Despite the process of trying to realize a creative project sometimes being recognized as 'an uphill struggle' [Film 67], the autonomy offers a privileged position: 'Instead of all the constant griping and complaining, I am incredibly fortunate in that I get to do what I want, create the work largely that I would like to do' [Film 67]. At the same time, creative producers reject the business aspects of industrial production and even the association with business:

> I love making things, but I am really terrible at running a business. I really respect people who can do it but I find it less creative. I find the constraints of what needs to be done to be mass-produced, would not suit me. I don't value mass-produced pieces. I am getting more and more inclined towards doing more art, one-off pieces. Things that make a bigger statement. I think the freedom of that and the excitement of that, for me, is much more important. I am kind of actually stepping away from anything being commercial. If someone said, 'I really like that piece, can you produce at least 10 more?' I would probably say, No. And I have said, No. This is terrible, but I am a really bad businesswoman. [Design 4]

The term entrepreneur is, therefore, replete with contradiction. While the figure of the self-entrepreneur is one of the key disciplining models of high modernity, the creative entrepreneur is a craftsperson who prizes autonomy and control and the attributes of preindustrial craftwork. Moreover, although creative producers prize their work for its ability to offer an element of relatively autonomous and meaningful labour, the circumstances of self-employment and microbusiness may seriously compromise that autonomy in practice. For example, McRobbie (2002) shows how aspirations for autonomy have led to disappointment, disillusion, and self-blaming among micro-businesses in the cultural sector. As Hesmondhalgh and Baker (2011: 66) note, 'debates about autonomy in the cultural industries have tended to focus heavily on artistic or "aesthetic" autonomy or a "professional" autonomy, where scarce and highly valued skills and expertise often grant those in these roles a high degree of autonomy.' Yet this autonomy, they conclude, is only ever partial: '[t]he intersection of the language of the market with film and television, especially from a writer's point of view, is never comfortable' [TV 59].

Further tensions arise from the commercial drive towards growth. Often, business and growth become synonymous, and business therefore contradicts the identity of the craftsperson: 'I am not a company that is interested in producing huge amounts. I am not a big company. It is just me, so I am interested in producing a very specific type of product. It is about handcrafted skills and it is also about expression, artistic expression. I am not too interested in having millions of pieces all over the place' [Design 5]. Decisions based on the difficulties encountered with larger-scale production are often reasons as to why designers choose to stay at a certain level, especially where growth brings with it responsibility to staff:

> I am not the business end of the company. I am totally not interested in it, which is probably why the company is just me. I don't ever want to be big enough to have a team to manage. It has to be me and one or two other people when I see a need for specialist stuff. Just now I can choose to do projects for other people. But if you have got somebody employed, you have to start worrying about paying them and I cannot do that. It is too limiting. [Film 72]

Employees present additional responsibilities: 'I got stuck in this trap before and basically ended up on this never-ending treadmill of having to find more projects to keep the people you have employed, employed. It is just horrible. I really don't want to get stuck in that again' [Games 50]. The speaker suggests that the managerial role of the identification and recruitment of labour, of devising payment structures and dealing with personnel administration, and organizing production, exacerbates the demands placed on the individual and detracts from the creative role. The managerial role is 'a treadmill... just horrible'. Indeed, there is resistance to expanding and becoming 'a business': 'I could produce a lot more if I did go down the line of having somebody in to help me. But I am just not generally organized enough. Because, that is the thing as well, being a manager' [Design 22].

As Murdock (2003: 33) notes, the 'oppositions between creativity and accountancy, personal autonomy and bureaucratic routine, have a long history in the professional ideologies of cultural production'. But while there is a tension, an uneasy accommodation, between the creative and the commercial side of a creative industries business, the exact nature of this tension is far more nuanced than a simple commercial/creative dichotomy would suggest. It has different facets and prompts different balances. Many interviewees do not define their work in opposition to business values, being critical of those who do not take the 'business side' seriously enough and understand commercial competence as a necessary precondition for artistic success: 'The decisions are always going to be about fiscal fluidity, creative control and ongoing business development' [Film 67]; artistic control and business development go hand in hand.

Within the creative industries, individual sectors have varying normative relations with commerce. There is, in the more commercially conscious arenas of games development and film production, criticism of those who are not sufficiently attentive to the business side of operations:

> I would say just remember it is a business. There are too many people in the creative industries [who] think more on the creative [side], rather than on the business, and that is very hard. I think the key to it is running it like a business. That is the main thing. You have to keep your costs down. [TV 60]

An excessive focus on the artistic or creative aspect contributing to the neglect of the business operations can be seen as self-indulgence. Once again, from the games sector:

> I think that the games industry needs to grow up and play like a business rather than people building beautiful things in their dark rooms. Very few companies have any sort of business acumen at all and that is why they go down so quick, because they are not managing their numbers. They are trying to make the game they always wanted to make. They are not watching their bottom line. They are not looking at their customers and they are not understanding project management. [Games 45]

The sector, characterized by a large number of smaller companies, is dogged by problems of 'scalability', stemming from a lack of interest in business skills: 'In terms of scalability, you see a lot of companies that have a reasonable success, but they cannot do very much with it' [Games 42]. Paying attention to business issues has a broader moral significance of needing to contribute to the overall state of the industry, as these two interviewees highlight:

> A lot of people don't want to be bothered with running companies. I have worked with a lot of producers who don't want to be bothered with that. But I am

> interested in ownership and how you pay people; what kind of working conditions there are and so forth. The industry is really unregulated at the moment. [TV 59]

> There is the myth that you cannot be business-minded and creative. The haggling is embarrassing. But I don't care. The more that I can take out of your pocket the more I am going to be employing my dancers. We are a business, of course we are. Let's stop apologising for wanting money. We want to make money. If we make money then we are happy and we can keep those dancers at the end of their contracts for longer and longer. When we go to Europe, we make money. We do the major theatres and we make money. We want to make money, of course we do. I remember a while ago people used to snub [X] when he started his commercial stuff. Everybody thought, 'Oh he is doing commercial work. He is on TV'. But he put his money straight back into making his dances. He did not pocket it. That is why his dancers were employed for so long. He put it straight back into his company. You look after a dancer and they generally look after you. [Dance 115]

The issue is complicated for arts organizations that rely on public subsidy, but even here there is the recognition that they function in a 'mixed economy'.

> Arts organizations struggle to reconcile an artistic driven organization with a business arm. You cannot run a commercial operation easily in harmony with an arts organization. Our expertise is not running bars and cafes. This business only survives on the back of the audiences coming in, so we have got to make sure that we have a healthy market going to the theatre. The need is to have a business head and to be much more aware of the mixed economy that you need to have to support these arts organizations. [Theatre 102]

Balance between artistic and commercial focus is also difficult in a practical sense. Microbusinesses and SMEs see the blending of managerial and creative roles:

> The difficult thing is having a holistic view over every area. You have got accounts. You have got design work. You have got production. You have got distribution. You have got marketing. There are so many different areas and I am sure a lot of small businesses find this so. You just think, 'Well, that in itself is a whole project, but actually I need to be in the studio. [F&T 35]

While some resist the tag of commerce, others criticize stereotypes of business-illiterate creative producers: 'I have always fought against the idea that artists are babies who don't understand things' [TV 59]. Ultimately, creative entrepreneurs recognize that the position of commercial ignorance is unviable:

> I think that I am kind of slowly but surely bridging that gap between conceptual artist work and commercial viability. There are so many artists that are brilliant at what they do with their work, but they don't know how to sell it, don't have a clue how to get their stuff out. [F&T 28]

Creative entrepreneurship is thus a highly ambivalent category. While critical scholars have understood the growth of individual enterprise as a disciplining subjectivity, others have made sense of IP rights as a framework of incentives for creative production. Our data suggest a more subtle picture: an ambiguity around entrepreneurship that struggles to marry the expectations of creative production as craft with the demands, and indeed responsibilities, of creative work in a market society. We now return to the central question of the constitution of economic agency among creative producers.

'Work' as Product

Business begins from the simple statement: 'Firms must produce products' (Aspers and Beckert 2011: 3). Equally, as Negus (2002: 118) notes, 'the possibility of gaining access to, participating in and becoming formally recognized within cultural production . . . is clearly dependent upon presenting a "marketable" product.' These simple statements, however, take the object 'product' as given, with the process of something becoming a product often overlooked. It involves, *inter alia*, the creation of an object *qua* object, thing, or entity. An entity must become stabilized such that its characteristics are understood and known within the community of potential purchasers: a product to be marketed. For creative producers the problem is particularly marked, as it is their labour—free, creative, and un-alienated—that must be transformed into products. The process of transforming creative labour into commercial product is enmeshed in dense social and cultural relations and is to a great extent mediated and structured by IP/IPR. We now explicate some of these processes from the perspectives of the creative producers.

'Ideas with Legs': Turning Ideas into Products

For creative entities to become 'goods', there is a process of 'pacification' (Çalışkan and Callon 2010). The pacification of goods entails 'objectification work' whereby entities become 'passive objects', objectified and detachable (Callon and Muniesa 2005). The transformation of 'objects' or 'things' into 'goods' involves detaching or disentangling them from their network of connections. As with any entity, each creative object is entangled in a network of relations, linked to the creator who creates it and the community, or the tradition, with which it engages. We argued in the previous chapter that creative producers work with symbols that have meanings in communities, drawing inspiration from their social context. IP/IPR occupies a liminal position between the acts of individual creatorship demanded by the law—for the law needs an individual to whom rights can be fastened—and the collective activity of the field that gives creative products their worth. A piece of textile, for example, is attached to the source of the yarns chosen to weave it;

the setting of the loom; the skill and aesthetic sensibilities of the weaver; the patterns used in its design. Pacification involves detaching the 'textile' from this entanglement such that it becomes a commodity fit for circulation and exchange and yet still retains the symbolic capital that gives it value. As Jones (2003: 149) notes, '[c]ommodification ... is clearly not a neutral process ... it is an active, transformational one', involving a series of active relationships dedicated to the conversion of original cultural material into a good. The law plays a role in this process of abstraction, constructing a legal entity and attaching property rights to it. Exchange requires the alienation of goods in the form of property: 'It is property rights which lie behind disentanglement—the key process which stabilizes products, detaches them from the networks from which they originate and allows for exchange—and which should be the focus of studies of the contemporary economy' (Slater 2002b: 237). Such is the foundation of economic and legal theory. Practice is different.

Markets thus rely on a process of abstraction, a degree of disentanglement, or reframing of products, such that they become alienable. 'Abstraction', however, is 'an action not an adjective' (Callon et al. 2007: 4). It is a process of disentangling and (re)framing, and the manner of this disentanglement (or reframing) is disputed: for Callon and Muniesa (2005), it is a result of calculation, not legislation. Artefacts become commodities when they are placed in a calculative space and compared with others. As one stage on the route of commoditization, pacification is a process of homogenization, the reduction of an object's value into an economic monetizable form.

Callon (1999: 189) writes: '[t]o turn something into a commodity it is necessary to cut the ties between this thing and other objects and human beings. It must be decontextualized, dissociated and detached.' For creative producers, disentangling a product may not be so easy: 'I think it is tricky for us as makers/designers because a lot of the pleasure is in making it, so it would be really hard to completely detach yourself from that part of the process. Although some people don't see that as a problem at all' [Design 22]. The difficulty of separating self from object is recognized by another designer, who talks about handing pieces to a gallery for sale: 'It is interesting, the whole gallery thing, because you do lose a bit of the ownership of the work and a lot of designers comment on that. You are handing over your work to a gallery and it is sort of *like giving away a bit of yourself*' [Design 19, emphasis added]. Recasting the product as IP is one way that creators are able to alienate their work. One games developer explains the process:

> Looking at [Game X] back when we started, it was obviously our baby. That was the first thing we ever did, and it was great. Nobody wanted to give the IP away. But now after having seen how it does and that we do need help, I am, and I think the rest of us as well, are more comfortable with just assigning part of the IP away. [Games 43]

The product, the first game created, is initially described as 'our baby'. Only later, when faced with the recognition that the company needs investment to be sustainable, is there the transition to describing product, firstly, as intellectual property, IP, and secondly, once it has achieved this status, seeing it as a form of property to be exchanged for financial support. The notion of IP facilitates a change from dependent offspring to alienable property. Perhaps this is not surprising. Appadurai (1986: 13) identifies 'commodity phase', 'commodity candidacy' (standards and criteria, symbolic, classificatory, and moral, that define the exchangeability of things), and 'commodity context' (in which things might be placed). Objects move in and out of the commodity state. It is just one phase in the life of some things:

> I took a lot of the designs that I had developed during my graduate collections and explored how to make them commercially viable. To make them relevant they have to be made up in fibres that can then be replicated and taken to the market. Where would I get the yarns from? Which mills would I use to weave them? How would that fit in with all those values that I had as a business? And how much would it cost? Are they commercially viable? Can I do the sustainable business thing? So there is a gap between the design and it being ready for the market and being viable. [F&T 32]

This quote nicely illustrates the moves made to overcome the 'gap' between 'design' and 'product'. This is echoed by another designer who makes the distinction between 'artistic creations' and 'products' in the description of her work: 'I think it is really encroaching more into artistic work. They are one-off pieces; they are not really products' [Design 4]. Here products are pieces that may be replicated, as distinct from 'one-off pieces'; products relate to production technique and *replication*. Yet the effective management of production requires its own set of skills:

> Production is not a complicated thing to understand. It is very complicated to do, and it is very difficult to execute, but it is not a complicated thing to understand. Get more things commissioned, make them so well that people want to come back for more, and that is fundamentally it. [TV 54]

There is, therefore, a distinction between ideas and the materialization of these into tangible, valuable, tradable products: 'Everybody always thinks, "Oh I had that idea. They have ripped that off". What we would say is that the IP is not just the idea. It is the spin and it is how you do it' [TV 56]. At the heart of the issue lies the distinction between 'ideas' and 'ideas with legs', or marketable ideas, the latter being those that have been made fit for market exchange.

> It will not be a perfect idea. They will have to go away and work it up. That is the difficult bit. A famous TV producer once said to me, 'We are not really interested in

> ideas. We have got loads of ideas'. I remember thinking, 'What is he talking about?' But I sort of know what he means now. Because it is difficult working an idea into a format and a thing that is going to work, and work in a timeslot. [TV 63]

Goods, be they high-fashion textiles or hour-long broadcasts of bakery competitions, must be stabilized, for position and 'fit' into the market. A product is the stabilized entity of a series of evaluations: 'the product, looked upon as an object, is the focus of evaluation and of negotiation between different stakeholders' (Berkeley 2003: 104).

In some sectors, the concept of a product is firmly established by the institutional practices that bring a creative product into being. A creative product does not begin its journey unless it is identified as a 'product' in some sense. In other words, its viability as a potential product is the determining factor as to whether it will begin the process of successful gestation and creation. If something is not seen as an incipient product, it will be starved of the wherewithal by which it may come to fruition. Broadcasting has such an understanding of new products:

> It is always market driven and it is never, 'Oh I would love to make a film about....' It is sometimes about that if you are working with an academic and the academic has a career on television, because the broadcaster wants the academic's next passion project. But most of the time it is not passion projects. Most of the time it is the result of a creative conversation. We will go in with ideas A, B and C, and they will like idea C. But they would actually like version C.1. That then becomes C.2 when we do it and then eventually it gets commissioned as Project D. So that is the kind of thing that happens. It is a product and a market for it, yes, because somebody pays you to make it. [TV 61]

Even here, once the idea has been understood as (potential) product, the production process may not be finalized, as this broadcaster explains:

> Even having ideas does not mean that companies are going to be commissioned to produce them, again because of the importance of the whole entity in ensuring the programme will be successful. Thus ideas, slightly modified, might be commissioned from other independent production companies because they have the skills to deliver [the programmes], either in terms of relationships with 'talent' that can ensure success, or occasionally, and more unscrupulously, because production companies have relationships with commissioning editors. [TV 56]

A product may be identified through interactions beyond the institutional practices of a firm, for example, with customers or potential users. The physicality of 'product' is so ingrained—even in the case of digital games design—that it may prevent producers identifying the 'real' product. In this example, a games designer explains how his understanding of product evolved from providing a quasi-publishing service that built games from user-generated content (UGC), to a development tool allowing others to build their own games:

> The business model was to convert user-generated content into games that we can shift, and if we can do it often enough to make a little bit of money, then a little bit of money in a lot of places makes a lot of money. But it then evolved. The business model of getting low-end games out and doing a small amount of sales—we were not expecting to get a hit; well, maybe one in twenty we might get a hit—but it was not working. You need to have a reasonable quality of product to get that 10 hits. To do that means we need to look at [a game] and go, 'Right—this needs a front end; that is the whole menu system; there needs to be a reward system within it; there needs to be structure to the game; there needs to be some form of competitiveness and replayability function within the game. You have to be able to monetize the game'.
>
> We were starting to realize that publishing had forced [Technical process X] into being a development tool. We started moving away from publishing, our core revenue stream, when we realized that our target was to move [X] from being an indie developer tool into a more professional developer tool. So when it was issued, we had the free version that had the basic functionality to allow you to make games, but they were limited. It gave you enough to make basic games or get an idea of how the tool worked. Then you had Standard, which allowed you to have a limited feature set. Then you had Professional, which started giving you all the features. [Games 51]

The physical concept of 'game' shaped how the company saw what it was producing. It was only after a period of time that it began to recognize its 'product' was the physical manifestation of the service they had been offering UGC producers. The ability to monetize products involved a 'rethink' of what the product was, a transition experienced by others in the same industry:

> If you have got a free game then you need to have lots of different ways for people to spend money on it. And you need to provide quite a lot up front and then constantly be updating. The games industry is now much more service-based rather than having this product that you buy. It needs to be maintained. The games have to change constantly. You still need to be maintaining the audience around that game. This is a service. Yes, we make products, but it is a service business. [Games 50]

Technology is also forcing more established creative industries to examine the concept of products, as this quote from publishing illustrates:

> Publishers are also experimenting in pushing the boundaries themselves. Children's publishers, for example, when they produce an app—is it an app? Is it

a book? Is it an app that draws on a book? Some publishers are producing books that come from apps. All of those things are challenging. [Publishing 74]

Stabilization: The Role of Categories

Having identified a creative output, transformed into IP/IPR as a product, the question then becomes, 'What type of product is it?' This is not self-evident. Callon et al. (2002: 197) distinguish between goods—where characteristics have been stabilized—and products, where the latter is 'an economic good seen from the point of view of its production, circulation and consumption'. The producer must produce something which will be recognized and understood, placed, or positioned vis-à-vis other goods, but is sufficiently differentiated to be understood as distinct. Differentiation is a 'grey area': an excess of distinctiveness has the danger of making a product uninterpretable by those who have to sell or purchase it (Caves 2000). There is a double movement: the producer must singularize a good, yet leave it comparable to others; new markets are constructed through extension and renewal of existing ones (Callon et al. 2002). The journey from creative output or offering to product involves the process of stabilizing the product through labelling an entity within a panoply of other products. Stabilization is a reflexive process shared between consumers and producers; in an industry where the construction of a saleable product, via the translations offered by IP/IPR, depends upon the reproduction and consumption of symbolic and social capital within the field, it is doubly so.

Classification is an important element of stabilizing a product: placing it in a category so that it might be easily located in relation to other products, establishing distinction and commensurability at the same time (Aspers and Beckert 2011: 16). Economic agents must learn the conventions of classification in the sector; classification upgrades a 'cabinet of curiosities to a body of objects sharing familial affinities' (Caves 2000: 329). As Aspers and Beckert (2011: 17) note, classification, or qualification, refers to 'the development of shared cognitive and normative understandings of the qualities of products exchanged'. Similarities are foregrounded, difference remains in the background, thereby carving out the 'homogeneous' within heterogeneity. This avoids too much 'splitting' (Kopytoff 1986). Too much 'lumping', appearing as direct equivalents of other commodities, and cultural commodities lose something of their uniqueness as individual artistic objects (Ryan 1992). Products have semiotic content and are reflexively qualified by producers and consumers: 'the technical, social, aesthetic etc. knowledge that goes into the production of a commodity', is also reflected in the knowledge that goes into 'the appropriate consumption of the commodity' (Appadurai 1986: 41).

In sum, 'commodities represent very complex, social forms and distributions of knowledge' (Appadurai 1986: 41).

Artistic language provides one means of structuring classifications in the field (Bourdieu 1987). 'First-order conventions' (core categories, poetry, fiction, or drama) are subdivided into 'second-order' (historical categories, e.g. rom com, jazz, or biography), with 'third-order' features and further subdivisions of second-order forms (Ryan 1992: 161). Yet concepts used to consider works of art, and particularly their classifications, are characterized by the most extreme indeterminacy (Becker 2008, Anand and Croidieu 2015). Terms for genres and forms are marked by vagueness and flexibility even when used by professionals. They are resistant to essentialist definition. Use and meaning depend on 'specific, historically and socially situated points of view of their users, linked to a situated and dated social universe, and also by the social position of users' (Bourdieu 1987: 206). The practical mastery of the specific knowledge, however, becomes part of the conditions of access into a field of production (Bourdieu 1987).

Most categories are institutionalized in industry conventions, as the following example from broadcasting illustrates:

> The BBC thinks of us as being specialist factual, whereas [Programme X] is not specialist factual. It is entertaining factual. The specialist factual stuff has a limited secondary market whereas the formatted factual—you know, you take a bunch of kids and stick them in a rehab place and film them for 10 days and turn it into 10 programmes—made us more distribution money than anything else ever has. [TV 56]

Within this example, the industry recognizes three different 'types' of 'factual' programmes, 'specialist', 'entertaining', and 'formatted', each with their own creative and content conventions, appeals, and audiences. These shorthand codes serve to communicate complex ideas quickly and efficiently (Beck 2003: 10); categories help producers, consumers, agents, and distributors navigate the market, and cope with the processes of disentangling and framing necessary to the realization of a market transaction.

Products are determined not only through relations of production, but also of circulation and consumption (Callon et al. 2002) to the extent that the product's identity is not immediately apparent even on final creation. Producers may impose classifications that may be accepted or rejected by consumers (Aspers and Beckert 2011: 16):

> We did a film with [comedian X] on his drug addiction recovery, and it did not sell as well as we thought. That was because, fundamentally, it was a current affairs story, and although it was funny in places, it was a serious film. I think that it was really about drugs policy in the UK and that is irrelevant to the rest of the world. [TV 61]

There are difficulties of ascribing 'bits of reality' into convenient labels. From the perspective of the company, the product was intended as a comedic and celebrity offering; in circulation and consumption, the film settled as a current affairs programme about drugs policy. From a commercial point of view the programme was unsuccessful for reasons out of control of the producer. Categories, therefore, are not self-evident, but best looked upon 'as a process of becoming rather than as an all-or-none state of being' (Kopytoff 1986: 73). As this example indicates, different product definitions delineate different markets, where 'each market/product definition is in fact a strategy' (Slater 2002a: 68). Redefining products alters the terms of competition.

Slater (2002a: 68) suggests that 'economic and cultural decisions have immediate consequences for each other; indeed, each is merely the reverse side of the other'. In contrast to economists taking 'products' for granted, and those culturist accounts seeing them as signs between readers and texts, it is important to see how things are stabilized or unstabilized, negotiated or contested, influenced by power relations and resource inequalities, the materiality of the object itself, and the economic and social structures through which it engages. Slater (2002a: 72) emphasizes the importance of 'the very notion of an object or product as a categorizable entity, to see how it can be fixed or unfixed, taken for granted or problematized'. Indeed 'destabilizing' particular products in order to re-institutionalize them around new product definitions is the function of a 'pitch' for the adoption of new artistic proposals (Bielby and Bielby 1994).

Classification and segmentation provide a means for creative producers to expand markets and develop new products, singularizing existing products by adapting them to different markets. They recognize that 'markets' are differentiated to match the categorizations of products. For example, this designer's original intention was to create different products for different segments:

> What I was intending originally was 'limited editions'. Then I would have the next category of products and they would be more retailable and would be batch produced. And then I would have wee things that would be really cheap, little things. So there would be a three-tiered product range. [Design 4]

Classifications of customers are heavily influenced by concepts of markets. Categories used to differentiate markets and their customers are largely imbibed from sector conventions and experience. Thus, there are 'casual' or 'hard core' gamers. Fashion may distinguish between 'trend' and 'modern heritage', the latter as:

> Someone who buys a more timeless piece. They are interested in design but it is more about detail, possibly yarn. It does not have to fit in with the trends. The

> other type of customer, the trend customer, is looking for new designs every season and we do that by offering different colour palettes and by also putting a lot of design into our collection. [F&T 33]

Customers may also be segmented by market participation and creative practice, as this example of a company making music databases for film makers illustrates:

> We have early adopters who are actually people who teach film and animation production. After that, we have prosumers who make films, and also consumers, individuals, but also companies, who produce a lot of film and videos as well. In the future we want to do versions for mobile devices, so like for tablet and smart phones, that will be the consumer mass market. [Music 85]

In sum, creative producers become sophisticated at identifying and working with the classificatory structures of their industry to stabilize IP/IPR objects and make them valuable. Product differentiation and market segmentation target specialized product lines to carefully delineated consumer segments. The ability to conduct this task of classification is simply the final aspect of a process of configuration of economic agency on the part of creative producers. Much of this economic capacity is distributed across socio-technical networks—the classifications that we have discussed, or the legal contracts involved in clearing and holding rights to exploit a creative work. Despite the limited evidence for the efficacy of economic measures in terms of incentivizing production, we have argued that they are unexpectedly performative and that the economic agency around which the incentive structures are designed emerges as a consequence of their implementation through the IP/IPR object. We also considered how, as creative producers become economic agents, they are incorporated in the disciplinary regime of 'entrepreneurship' and how their attitudes to business practices are often ambiguous. We now move to consider the role of IP/IPR in managing the uncertainty of creative production.

4

Nobody Knows

Managing Uncertainty

As we noted in Chapter 1, interest in creative labour has been informed by the insecurities and uncertainties that come with the loss of (organizational) boundaries as more and more individuals are 'encouraged to perform as "Me & Co"' and embrace uncertainty and entrepreneurial projects (Beck 2000: 3). Such experience is reflective of a broader transformation in the societal place of risk: greater levels of risk and increased uncertainty have been identified as the defining spirit of 'reflexive modernization' and the 'risk society' (Beck 1992, Beck 2000). In general, debate emphasizes the harmful aspects of uncertainty but in the strictest Knightian (1921) sense, uncertainty is not only a source of possible harm, but a wellspring of profitable opportunity. Indeed, the entrepreneur, for Knight (1942), earns rents through the exploitation of uncertainty.

Uncertainty has a historical trajectory and is a social construction linked to broader understandings of the field in which it circulates (Adams 1995, Tellmann 2016). In the culture of financialization, for example, an emphasis on the destructive effects of uncertainty promotes 'technologies of harm reduction', which serve to render uncertainty statistically tractable and economically valuable. Uncertainty becomes the basis of a market comprising the production and consumption of technologies for managing the ratio between risk and reward—in common parlance, insurance (see, e.g. McFall 2011, Fourcade and Healy 2013, Lehtonen and Van Hoyweghen 2014, Van Hoyweghen 2014). Uncertainty is thus made tractable, 'reduced' to risk, and, by making uncertainty 'known' or knowable, rendered productive, tied to an opportunity for profit.

Risk, in the creative industries and elsewhere, is itself culturally constructed: as Neff (2012: 13) notes, 'how risk is framed concretely shapes social practices'. The converse is also true, social practices shape understandings of risk

(Adams 1995: 81). More generally, it is well recognized that 'artistic labour is shaped by uncertainty,' (Menger 2014: 3). Caves' (2000) important study of the role of contracts and the organization of creative industries is underpinned by the aphorism that 'nobody knows', a quotation borrowed from William Goldman's (1983) experience as a screenwriter in Hollywood, referring to the unknown reception of creative products. The creative process itself entails great uncertainty, not least in the artistic project of 'pushing boundaries' or establishing a distinctive voice: 'Great art risks failure. But to be boring, predictable and safe is to guarantee failure' (Adams 1995: 2). Caves (2000) identifies two further factors that introduce uncertainty to the sector. Along with 'nobody knows' is what he terms the 'arts for art's sake' property of creative work: '[t]he creator... cares vitally about the originality displayed, the technical prowess demonstrated, the resolution and harmony achieved in the creative act' (Caves 2000: 4). Having motivations and values other than the merely pecuniary engenders the problem of 'coupling creative effort with humdrum commerce' (Caves 2000: 4). Allied to this, or exaggerating it, is the image of the creative process and creative producer inherited from Romanticism, with its refusal to compromise with non-artistic imperatives. In the creative arena, then, risk implies an inherent characteristic of the artistic endeavour, one that is understood and responded to intuitively and emotionally, 'following one's oeuvre'; whilst in the latter [i.e. commerce], risk comes hedged in approximations, allied to calculation it becomes translated into probabilistic outcomes, a quasi-measurable phenomenon.

Caves is perhaps guilty of two over-simplistic dualisms: between art for art's sake and the humdrum activities of commerce, and between overwhelming artistic uncertainty and a manageable commercial risk. We have already begun to problematize these distinctions. Our previous two chapters explored how the IP/IPR nexus gives rise to creative products and calculative agencies. This 'market device' (Callon et al. 2007) mediates between the individual and collective field, disentangling creative products and domesticating them for exchange, while at the same time maintaining the rich symbolic links to the field that give such products worth. Just as it performs creative products, so it constructs creative producers, allowing them to calculate temporality and work with classifications within the field. We also explored the ambivalence around creative enterprise and its disciplining of the entrepreneurial individual. The previous two chapters have, therefore, established that actors are always calculative and that their calculations are embedded in the socio-technical arrangements of the field (Çalışkan and Callon 2010). Art for art's sake and humdrum commerce exist not in opposition but in unstable, multifarious relations, a dialectic mediated by IP/IPR.

The present chapter extends this argument to explore how creative producers work with uncertainty, both to limit harm and to generate opportunity.

We show that risk and uncertainty are managed through the same processes of symbolic production that give rise to creative goods and creative agency, mediated by the IP/IPR nexus; as creative products solidify into market goods so the uncertainties are transformed—at least in part—into risks, and uncertainty management through the social relations of the field develops into the legalistic protection of intellectual property rights. We first of all consider the relationship between creativity, uncertainty, and entrepreneurship, before examining in turn how IP and IPR offer strategies for managing and exploiting the uncertainty of creative production.

Creativity, Uncertainty, and Entrepreneurship

The previous chapter explored the ambivalent nature of creative enterprise, as creative producers struggled to articulate the closely linked, but differing, concerns of business and creative agency. We showed how the responsibilities of Me & Co act as a form of discipline under late modernity, yet sit alongside the creative entrepreneur *qua* craftsperson. Discourses of risk and risk-taking are crucial here. The notion of 'risk-taking' has become synonymous with 'entrepreneur'. While the classical tradition associates entrepreneurs with the creation of 'new combinations' (Schumpeter 1934), Weber emphasizes the importance of risk, with entrepreneurship directed by 'the sake of making a profit, at one's own economic risk' (Swedberg 2006: 251). Entrepreneurial activity is allied with risk and uncertainty. For Knight (1942), it is under conditions of 'true uncertainty', where the future is both unknown and unknowable, that the individual entrepreneur takes risk and assumes the profit if successful. Making for 'future' demand in the market and bearing the financial risks involved in this production, the entrepreneur is 'simply a specialist in risk taking or uncertainty bearing' (Knight 1942: 129 quoted in Bröckling 2016: 72). Entrepreneurial activity exploits uncertainty and manages its incalculability (Sarasvathy 2002). This depiction also serves to construct the individual in a particular way. Risk is seen as being equivalent to choice, or taking chances, being active rather than passive; risk gives the 'appearance of choice, power and individual agency' (Neff 2012: 37).

Within this context, the creative producer has rightly been identified as an entrepreneur; when Caves (2000: 59) describes the decision to accept a manuscript, he suggests that the editor is 'playing an entrepreneurial role'. Hirsch (1972: 651) identifies the 'environmental uncertainties' of creative industries that function to create high risk: fundamentally the field is characterized by 'uncertainty over cause and effect relations'.

Lampel et al. (2000: 263) identify five 'polarities' that characterize this high level of uncertainty. These are the need to 'reconcile expressions of artistic values with the economics of mass entertainment' (see also Glynn 2000, Voss et al. 2000); the need for novelty that 'differentiates' without making something that is 'fundamentally different' from those within the same category (novelty ensures difference, but familiarity enables the audience to understand what is offered) (Mezias and Mezias 2000, Wijnberg and Gemser 2000); the need to satisfy existing demand 'while using imagination to extend and transform the market'; the difficulty of balancing vertical integration with flexible specialization in order to ensure the flow of creative product; and finally, the need to 'create systems to support and market' cultural products while ensuring that this does not 'suppress individual inspiration which is ultimately at the root of creating value in creative industries'.

The creative industries have traditionally addressed these polarities with a bifurcated industry structure: 'small-scale pickers that concentrate on selection and development of creative talents', while 'large-scale promotors, working with developed and tested creative inputs... undertake the packaging and widespread distribution of creative goods in pursuit of winner-take-all successes' (Caves 2000: 364). Partly this reflects the different management styles necessary for each stage in production; more important, it constitutes risk management in terms of who pays for what and when, thus determining who bears the greatest risk in the creative production process. As Banks (2007: 129) notes, '[f]or the major corporation, subcontracting or outsourcing enables the offloading of risk and development costs to the independent while maintaining control over distribution and intellectual ownership—key profit centres'. Thus, much of the work of creative development and management is carried out by an 'independent periphery' (Ryan 1992: 106). Outsourcing of production to sole-operators or medium-sized companies spreads not only creative but also financial risk in production. While corporations can pick and choose without bearing the financial costs of creative experimentation (Ryan 1992: 152), creators bear the costs of producing commodities that are 'high risk, likely to fail, and involve considerable conception costs' (Miège 1989, McGuigan 2010, Hesmondhalgh and Baker 2011). Although this bifurcation of creative production from promotion and distribution began early in the history of entertainment (Hirsch 2000), the recent 'vertical disintegration' of large companies, particularly in broadcasting, has spread the investment risk to the smaller and micro-enterprises, to the point where risk is a personal responsibility (Towse 2002: 10). Given the low chances of success, individual investment in training is 'highly risk-loving' (Caves 2000: 24); in the case of musicians, writes Toynbee (2003: 52), individuals 'carry the burden of buying their own equipment, or writing and rehearsing, and then absorb the risks of an uncertain (proto-) market until the unlikely event that they are recruited by a record company'.

Managing Uncertainty through IP

The Experience of Risk

Uncertainty surrounding the commercial exploitation of creative products also results from their property of 'infinite variety', for such goods display both vertical and horizontal differentiation (Caves 2000: 6). While vertical differentiation implies that one good is superior to a similar other, horizontal differentiation among goods is mapped by traits, moods, and styles. Uncertainty also results from the truncated product cycle of cultural commodities (Ryan 1992): where cultural goods become popular quickly, increased familiarity and popularity undermines their perceived value, thus adding to their decline and introducing a continual need to update and replenish. There is, as a consequence, a recurrent cycle of production and a constant reinvestment in artistic labour. Not only is unpredictability inherent to the product, it is also dependent on timing: '[c]ultural commodities are caught in the ebb and flow of fashion, with market demand constantly shifting under the impact of competition and the flood of new releases it generates' (Ryan 1992: 59). Just as the creative process is inherently uncertain, so the response of a future audience is also difficult to calculate:

> You might come up with a game and spend a year making it and it flops, and so there is no value in the IP. Or it does an *Angry Birds*. It is quite intangible. I mean, what do you need to have a hit game? *No-one really knows*. It is like the lottery. I mean, the chances of succeeding are very, very small.
>
> [Games 42, emphasis added]

In art forms that are considered more challenging, audience unknowability is enhanced, as in this example from a contemporary music ensemble, which holds performances in different 'non-traditional' venues such as museums and castles:

> The thing about our particular branch of music is that *you do not know* what is going to be a hit and that is problematic. I think me and the promoter sat down and reckoned that we would get an audience of 400 for [X] event. Maximum. Looked at before the event, that looked like a pretty vicious target. 1,400 people turned up. There is no way you can predict that. You don't know. You just don't know. Every single show you are not comparing like with like. It is not like going, '50 people turn up today', and 50 people will turn up. It just does not work like that. [Music 90, emphasis added]

Nobody knows indeed. While asymmetrical information between producers and consumers is well recognized in economics (Akerlov 1970), Caves (2000: 14) sees creative products as entailing a different type of asymmetry: 'symmetrical ignorance'. But this is not entirely the case. Creative producers work to develop IP. But this production is embedded in the social relations and symbolic structures of the field that helps creative producers singularize their goods: although it is true that 'nobody knows', it is certainly not the case that 'anything goes'. The social relations and constructions of the field provide a means for creative producers to manage risk involved in creative production. While risk is borne by cultural producers, there are patterns and consistencies of a field that help develop a degree of expertise in coping with uncertainty. Fields develop their own mechanisms, 'rules of the game', for calculating risk (Bourdieu 1993). Individuals make sense of the field's uncertainty by using the tools and language available within it, along with its mechanisms of calculating 'reward' or worth (Neff 2012). Uncertainty is guided by tacit knowledge of the fields' conventions. 'Rules of the game' signal a strategy of adaptive processes and experimentation, a process of learning over time as a means of adapting to uncertainty and risk.

Even the creation of 'an original', the beginning of creative production and inherently uncertain, is guided by the conventions of the canon (Becker 2008). Genres act as a 'kind of institutionalisation and routinisation in a highly uncertain production interpretive world' (Hesmondhalgh and Baker 2011: 14), part of the cultural conventions underlying the general form of work. Recognizable characters, plots, relations, and settings form a 'collection of cultural rules which operate at the level of form and stylistic variation derived from the past and applied to the present as a template for creativity'; they are 'operational rules' for working on an artistic product, to maintain 'continuity and style' (Ryan 1992: 173). Conventions help mediate the insecurity of uncertainty in creative production. They constitute the foundations of claims to 'truth' and 'authenticity'. Zoellner (2009: 531) also sees conventions 'as professional codes supporting a particular ideology of professionalism', for example, adherence to professional standards that ensures that commercial concerns do not entirely pre-empt artistic standards.

Creative producers do not often use the term 'risk' in relation to the creative act itself. As we have seen in Chapter 2, they appeal rather to the integrity of the creative product. Where 'risk' is used, it is a borrowed term, a language absorbed from other fields and contexts. In this example of a theatre focusing on the production of new work, the language of business, 'R&D' (research and development), has been absorbed and transposed into the explanation of the functioning of the art form:

> Our type of business, because it is research and development, is at the cutting edge and we do take risks. I think the argument for public subsidy can be made in a much more robust fashion for our kind of work. Being at the cutting edge, taking the risks, how do we make sure that we get some kind of royalty or return on that investment? This organization is not only to take risks in terms of the work. We also take risks in terms of staff. We have got a lot of the team who are learning on

> the job, for example, production, education, marketing. That means that they are not always going to get it right. Each thing we do, if I had a risk ladder, is extremely high, because it is R&D. [Theatre 102]

There is, however, a big distinction to be made between the 'risk' involved in the creative act, and the risk for the individual in the creative industries (Ekinsmyth 2002). The Romantic myth disguises the extent to which risk necessarily carries a financial component. Risk is never either artistic or commercial: the two are necessarily intricately related. Livelihood in the sector requires financial wherewithal; economic resources are an important aspect of any cultural 'breakthrough'. As Caves (2000: 50) remarks, 'for a new style to be disseminated, it must command enough economic resources to keep its artists from starving and the dealers in business' (see also Bourdieu 1993).

One element of risk is the inevitably high degree of sunk costs involved in creative production (Caves 2000, Bakker 2015). While failure or success is determined retrospectively, decisions about what is produced have to be taken prospectively (Berkeley 2003). Caves' (2000) own examples come from large-scale enterprises such as film and commercial theatre, but his comment applies even more to small producers:

> Doing any trade fair is a big gamble. It is the cost and fear factor of basically spending months investing time, stress, and money into something and then spending two weeks standing somewhere, hoping that they will come and buy. If they don't, that is half your year's income gone. [Design 22]

Small-scale creative enterprises lack the financial reserves to speculate carelessly with half a year's income, and taking such risks compounds existing difficulties of maintaining cash flow. One fashion designer explains the dilemmas that come with investments of time and imagination:

> If you don't have the money behind you at the start, you are not doomed from the start, but it is very difficult, if you make a kind of big-money mistake. I developed a collection which did not sell as well as I wanted it to, so the money that I assumed I would get, did not come through. It was like, 'Well, now what? I don't have any money. Do I put it on hold and work and try to get the money? Or do I try to get investors? Or do I try out different things, things that don't cost as much but will bring in small revenue'. If you can keep that coming then that builds up and gets capital. It is a very capital-rich industry—you have to have the money first, and to get that is very difficult. Unless you have got money behind you—backing behind you—it is hard to raise and especially hard to raise that within the business. [F&T 28]

As we saw in the last chapter, IP/IPR configures the economic agency of creative producers, allowing them, among other things, to appreciate the temporal dimension of their work. This dimension of time is also closely connected to the risk of a project, and a close understanding of the mechanisms of the field is essential for managing this risk. Each sector has its own timelines for the point at which it becomes clear that something is 'not going to fly', a problem that may be compounded by slow or unpredictable audience feedback:

> There are games that have huge long tails. We have games that will sit, and have sat, for long periods, and they will still be generating reasonable revenue three years later. Then there are other games that come out and peak for a couple of weeks and then do virtually nothing thereafter. It does vary dramatically.
>
> [Games 49]

Being able to support a product over time produces serendipitous opportunities: 'You are aware that e-books trickle along, and then suddenly something will happen either with you, or out in the world, and the sales will pick up enormously' [Publishing 80]. Of course, such opportunities only stem from the durable revenues afforded by IP rights, the *ars longa* as Caves (2000) terms them. But maintaining content with such long tails involves costs, lower in some sectors than others. Porting content between platforms in games may be more problematic than, for example, in publishing. Orientation to time is also seen in estimations that are made of 'payback' or returns, as in this example from publishing where a more long-term view of the publisher's relationship with the writer is outlined:

> I think I would say that we are very different to most publishers in that we are very much playing the long game. I want to work with sustainable writers that in five or ten years' time are really coming to their own—so looking to the long term. Some of those will fall away and it is very much the Parable of the Talents. You have to gather together quite a big group of people and out of those you would hope that one or two would maybe become major players, long-term. You need a portfolio of authors and then it is very much down to the individual writers in terms of how they develop and how motivated they are. Some writers will write two books and then get discouraged and go off and do something else. Others will stick at it. Others might do one or two and then have a 10-year break and then come back. It is about building a relationship and is very much what publishing was like 30 years ago. That is one of the good things about the recession, because it has stripped away a lot of the fast bucks. People are having to go back to more traditional values, back to basics. [Publishing 77]

The existence of IP, as we saw in the last chapter, allows creative producers an orientation to the future, and this comprises a first step in developing a calculative apparatus necessary to disentangle risk from uncertainty. For many, though, 'success' remains a variable target. For many small businesses, the important factor is the ability to stay in business: 'I still have never had a hit. I suppose the first step is to make sure that you can make a living and then worry about the hits' [Games 50].

Choosing Projects and Portfolio Production

Knight (1921) suggests that where the future is to an extent known, for example, where decisions involve calculating the (rough) odds of particular outcomes, a strategy of portfolio management or product diversification may manage risk. A portfolio of projects is common in the creative sector as a whole, 'a rational response in an environment of low capital investments and demand uncertainty' (Hirsch 1972: 652). Both overproduction and the differential promotion of new items are designed to cope with the high ambiguity of cultural production. Creative producers seek to blend their most imaginative—and therefore most risky—work with outputs more closely linked to the institutional conventions and patterns of their field. A dancer, for example, might hedge the risk of exciting novelty with also working in collaborations with well-recognized names in the field. In other words, she can draw on well-known performers' own symbolic and social relationships in the field to manage the potential uncertainty of new IP production:

> Generally, I work with people who excite me. [That's] number one, whether they are new and upcoming and excite me. Number two, whether they are established and I pretty well know what I am going to get. It is a balancing of the risk.
>
> [Dance 115]

This quotation shows the blending of artistic and economic calculation as the dance producer assesses the potential risk and return of a portfolio of ventures. Such uncertainty management comes at an economic cost, at least in terms of sacrificing short-term economic reward for longer term creative gain, however, and relationships may be hit-or-miss:

> You can find co-production partners with whom you get on very well and it feels like you are all working in the same company and for the same ends. And you can find co-production partners who are not really interested in that long-term relationship and just want to make as much money as they can on that deal. [TV 61]

Knowledge of the field renders new projects calculable. A small games producer describes deciding to invest time and resources in a project: 'How do you choose which project to invest in, because there is never a shortage of ideas? It is not a gamble as such, but there is a calculated risk involved in whatever project you do' [Games 50]. The development of new ideas is expensive, and many producers in the games sector balance their output between self-publishing and contract work: 'I mean that is the dream—to work on your own stuff—but it is an expensive business and very risky' [Games 52]. Paid-for work—where the risk is directly offset by the legal structures of IP rights and contracts—may be seen as essential to maintain the viability of the company, particularly in view of the speculative nature of self-published work:

> We are a video game developer and self-publisher, so there are two main strands to the business strategy and the operation. One strand is self-publishing: We concept, create, and take to market our own games and we publish those ourselves direct on to, mainly, the Apple App Store and also Google Play Store, Nintendo, and Sony's digital stores as well. That is a high-risk and potentially high-reward part of the business and you get a lot of failure in that. Maybe 9 out of 10 games are complete, abject failures and you get virtually nothing and there is the odd game that does particularly well. We obviously retain our own IP in that, which is great. [Working for] the large game publishers, television, broadcast, school companies, brand owners, pretty much anyone that wants a game made to promote their brand, their property, or wants to take a game from one platform to mobile for the first time, or just wants a bespoke game made for them—that is relatively low risk. But you have got to go out and find the work. It would be fairly similar to most kinds of business that are service-based: there is a period where you respond to the brief and you then go and pitch for that, and you get it based on a combination of talent, quality of pitch, price. [Games 42]

Even contract work, or 'work-for-hire', brings a 'longstanding tradition of feast-and-famine livelihoods' (Ross 2013: 177); it must be stabilized through good relationships in the field and it remains uncertain. 'Contract work is safe and steady, but at the same time it is not safe. It is safe when you have it. But then you get paid and then there is nothing' [Games 43]. A portfolio strategy raises the issue of opportunity costs, which must once again be calculated:

> We are in this to make our own IP and so the challenge is getting that balance right. Ideally for us we would already have released [X game] by now, and [Y game] would be further ahead in development. But the nature of this business is that you have got bills to pay, so you have to get work-for-hire sooner. That balancing act starts much sooner. [Games 44]

The publishing industry provides a similar example of such calculation. Costs are spread across a catalogue or repertoire so that the few hits cancel out many misses (Hesmondhalgh and Baker 2011). 'A wise publisher will hedge his bets... It is more efficient to produce many failures for each success than to sponsor fewer items and pre-test each on a massive scale' (Hirsch 1972: 652). On the basis of 'nobody knows', publishers have no guarantee that a book will be successful:

> The publishers take on the risk by putting up the money to publish the book in the first place. If the book doesn't do well, then it is not the author who loses money. It is the publisher who loses money. I mean, obviously, the author loses it in terms of lost revenue. But they haven't put the money out in the first place. [Publishing 79]

This publisher's commercial estimates of risk fail to acknowledge that authors, unless they are lucky to receive advances, also take risk, having to support themselves during the creative process. Yet publishers do not engage with authors at random and let the algorithm of the market determine their success, as Hirsch's (1972) quotation might suggest. Skilled creative producers have an understanding of their field and can, despite residual uncertainty, judge that some books are likely to succeed where others are not. The same publisher speaks of 'bread and butter' titles, less exciting but more predictable than the risky ventures:

> Publishers have got their so-called 'bread and butter' titles. Say they are publishing 10 titles—two of them might do really well, but the other eight may well do less well. They often rely on that kind of balance to subsidize, perhaps, some of the other parts of their list. [Publishing 79]

Structural changes in the field, however, have introduced risks beyond commonly accepted levels. Publishers complain that margins are being eroded:

> The level of risk you are taking on has increased over time, because it is more and more difficult to make money from publishing books. Actually what you are doing is taking on more risk and if you increase the risk, then you need to increase the rewards. [Publishing 76]

Christopherson (2008) illustrates how the concentration of global conglomerates in the television industry has resulted in a more globalized television system with interconnected broadcasters, producers, and distributors, while the fragmentation of channels has increased demand for cheap programming to fill airtime. Multi-channel, multi-platform production, distribution, and consumption and a growing fragmentation of audiences (and advertisers) have emphasized a more commercial focus at both commercial and public service broadcasters (Zoellner 2009). Production for TV is increasingly organized in a vertically disintegrated system based on specific projects, where the risk falls on the independent producer. Risk-handling strategies include an economized strategy of low-cost production or adopting an 'upmarket' strategy—in other words, one based on symbolic understanding of the field—using well-known industry workers (Christopherson 2008: 82). Changing industry structure has had a direct impact on the type and diversity of products that are made (Zoellner 2009; for music see Peterson and Berger 1971, 1975). Drama, entertainment, and 'factual entertainment' are more easily exploited internationally, one-off programmes are increasingly seen as high-risk, while documentaries are viewed as difficult programming (Zoellner 2009).

Within the UK, there is an increased dependency on the 'broadcaster-publisher system', with the BBC, ITV, and Channels 4 and 5 commissioning programmes and providing the main source of funding for independent producers. The UK Communications Act 2003 stipulates that 25 per cent of all programmes are to be sourced from independents. As Berkeley (2003: 110) notes, '[t]he 25 per cent quota obligation... has led to an excessive increase in the number of independent producers.' These structural changes have been accompanied by a transfer of risk, previously borne by larger broadcasting companies, to the independent producers. As risk is outsourced to producers, production becomes more 'flexible', reduced to an essential core, with risk further outsourced to self-employed and temporary workers used as needed (Ekinsmyth 2002, Coe and Johns 2004). Costs and uncertainties are now absorbed by independents who are expected to carry out a substantial amount of work on a project, even before the stage of pitching to a broadcaster (Ursell 1998, Berkeley 2003, McGuigan 2010):

> The BBC don't do their own version of *Book of the Week*. They go to an outside production company and would expect that to have all been produced and packaged and abridged and so on to suit the format. Somebody now is paying money to do that before making the pitch. It is a changing landscape.
>
> [Publishing 84]

Nor is commissioned work without risks for producers, in terms of trying to balance what the company is known for:

> With one-person indies, you have to be very get-up-and-goey and be interested in a lot of different things. If you are [saying], 'I am only going to do this', then I think you are dead in the water. Yet, you have to be not so eclectic that people don't know what your brand is. [Film 72]

The time that may be invested in speculative projects, with no guarantee that investment in R&D will be recompensed through the project being adopted, has implications for cashflow and capital. Creative producers must constantly calculate trade-offs between expenditure of money and time, and the potential upside of a project. In the following example, one company considering filming a programme about a school for stammerers (on the back of the film, *The Kings Speech*), was forced to make calculations about the best way to spend time, clearly a finite resource for an independent production company:

> We could not afford to sit down there for a month in an expensive part of London endlessly filming people. Because broadcasters require very solid test tapes now before they will go with characters. You need to almost make a mini-film. I have seen briefings where [the test tape] is actually transmittable. Again that takes a lot of time and energy if you are competing with 10 other companies. You are saying, 'Is this a good way to be spending our time?' That is something you constantly have to factor in if you are a small company—saying how you are going to spend your time.
>
> [TV 53]

As we saw in Chapter 3, the calculation of time is facilitated by the structures of IP/IPR classification which make (the possibility of) future revenues more concrete, as compared to the blend of commercial risk and symbolic knowledge in the field that must be applied to some kinds of specialist production:

> History [programming] is tricky. You have to have either a very big face or a completely new twist and in some cases, that requires exclusive access to a writer, which requires chequebooks. Sometimes, somebody has written a book and they have just researched something new and have got new material. The problem with that is there are big companies in London who have departments that do nothing else. You have to speak to the publisher for six months, or a year ahead, and that is almost a full-time job. How do you get that material before anybody else knows about it? Once it is in the papers forget it—somebody else has already got their mitts on it. We cannot always compete. I know a company who actually packed it in because they had had a successful run of a certain kind of programming and they were offered a story, and they pitched to a broadcaster and the broadcaster said, 'I would not bother because big company A, big company C, big company D, big company E are already getting on planes to Moscow with chequebooks to get that person to sign to them exclusively, and I would not bother if I were you'. Money really talks when you are trying to get access to things, even to stories.
>
> [TV 53]

This example shows how an independent producer may, under the circumstances, simply decide to give up amid unequal competition.

Matters are made worse when the specialized knowledge of the creative field, which does so much to underwrite judgements concerning uncertainty and render them calculable, becomes valueless in the face of other forms of justification (Boltanski and Thévenot 2006). Large corporations, and some large independents, have management structures accountable to primarily economic concerns (Faulkner et al. 2008). Programme commissioners now have responsibility for a much larger number of programmes, while the financial aspect of risk has increased risk management, in some cases translating into risk aversion. As creative producers have moved to independent firms, so they have been replaced by business school-trained administrators and accountants (Murdock 2003). Understandings of risk in the IP, guided by the symbolic knowledge of the field, have been replaced by understandings of risk based on audience size and programme 'acceptability' (McGuigan 2010). Playing safe is one of the 'unspoken "rules of engagement"' within TV production (Berkeley 2003: 115).

> The other thing with the major broadcasters is you have so many layers of management. I have had good stories, and spent a lot of time getting access to a good story, and people half-way up the tree can't make up their mind as they are frightened they get blamed for a decision. 'I am not sure that it is going to work'. Then they drop it, and somebody else makes it, and then you hear that the channel controller sees it on another channel and says, 'Why did we not get that? That is a good story'. How do you protect yourself against that kind of nonsense? [TV 53]

One possible solution to managing risk is interpersonal trust (Raffo et al. 2000b). Following Granovetter (1985), economic sociology has identified trust as an essential mechanism in keeping markets running. In the creative industries, Christopherson (2008: 82) notes the 'persistence of "hard-wired" social and economic networks that reduce risk', but it is often the case that such networks serve to reinforce exclusion along gender and ethnic lines (Grugulis and Stoyanova 2012). Creative producers see trust and relationships as managing risk (Zoellner 2009):

> The process of winning [commissions]—it is not as simple as [developing our own] ideas. It is all about trust and winning that trust. That is why they call us 'luvvies', because we have to be good at parties. You have to do an enormous amount of sucking up and in a way, you cannot blame the guys, because how do you define the ethos of a programme? It is affected by the mind-set, the world view of the person who is in charge of it, and although television is made by teams, the choice of people that you have around you, that team is affected by your vision. So, the relationship between the executive and the commissioning editor is absolutely crucial. We are essentially going to them with some bits of paper or a chat over a drink and saying, 'How about you give us £150,000; £1.5 million? And by the way, if this all goes wrong, yes, our reputation will not do well out of it, but neither will yours, and you have next to no power over it except to trust us to get it right for you'. [TV 56]

Yet, there is a danger that scholars simply use trust as 'an undifferentiated explanation of coordination that black-boxes maintenance operations and socio-technical devices' (Çalışkan and Callon 2010: 21). The quotation above displays the dense entanglement of the producer and commissioner with the social and symbolic structures of the field. It mentions ethos and vision, as well as reputation; it describes the commission as a gift embedded in a reciprocal relationship and secured by reputation. These things make sense only within a field of symbolic production that informs the understanding and production of IP structuring the field. Proven track records demonstrating an ability to cooperate and 'deliver' show the historical context of the field (Zoellner 2009, Hesmondhalgh and Baker 2011). Independents have to be aware of a commissioning broadcaster's preferences regarding audience makeup and expectations, channel profile, scheduling, budgets, target audiences, and 'slot requirements'—cultural capital that is only convertible into economic capital through the commissioning process (Zoellner 2009). Yet this very convertibility forces another calculative act regarding risk. Here, one firm is forced to compare the economic cost of buying in cultural capital—in this case the 'credentials' and 'network' of a well-regarded producer—with the possible benefit of commissions he might bring:

> You have to have a showcase [proto programming], which costs money to make. We have recruited a London-based development producer who left a big indie

> down there. He's working for us now, so that is a bit of a gamble. He is not cheap. It is a hope that his credentials and his network are very strong so that will be a quicker route for us getting to where we want to go. [TV 58]

'Packaging' and Formatting

Another solution to uncertainty takes the form of 'packaging'. As we argued in Chapter 2, a viable product demands more than ideas: 'An idea is no longer enough unless you are very much the company of the moment who has just had a huge hit. You do need to bring other factors into the mix. It is very tough' [TV 53]. A product requires an ensemble—'talent' or presenters, big names who can draw on their symbolic resources, or specialist crew who have a 'track record'—with an aim of building target audiences for advertisers or co-production for export and to accommodate programme commissioners' requirements for predictability. Independents develop packages geared towards reducing risk: 'Everybody can use the same idea at once,' says one television executive. 'How many cop dramas, hospital dramas, rom-coms can you get? Essentially the idea is possibly going to be similar but what I attach to it is the right to arrange a creative team' [TV 72]. Such packaging may be a double-edged sword, however, as the 'owners' of popularity with the audience compete with other creative producers for the lion's share of the rewards:

> You take a well-known presenter to a meeting with broadcasters in order to let him feel that he is part of it and let them feel that they are talking directly to your guy. The next thing you know he is turning 'round and saying, 'Well it is my idea. You would never have got it if it was not for me'. You have a broadcaster meeting, and the next thing you know his agent is saying, 'Well we might do this project with you and we might do this project with somebody else'. [TV 56]

Such competition inevitably develops into a bidding war for talent between those trying to develop 'packages' that can be expensive and difficult: 'We have found talent and people have tried to nick them. People say, "Why did you not sign them up exclusively?" which would be more expensive. It is very difficult. It is dog-eat-dog out there' [TV 60]

An alternative—or perhaps complementary—response is to seek to eliminate uncertainty through the pursuit of formulaic production or 'formatting'. With a high value on predictability, one strategy is to produce creative products that are already known (DiMaggio 1977): 'Commercial thinking presumes that the strongest predictor of success is to repeat the formula' (Ryan 1992: 157). Current audience taste, indexed by existing patterns, dictates creation, so that 'formatting transforms the usual rules of a form into a necessity' (Ryan 1992: 172). It is an attempt to 'discipline the creative process' (Banks 2007: 76).

Characterizations, narrative structure, and plot are strategized, as 'each different format of TV drama carries its own assumptions about its target audience' (Berkeley 2003: 105). It is also a form of cost-cutting, lowering the economic exposure of any new venture. Production formats reduce skilled inputs; reality TV exploits the 'attention economy' (Ross 2013: 179), replacing actors with 'participants' and writers with 'programme planners'. Worst of all, at least in the eyes of the creative producers themselves, formatting 'runs contrary to the freshness and originality necessary for creating hits' (Lampel et al. 2006: 11), and prompts broader concerns with 'mass culture', 'homogeneity, blandness and triviality' (DiMaggio 1977: 436).

> Ripping off formats is certainly on the increase because people are more and more risk-averse. If you can see something has been a huge success.... When you look at the UK market, this winter we have got *Strictly Come Dancing* on BBC and we have got *Dancing on Ice* on ITV. The difference is that it is two celebs dancing together on ITV, so it is derivative. [TV 54]

Formats, such as reality programmes and game shows, are a means of embedding a creative idea in a broad nexus of IPR. Kretschmer et al. (2009) point to the use of trade secrets in these formats, where the licensee of the format receives comprehensive documentation, the 'production bible' of know-how associated with production (how to find appropriate contestants and audience organization, for example), and copyrighted themed music. Big names such as *MasterChef* and *Who Wants to Be A Millionaire?* are important, trademark-protected brands, allowing exploitation of the format through sales to overseas markets and merchandising, protecting value and offering the guarantee of income for as long as the format remains popular.

This kind of programme is inevitably less exciting for creative-minded producers, but is regarded as a necessary means of staying in business. Independents attempt to get a balance between projects that pay the bills but offer less in terms of reputation, and riskier pieces that might create notice:

> We try to earn our money through television commissions and then take a risk on projects which are less commercial for the rest of the time. Format shows keep on bringing money into the building and that pays for the photocopies and the development staff and all that stuff. That means that the staff might be able to try to get away smaller programmes which are more about their reputation and less about revenue. It isn't going to make them a fortune but it is going to make people think, 'Oh, that is interesting'. [TV 63]

It is a balance that not all feel able to achieve: 'I suppose from a business point of view you should not do the kind of things that I do, which are sort of one-offs about the arts and cultural. You should think of popular TV formats that you can sell around the world. But I am not able to do that' [Film 68].

Creative production is fraught with uncertainty. In this section we have sketched out how IP—understood as the text or the ideational object—offers creative producers a mechanism through which this uncertainty may be managed, and even codified into calculable, exploitable risk. IP allows the symbolic knowledge of the field, in terms of conventions of production and recognized forms of value, to interact with the accounting measures and classificatory regimes that structure the economic aspects of the field. Conventions of value embedded in the field, along with social relations, allow the creative producer to judge the many economic and artistic trade-offs that producing IP demands. Once again IP—the creative work—provides a means for market agents to operate as market agents.

Managing Risk through IPR

IPR, we argued in Chapter 2, comprises the legal properties that singularize creative goods, allowing them to circulate in a marketplace. It offers producers a 'legally regulated, artificially created monopoly', and in doing so performs certain kinds of (individual) ownership of a creative 'work' (George 2012: 6). IPR also offers creative producers a means of managing uncertainty and risk through contracts that specify the nature of potential issues and attempt to remove them. Contracts are a form of security to prevent partners behaving opportunistically (Bröckling 2016). Transactions are based on contracts, or rather contracts have a transactional property: 'a contract is the agreement that governs the conduct of any economic transaction, defining what each part brings . . . and takes . . . from the transaction' (Caves 2000: 11). The role of contracts is prominent in economic theory. Williamson (1985) identifies trade-offs between transaction costs, via contract or internal to the firm, as the reason for the existence of firms in the first instance. In the case of creative industries Caves' (2000) analysis identifies contracts managing risk as the principal property impacting the organization and structure of the creative industries.

Although economists view profits as the reward for risk taking, this is only meaningful if risk is also attached to property rights. Property rights enshrined in contracts, in the eyes of economics and of the law, guarantee market participants' legal security. The contract is 'transaction, production and debt relation all at once' (Bröckling 2016: 85). The freedom to contract, meaning that individuals have the right to determine with whom to contract and the terms of contract, is another core tenet of law. A contract therefore signifies an implied, even if not a real, equality of partners, a transaction 'truly and freely' entered into. This assumed formal equality overrides and legitimates any material inequality. Contracts work to organize the market in a particular way with the danger of contractual reason establishing itself as the primary model of social relations. As Bröckling (2016: 81–2) notes, '[f]raming all action as market action involving contracts between market participants... makes the contract appear as the fundamental social institution', subjugating social relations via the performative role of the contract to economic explanations.

Market participants recognize that the contract is a form of exchange to be distinguished from relationships based on cooperation or a commonality of interests: market-governed relations are distinct from social relations. Yet IP/IPR occupies a liminal state where social and market relations intertwine, and tensions are often evident, as is illustrated in the following example from dance, where permission to use music for a dance, accessed through an informal relationship, was given, only for it later to be seen as a source of revenue:

> One choreographer sampled other people's music. He sampled a friend of one of the dancers and this guy verbally agreed for him to use the music. There were three of us who remember that. But we did not put it in writing. We should have done because he came back a few years later and said, 'Okay, this [dance] piece is still touring. Where are my rights?' He accepted in the end that actually he had verbally given us the rights. But that was a real lesson for us. Put it in writing, 'Thank you for agreeing to blah blah blah,' and get him to sign it. [Dance 122]

This example illustrates how the creation of IP, the music, also creates IPR, the rights to use the music and, with this, claims for compensation of some kind. It also illustrates the problematic balance between informality and formality in managing relationships. The expected reciprocity of the informal relationship is obviated as the informal agreement is taken as an implied contract. Market relationships determined by contract take precedence.

Contracts in the Field

Our previous discussion of strategies around IP as means of managing uncertainty highlighted the role of practice in the organization of the creative industries. Practices continue to be important in the realm of contract where social norms enforce verbal or unspoken agreements. Entering into formal, written contracts can incur costs, not all of which are economic: contracts may change the dynamics of a creative partnership. Contractual relations objectify a relationship (Bröckling 2016), and are often viewed as unnecessary or alien. As a result, contractual relations tend to become more formal as social relations become weaker. Contracts are for 'people you don't know':

> I have never signed a contract with the company, and I have been here nearly one year now. I know the guys. They know me. I know what I can do with the engine. I am not going to do anything that would damage them or anything like that. I know what they expect of me and I know that I have got no claims on the games that I work on when I am here. I could walk out and make a big fuss about it but

> that would just be me being an idiot. I know the basis [of] why I am here and they know that I am going to be sensible. It is fine. But it is when you are working with people in America or the people you don't know, then you get the problems. [Games 52]

Where collaborations are fruitful liaisons, contracts and IPR can be seen as an intrusion but experience teaches participants that this may often change. Creative producers may learn to develop semiformal written agreements covering various potential outcomes:

> Agreements are really good because they give clarity to the situation. How can you know what somebody else is thinking? You can't. The only way you can do it is to reach an agreement, which is written down and clear. Two years ago, I would not have said that. I would have been on the trust-basis side of things. [F&T 34]

This designer's experience has clearly steered her towards future caution, a wisdom that is echoed elsewhere. It may be the case that the closer the social tie, the more potential for difficulty in the case of unexpected problems:

> You know that saying about businesses with friends. You just never know where things can go wrong. I think that it is probably wise to have contracts for everything. [F&T 32]

Informal, written contracts, as opposed to legalistic agreements, are thus seen as a means of managing potential issues, specifying the protection of input and potential returns in collaborative projects:

> The first thing that I do is write something down that covers all the possible bases that I could imagine. Normally I will just say, 'We should have an agreement. Why don't I write something down and you write something down and then we can check it?' That is what we do. It is really quick and it is just a written agreement. No lawyers. Nothing complicated. [Design 13]

Born out of relationships, a contract in this sense is seen as a document that both parties construct, rather than something imposed by market forces:

> I think there is a misrepresentation in many creative sectors that a contract should just be verbal and based on trust. I think it is very important to say that the contract is there for both parties so that they know where they stand. Everyone should be happy with it and it should work for both parties. It is not just about you signing over your rights. [Dance 120]

These quotations show a consistent attitude towards some kind of straightforward contracting as a means of managing and reinforcing social relations. Creative producers are simultaneously reliant upon trust and wary of its limitations; it appears that the ability of trust to lubricate the engine of the creative economy is limited to stretches of clear and smooth road. Putting something in writing, even in an informal manner, offers protection to both parties; a failsafe that, it is hoped, will never be needed:

> In the five films that I have produced, never once have I had to withdraw the contract out of the filing cabinet. Ultimately there could be a point, where, if things go awry, you need to know where the buck stops—where does everything lie when things go wrong? [Film 69]

We noted in Chapter 2 that the right to exclude is a crucial tenet of intellectual property rights such as copyright. We might speculate that a vital difference between IP maintained through social relations in the field and IP secured through a formal contract—even of a non-legalistic variety—is the ability to exclude future courses of action. Where informal relations may provide permission to follow certain courses of use, IPR allows a blanket exclusion. The following quotation shows a choreographer struggling with the limits of the informal route in preventing certain courses of action. Here the concerns lie in the integrity of the work to be produced elsewhere:

> With a production I worked on recently at the opera, I was the choreographer and movement director. This production is now going abroad to the States and I had no say in that at all. I was consulted about what I thought the needs were, movement wise, and so on. But I have not been asked to go and re-stage it. They will be using my choreography and movement direction. But it will be somebody else who will be doing it who I have never met. The contract does not say that they are allowed to. But it does not say that they are not allowed to. But it is my intellectual property. It made me realise that I probably should have something put in my contract. I would say, should it go on to other productions or get bought by a third party that I have the right to oversee the work, and if I cannot, I have the right to be consulted about who will oversee the work and how that will be carried out. But it would be interesting to see how that would play out in the negotiation because of the sort of leverage the larger companies have. They could then go, 'Well, we will get someone else to do the work'. [Dance 116]

The choreographer's concerns centre on the maintenance of rights to control her IP. These rights are embedded in authorship of intellectual property, but have not been transferred to more formal contractual right of control. This is a common problem and pertinent concern. Contracts raise issues of when in the relationship they should be drawn up, when it is necessary to 'put something in writing'. One film director speaks of contracts as being emergent from existing relationships:

> You should always try to have the contract emerge from the relationship rather than get into something where you have in your mind a fixed idea of what a co-production might look like and try to apply it to a relationship. You find a relationship and then let the contract emerge from there. [Film 69]

This reflects the view that the relationship is particularly important, particularly at the early stages of a project, with ideas still not clearly articulated, risks high, and rewards uncertain. It is only when ideas are more developed that contributions can be 'coded' in more formal mechanisms. At the same time, contracts can undermine the norms of fairness by shifting ownership of copyright. While authorship is determined by contribution to the work and does not vary by contract, ownership of the copyright can and does. Contracts, or lack thereof, impact who ultimately owns a creative work. McRobbie (2016) illustrates how independent fashion production can be undermined by the large retailers through sub-contractual terms and conditions or find their products adopted as their own. The relatively low level of IPR awareness and sophistication can exacerbate inequalities, with a failure to specify ownership of IP early, leading to a failure to adequately protect work, as seen here:

> I produced all of this work. I produced lots of models, did digital renderings, costings, and sourced manufacturers, and presented it to them. Then it just kind of dried up. They were saying, 'We are not happy with this', etc. Then you think, 'Okay'. So I billed them for what I had done so far. They paid me for the work that was done. Then it began to come through in their range of work, or as part of their range of work. [Design 5]

Where contracts are used, the contract is likely to reflect the bargaining power of the parties, notwithstanding the legal niceties of 'freedom of contract'. For example, an independent games developer working with a large publisher under a work-for-hire contract will have almost certainly assigned the copyrights to the publisher or have punitive clauses as part of the contract:

> I would say that we have been quite lucky, but we have never really had many delays in any of our work, and delays are something that can come about quite easily in the games industry because sometimes things just crop up that you could not plan for and they take a long time to fix. The only time that I could actually see a contract going quite bad, or severing slightly, is if there is a delay that was not planned for, but so far we have been pretty good in that we have not had to delay anything really. Because a lot of the time with contracts, there are sometimes punitive clauses, so if you fail to deliver, the contract changes. A lot of the time if you fail you lose access to this IP, to this code base, and you no longer have the right to use the perpetuity with different customers. So delays can often have an impact on the IP ownership. [Games 43]

Managing Risk in Creative Product Development

Caves (2000) shows how, in theory at least, contracts are used to manage specific risks as projects develop. Contracts offer a variety of legal strategies aimed at protecting all steps in the journey from the initial idea generation, through options on creative development, managing the financial element of risk by compensation mechanisms, to final sale. Yet in practice contracts evolve from informal agreements through to formal contracts as the project develops. Eventually commercial constraints will require contractual proof of ownership of a product that has been sufficiently alienated from its producers to be an object of transaction, but the early stages rarely demand such legal framing:

> I say to people, 'Let's work on this together, and it is 50: 50'. We don't have a contract from the outset. But to get the last bit of money from a broadcaster I will need one. You can get quite a long way down the line without one in place. But it is not something lawyers would recommend doing. [Film 72]

As ideas develop, so they will be codified into intellectual property rights. One mechanism for protecting an extended period spent working up an idea is an options contract, as is explained in this example from film:

> I am developing a script with a young theatre director who wants to move into film. He came to me with a worked-through idea and I talked to him about it. I was willing to participate in that in an unprotected way at that stage to allow a number of things to happen, for us to see if we could work together, which in a sense comes into the intellectual part of the IP statement. Because one of the things which I am always keen to do is to have a creative engagement with the idea. He and I got on very well in that process and he was amenable to debate on what this thing would be like.
>
> Once that had got to a certain stage, I then contracted with him the option on the ownership. You can buy things outright; although it is a one-off process, it can be too expensive. That is too much of a risk. An option is defined within certain characteristics, mostly it is to do with time and money, and then you would define the point at which you would exercise that option and in fact own the rights to the particular piece. That is often at a much later stage. With the theatre director I have an 18-month option, automatically renewable after another 18 months. That 3-year period can sound like a long time. But it is not. In film, it can take quite a long time. If he took the property to a third party, the contract between him and me would dictate that the third party would then be obliged, again in certain circumstances which would be contractually defined, to repay me my expenditure, and so on. [Film 69]

In this scenario the director presents an idea that is already 'worked through' to a state where it can be talked about. The producer is willing to work without legal protection 'to allow a number of things to happen', the implication being that contracts will impede the creative process. Beyond a certain stage, however, the developed intellectual property is worth protecting and the speaker takes an option on the film. The option transforms the nature of the project. Its changes from an idea embedded in conversation between two creative producers into a legally bounded object of work with ascribed ownership. The property—as it is now described—cannot be sold elsewhere without recompensing the existing parties appropriately. Conversely, the danger of *not* having a legal contract is that someone else might develop the project. Risk here is undertaken without property rights because the work is out of copyright:

> As it happens, at the moment I do have one film which I am developing which is based on a novel, but the novel is actually out of copyright. Now the issue with that, of course, means that the underlying text isn't protected—someone else could legitimately come along and start to work on this piece. [Film 69]

The staged production of complex creative products, with each stage demanding a different type of input from different type of personnel, means that option contracts are a common feature of the production process. For example, in scriptwriting, following the 'pitch', the first stage might be a 'treatment' involving a summary plot and sample dialogue, followed by a complete draft, which may then be further rewritten or 'polished', with each stage usually accompanied by a contract and stipend (Caves 2000, Coe and Johns 2004). Option contracts also occur in publishing and music, with the 'options' to future creative production, in part to defray the costs of original promotion, although with no obligation to produce it. For example, a publisher may sign a contract with an author that includes a call option for the author's future work. However, option contracts may also be used for purely commercial purposes as a strategy of clearing competition:

> With a very hot novel or play, the kind of scrummage to option a hot project is massive. What would happen is that companies just option stuff to keep it off the market. If it is a particular author, the sale will already be set up and will already be optioned before someone like me would ever see it anyway. It is often the real big boys—it used to be Miramax—just clear the shops even if they don't want to do anything with it. [Film 72]

There are other legal mechanisms for protecting IP before it is developed into a viable product. Non-disclosure agreements (NDAs) may be used, as for example, by games developers when pitching their products to potential corporate adopters. The use of legal arrangements, however, is subject to complex norms within the field, the contravention of which may be indicative of naïveté or worse, as is shown here:

> I had recently a couple of writers who have done nothing, literally nothing, and who have just come out of university, sending me non-disclosure agreements. I am like, 'What the fuck? Really? Come on!' This, before I see their glorious script. I am saying, 'I work with some massive writers and no-one has ever sent me one of

> these before and I am not signing it. If you want me to look at it I need to be able to look at it and talk about it'. They are saying, 'Anytime you talk about it I have to be in the meeting', and it doesn't work like that. When I am pitching ideas it is very rare that I have the writer with me at the first round because, quite often, the writer will not want to hear what the commissioner is saying about it. [TV 72]

In this context, insisting upon contracts at an early stage signifies a lack of understanding of the rules of the game and potentially, personality traits that a more established creative producer might wish to avoid:

> Personally, I would worry about that at the beginning of a relationship. Because I would be thinking, 'Look, if you don't trust me then there is no way. You have done nothing. I have done quite a lot'. You know it would be different if it was [internationally known author X] saying to me, 'Sign this'. No-one of that nature has ever got me to sign anything like that. A big massive writer. Blimey. But not for someone just coming out of university. You are bloody lucky that I am even looking at it, far less signing a legal document. I think that it sets you up to be a bit of a wanker if I am being honest. I don't know anyone who would not think that was a bit wanky. Because it is just not practice. It is not what you do. [TV 72]

The speaker continues, stating that even writers' agents—those whose very existence in the sector is that of contractual brokers—have never asked for such a document. The demand and all it signifies is likely to curtail the prospects of the young hopefuls:

> But even an agent...no agent has ever asked me to sign one. You know, massive agents. So, a writer who is coming out from university and who has not got an agent, he has got a script and sending something like that NDA out. No. [TV 72]

The response above is not so much prompted by concerns with status, although these clearly play a part, but by ignorance over the workings of the industry. Crucially, as the discussion about options for a film project also indicated, formal IPR gets in the way of the processes of creative production within the field. The social relations of the field allow creative producers to develop IP collectively through discussions with others, vital in allowing the testing of ideas on potential buyers without the risk of developing them as formal commercial propositions. For example:

> There are specific things that you see, you get an idea and you are thinking, 'There is one person I think that might get this. Can I talk to them about this? If that person does not get it, seriously, put it in your pile marked "people aren't ready" and come back when people are'. There are plenty of ideas like that. [TV 72]

Collaborations inevitably raise issues of ownership and IPR. As intellectual property solidifies into legal rights, collaborators must decide how these rights are assigned. Again, this decision is embedded in social norms within the field.

Though 'very much a grey area' [Film 67], the division of IPR is usually based on some notion of how much each has brought to a piece:

> I think as with most other producers, if somebody comes to me with a project, with a script, and I like it, and it is in an inchoate state of development, it depends upon what extent we become involved in developing that project that we will take ownership, according to our influence on those underlying rights at that point in time. It may be that it is 100 per cent, or 50:50, or we feel that the material, the adaptation that we have done is so based on the original sourced material that we will own none. It can be anything across the broad spectrum from 0 to 100 per cent ownership of IP. [Film 67]

Often, as a product is developed it is tested to see if indeed there is market for it. This also stimulates a number of mechanisms to ensure that creative product is not 'lost'. Time-limited licence agreements are used to protect the IP created but not yet sold as a viable product, as shown in this example of music produced for TV production, where in the attempt to maintain control of the sunk costs of production, ownership is released only on a time-related basis:

> We might do a pitch for a programme and they might normally do one or two episodes as a kind of demonstrator for different channels and try to sell that idea to the channels or, if not, sell it to other programme makers. It is in our interest that we would do the best that we can for that, knowing that if this gets sold we will be the company who will produce the music. We want to help them to sell their idea. Therefore we will do the best music possible and we will do an entire full package of it. But for us obviously it is very little money up front and you are doing essentially all the work. They are essentially getting all of the work for a demo fee. In those instances, we say, 'Right you have this much time, a year, 18 months, to sell this idea for a TV series with our music attached to it. If you don't then we get our music back'. If they cannot sell that within a year and a half then there is something wrong with the actual idea of the programme. It will never sell essentially. At least it gives us a little bit of freedom. It reverts back to us and we will maybe have a look elsewhere. We can then try to sell it on or make changes to it. [Music 88]

When creative product is finished there remains a balance of risk for sellers and buyers of the IPR. The outright selling of IPR, selling copyright for an up-front fee, defrays risk and uncertainties associated with the future financial performance of the copyrighted works, as exploitation rights transfer from the seller to the buyer. The direct purchase of IPR, however, carries risk, as this dance director explains: 'We tend to do a buy-out [directly buying rights from the choreographer], especially if it is a commissioned work. Then we take that risk. We have bought a few works that have just panned, so it is not always in our interest' [Dance 115]. Alternatively, licensing is used to spread risk. Royalty contracts, for example, transfer some risk from the licensor to the licensee, with the licensee incurring the uncertainty and costs associated with marketing, distributing, and selling the work. Up-front payments or advances also reduce the risk to the licensor. Some risk and uncertainty remain shared, however, as both parties cannot predict sales. With untested work an important element is protecting future options. In recognition of the potential risks associated with direct IPR purchase, many contracts are designed to safeguard against the financial risk while still maintaining the option to exploit the work, should it prove successful, as is seen in this example from dance:

> We give an option. We have got a licence for X amount of time, but we will give you X more for the rights to the work. We negotiate after we see what the work is like. We have a choice of first refusal. If it is good they will get that extra percentage and if it is not good then they can have it back after the two years. It is a gamble on both sides. Also, it frees us up from paying royalties every time it is performed.
> [Dance 115]

In sum, as a creative work develops, the legal rights around it solidify from an IP enforced by social relations to formal IPR that allows it to circulate in the marketplace. The IP/IPR nexus allows creative producers to manage the uncertainty and risk around their products. First, knowledge of the field and social relations within it help creative producers manage the uncertainty endemic in creative production, the 'nobody knows' property. To help mitigate the risk of creation, creative producers can embed their projects into networks of symbolic capital, for example by recruiting a celebrity name or known production talent, or by making use of recognized genres or formats in the field. Informal relationships, unencumbered by contract, allow producers to test the reception of novel projects among potential consumers. In doing such things they not only reduce uncertainty but also render projects more calculable, enabling economic costs and potential rewards to attach to any new project. Against a pattern of structural changes in the creative industries that see ever more risk being outsourced to independent producers, usually small and micro businesses, such mechanisms are vital to the survival of the sector. As projects develop, so risks become more easily codified into intellectual property rights and contracts increasingly come into force. The market objects singularized by contract may now have specific risks attached—ranging from use of assigned ownership to financial collapse—with contracts seeking to prevent these through sanctions and exclusionary arrangements. The management of risk, then, is worked out through the IP/IPR nexus along a continuum similar to the mechanisms of product singularization and construction of economic agency discussed in the previous two chapters. Uncertainty and risk are seen to exist in a continuum, and in a complex, unstable relationship with each other; for creative producers they are both the source of possible opportunity and of considerable financial and personal harm.

5

Constructing Value

We have argued that IP/IPR frames and alienates creative products so that they might circulate in the market, performing a particular understanding of their individual ownership while at the same time ensuring they remain embedded in a network of symbolic production. We considered how IP/IPR functions as a market device to configure producers' market agency, facilitating a temporal orientation, dealing with the ambivalence of creative enterprise, and ordering creative work as a product. We then saw how IP/IPR offers mechanisms to help market participants manage the uncertainty endemic to creative production. The present chapter draws on recent advances in the sociology of valuation (Dussauge et al. 2015, Kornberger et al. 2015) to explore how IP/IPR acts as a mechanism through which creative works are rendered valuable. We suggest that the IP/IPR nexus orders and stabilizes the multiple evaluative principles at play in creative production, and bounds and singularizes goods.

Value remains a contested topic in the literature. Historically, economics has tackled value and sociology 'values', a mid-twentieth century division of economic and social worlds between the social sciences often attributed to Harvard sociologist Talcott Parsons (Stark 2011). Much of the debate around creative production follows this route, with economic value sharply distinguished from other kinds of aesthetic or cultural worth. Even Caves' (2000) ground-breaking economic study follows the same trajectory, lumping non-economic cultural motivations into 'exogenous factors' responsible for the uncertainty of creative production. More recently economists, notably Becker (1964), have sought to reduce a plurality of motivations to a single value calculus of returns against costs, echoing Bentham's 'calculus of utiles' (Kornberger et al. 2015).

Sociological approaches, on the other hand, have tended to take non-economic value structures as pre-existent, or at least shaped by the social structures of existing fields, 'artistic' or social. For example, Boltanski and Thévenot (2006) present a taxonomy of rival orders of worth and investigate their interfaces, but offer little in terms of an account of how such regimes of value come into being. But orders of worth need to be assembled and agreed in the community surrounding any goods (e.g. Coslor and Spaenjers 2016). Discussing art markets, Velthuis (2011: 183) writes: '[b]efore exchange can take place, a market order needs to be established including . . . the standards of value by which the works of art should be appreciated.'

Recent advances in the sociology of valuation have started to focus on how orders of worth are constructed. Following Dewey's 'flank movement' in valuation (Muniesa 2011), sociologists take a pragmatic approach and examine the social and material practices through which things may be 'praised, prized and priced' (Stark 2011). Creative works may be judged according to different and sometimes conflicting criteria, reflecting the many and varied actions of producers, sellers, experts, journalists, industry associations, marketing specialists, and consumers that participate in the making of artistic worth (Rösell and Beckert 2013). Trade fairs and festivals act as venues where standards are negotiated, knowledge is created and disseminated, and hierarchies are confirmed or subverted (Moeran and Strandgaard Pedersen 2011, Kuipers 2014). Valuation practices also have an epistemic content, constituting knowledge itself as valuable, separating what needs to be known from what does not (Dussauge et al. 2015), while concomitantly, though not necessarily overtly, embodying distinct understandings of ethical practice (Roscoe 2015).

There are, therefore, multiple, sometimes contradictory framings for basing calculations of value (Holden 2004), with goods often lying at the intersection of several valuations (Slater 2002a, Banks 2015) or 'regimes of value' (Appadurai 1986). Stark (2009) uses 'worth' as a concept encompassing the different scales through which the value of an object may be assessed; he associates entrepreneurship with 'the ability to keep multiple evaluative principles in play and to exploit the resulting friction of their interplay' (Stark 2009: 15). Readers already will have noticed such frictions and interplays at work in our interviews. Multiple understandings of worth are ever-present in the voices of our creative producers. Producers are consistently calculative and strategically aware; economic value and symbolic worth are inseparable in their accounts. In this chapter we contend that the IP/IPR nexus is the mechanism through which creative products are constructed as valuable: that it orders and settles the multiple, evaluative principles at play in creative production, that it bounds and singularizes goods. IP/IPR is constituted by valuations as diverse as knowledge, networks, or legal stratagems. Inevitably such settlements are only temporary but they are vital in the operation of markets for creative products. Subsequent chapters will explore how this market object can then be exploited as a source of revenue.

Symbolic Value and Economic Worth

Creative goods circulate in markets for 'singularities' or 'status markets' (as distinct from 'standard' goods and markets), where the value of creative products rests 'primarily on their symbolic content and the ways in which it stimulates the experiential reactions' (Power and Scott 2004: 3). The main coordinator between demand and supply in such markets is quality (Karpik 2010). And, just as symbolic production takes place within a specific artistic community, the construction of value is also embedded in this community. Quality reflects the symbolic orders of worth circulating in the field.

Bourdieu (1987) argues that a product has no integral or inherent value of its own, seeing it rather as ascribed by the prevailing discourse of the field. Value thus reflects the agents engaged in the field and the practices they employ. He writes:

> An entire set of the specific institutions are a necessary condition for the functioning of the economy of cultural goods. These include: places of visit; institutions of consecration and sanction; instances of reproduction of producers and consumers, specialized agents, all of whom are endowed with the dispositions objectively required by the field and the specific categories of perception and appreciation .... Among these are producers of works classified as artists, critics, collectors, middlemen, curators, etc., in short all who have ties with art, who live for art and who, to varying degrees, live from it, and who confront each other in struggles where the imposition of, not only a world view, but also a vision of the art world is at stake, and who through these struggles, participate in the production of the value of the artist and of art. (Bourdieu 1987: 205)

The relative autonomy of the field of production supports what Bourdieu terms 'an act of consecration', the power to produce and impose legitimate categories of perception and evaluative structures through which cultural value is constructed (Bourdieu 1979, 1989). Such consecration establishes a definition of artistic value largely autonomous of the economic (Bourdieu 1987). Value construction is a collective production. Non-linear, iterative, and distributed, it is continually recognized and reproduced by a network of producers and knowledgeable consumers (Pasquinelli 2007, Khaire 2017).

Within the field, creative production is measured by its own norms, based on the exploration and experimentation with an art form. Value, by this account, exists independently within the field, its creation central to the rationale of those working within it. This understanding constructs the boundaries of the field, leading to intense debates as to who is in and who is out, who has the right to participate, and what symbols are acknowledgeable and recognized as legitimate (Mears 2011). From this, it follows that cultural goods should display the originality expected of a singularized product:

unique, original, and authentic. Yet even when creative producers speak of originality as the source of value, their judgement remains intertwined with market values, as in this quotation which combines claims of originality and uniqueness, with notions of exchange and market:

> I think the customers must definitely recognize it as being an original design. I worked quite hard at researching what is in the market so that I know what I am doing is something different. It is really unique. [F&T 31]

'Authenticity' stands alongside originality as an important element of value (Jones et al. 2005). Stemming from the Romantic ideal of the symbolic unity of the creative work with its producer, authenticity reflects the aura of the original (Benjamin 1968). Value comes from creators 'investing' themselves in the creative production (Ryan 1992, Banks 2014), an act, as we have seen, at once psychological, through authorship, and financial, through opportunity cost. Products need to be the work of a recognizable artist: '[e]very book must have an author, every score a composer, every film a writer, director and cast of actors' (Ryan 1992: 45). In this, creative workers are unusual in having their names publicly assigned to their work, a veneration of 'sovereign talent' leading to the auteur relation identified in some art forms (Hesmondhalgh and Baker 2011).

From the intuitive understanding that a creator must develop her own authentic voice comes the more formalized process of differentiation, the need to distinguish one's creation from others. Although producers in the same market share an identity, their reciprocal orientation towards each other results in different identities emerging, as they employ strategies of differentiation to establish and attribute value (Bourdieu 1984, Aspers and Beckert 2011). Value comes from distinction and differentiation: singularity is expressed through difference. This may be the specific focus of artistic production, as seen in this example from a theatre, where the signifier 'women's theatre' is considered insufficient to mark distinction:

> I felt even more that the company needed to find other ways to remain relevant. Not to be seen as, 'just an old-fashioned women's theatre company'. I wanted the brand to be a company that innovates as well as a company that is about equalities. The company's key thing is that it is equality-based, and we all hope that ultimately that 'equalities remit' becomes obsolete. [Theatre 103]

Within the field, value is also expressed in terms of quality, variously understood as well-crafted, displaying high levels of skill and execution: excellent work according to the standards of the practice. Knowledge, skill, uniqueness, and provenance ensure the value of a creative product, meaning that symbolic value is an experientially based, embodied understanding. Professional creators thus make reference to the 'experienced eye', an appreciation of what is involved, often gained through trying to work in the same medium as, or to replicate the work done by, others:

> I will throw a pot and then look at a piece like [X]'s and think, 'Shit. How does he do that?' Look at my pot. I am thinking more highly of the value of the professional maker, your understanding when you go and buy a piece of ceramic from a professional maker, the actual skill and experience that is behind that. [Design 11]

Symbolic value can be displayed by progress within the field, in finding new ways of addressing challenges raised by the artistic form (Hesmondhalgh and Baker 2011). But the recognition of value must travel beyond experts. Successful economic exploitation of the creative work requires as wide an understanding of the structures of symbolic value as possible. To this end, a designer making high-quality wood products sees his remit as including educating potential consumers:

> I show people 'round. We do workshop tours. People come in and they can see all that is involved. How it goes, from the slices of trees through the whole process. I spend quite a lot of time talking to people about the design process, how it takes time and all that stuff. [Design 1]

By this account, the recognition of distinction and differentiation—of value—depends on the 'aesthete's eye'. For Bourdieu (1987: 202–3), the aesthete's eye is fundamental for acknowledging value in the creation:

> The work of art exists as such only if it is apprehended by spectators possessing the disposition and the aesthetic competence which are tacitly required.... It is the aesthete's eye which constitutes the work of art as a work of art.... The pure gaze, capable of apprehending a work of art as it demands to be apprehended...is inseparable from the appearance of producers of art motivated by a pure artistic intention, which is itself inseparable from the emergence of an autonomous artistic field capable of formulating and imposing its own ends against external demands.

Meaning and value are therefore the consequence of two mutual constructions: the cultured habitus and the artistic field. The artistic field creates an aesthetic disposition without which it could not function (Bourdieu 1987). Such an understanding of value as appreciable only by the expert gaze underpins assessments of value in fashion textiles, for example:

> The nature of the type of process that I use...it is a technique, and it is quite tricky to do and not very many people are doing it. To the untrained eye, the process looks digitally produced, like something they could replicate. But people who know can tell the difference between digital printing and silkscreen printing. [F&T 37]

The 'aesthete's eye' denotes cultural capital, 'the possession of cognitive, affective and bodily means for appropriating meanings associated with art and other objects with complex aesthetic properties' (Ravasi et al. 2011: 302). Expertise—an ability to read the symbolic capital within the field—is considered essential in terms of distinguishing the value of creative goods, seen in Gans' (1974) distinction between high and popular culture, or Greenberg's (1961 in Caves 2000) 'avant-garde' and 'kitsch'. Becker (2008), for example, distinguishes between 'knowledgeable' and 'occasional' audience members. Caves (2000: 185) writes of 'casuals' and 'buffs', again reflecting levels of involvement, where buffs 'cultivate extensive knowledge of the activity and likely possess some training or serious experience in creative activity. Their viewpoint and interest lie close to those of the practicing creative artist, critics, and others professionally involved.' The development of taste, the aesthete's eye, however, reflects distinct investment processes, necessarily requiring time and concomitant economic resource to acquire.

Some aspects of symbolic value do appear to defy economic valuations. Just as the search for 'value' in individual practice benefits the practice and the community of creative practitioners, value incorporates some concept of the common good (Banks 2007, Hesmondhalgh and Baker 2011):

> Obviously, there is an extensive, wide-reaching, and diverse programme of participation, learning and outreach, working with communities such as young people, older people, drug offenders, offenders. Working in prisons, working with homeless and vulnerable women, working with young, unemployed people and an increasing emphasis on working with disabled people—particularly with the deaf community, training practitioners around working in accessible practice, working with adults with learning disabilities. [Theatre 107]

This example from theatre detailing examples of its outreach, encompasses voluntary and revenue activity, stimulated in part by the need to diversify revenue sources, but also by the widely held ethos that 'theatre is for everyone'. There is thus a political nature to the understanding of cultural experience as a public good.[1] It recognizes the transformative power of an imaginative performance or good, valued for the 'of-the-moment' experience it delivers (Holden 2004). It offers an artistic critique that 'stands opposed to the commodification of other forms of values which money will never be able to take into account: artistic value, aesthetic value, intellectual value and... cultural value' (Chiapello 2004: 593). It is the explicit recognition that cultural products have a value above and beyond any extrinsic or economic value; that 'culture does not simply produce value, it embodies value' (Holden 2004: 49). Such activity, however, is necessarily circumscribed by the requirement to be supported by a revenue source. Values are necessarily entangled.

[1] The public good argument should not be confused with public policy agendas for the arts, with their focus on 'impact', social inclusion, learning etc., allied as they usually are with increased bureaucratization and evidence of 'linear' outcomes.

We have suggested that symbolic value can never exist entirely independently of economic projects. The economic remains intertwined with the symbolic; even where there is little financial motivation available, it is noticed by its absence. We must now further develop the argument that the process of value construction is distributed across the socio-material networks through which creative goods circulate.

Cultural Intermediaries and Economies of Qualification

As we have noticed, consuming symbolic capital is hard work. Consumers may need the assistance of cultural intermediaries to provide understanding of creative products' qualities and value (Ravasi et al. 2011). Their function depends heavily on the theorizing of production's relation to consumption (Matthews and Smith Maguire 2014). For economists, they play a role in reducing information asymmetries, providing the pre-purchase information particularly pertinent for experience goods. In the creative sector, however, quality uncertainty rarely reflects information asymmetries, but rather the elusiveness of what constitutes 'quality' (Beckert and Musselin 2013, Rösell and Beckert 2013).

Cultural intermediaries play an important commentary role, policing the boundaries of style (Matthews and Smith Maguire 2014). In Bourdieu's work (1984, 1993), they bridge the gap in cultural capital between producers and consumers, placing the product in context, explaining its cultural value and attributes, and the evaluative schema and standards that are used as the criteria for judgement (Khaire 2017). Mediators within the 'babel of assertion' (Jones 2003: 150), they translate cultural meaning from one level of discourse to another (Negus 2002), 'making the new less unfamiliar' (Khaire 2017: 36). The role is associated with critics and those in curatorial and brokerage positions (Wright 2005, Foster and Ocejo 2015), as well as occupations whose explicit function is promotion and 'talking up' reputation (Wijnberg and Gemser 2000). Greatest credibility devolves to independent certifiers whose critical opinions depend on their 'mental or even material archives' of successive observations over time (Hirsch 1972, Caves 2000, Hutter 2011, Khaire 2017).

Yet an account of value as produced and consumed by experts, while the public looks on and learns, fails to acknowledge the complex interrelations of symbolic and market value inhabiting overlapping worlds. As McFall (2014) notes, cultural intermediaries are but one type of actor among many involved in the qualification of goods: they are the 'professionals of qualification' (Callon et al. 2002: 206). To concentrate on their role alone ignores the actions of other material and non-material actors and intermediaries whereby things are rendered valuable. Diverse mechanisms of valuation bring order and stability to the uncertainty endemic in the creative industries, providing the categories and tools that allow individuals to 'appraise, compare and classify' (van Zanten 2013: 79). Judgement devices, both social and material, characterize singularities in opaque markets, allowing consumers to make choices (Karpik 2010). As heuristic devices, they enable comparison through networks (personal, trade, and practitioner); appellations (names that define singular products, e.g. labels, certifications, product brands, etc.); cicerones (critics and guides offering specific evaluations, embodying symbolic authority); rankings (hierarchical according to one or several criteria); and confluences (techniques designed to channel consumers) (Karpik 2010: 45). All these instruments act to reduce uncertainty about quality; all are the paraphernalia of the modern consumer market ensuring a 'reasonable choice'.

Through such mechanisms, goods are rendered valuable relative to others, made commensurate by technologies of classification and the formation of categories (Espeland and Stevens 1998, Bowker and Starr 1999). Quality not only implies difference, but positionality, as it serves to rank objects against one another (Aspers and Beckert 2011). Despite creative producers dealing in values that are not amenable to quantification, numbers and rankings have become prevalent instruments of commensuration: 'value depends on the metric' (Lampel et al. 2006: 11). Sales figures, box office receipts, weekly totals of radio listeners, best-seller lists, and TV audience sizes act as 'cues to producers and disseminators . . . as to which experiments may be imitated profitably and which should probably be dropped' (Hirsch 1972: 649, Taylor 2003, Rösell and Beckert 2013, Kuipers 2014). Valuations from 'certification'—prizes, awards, and organized competitions—provide the imprimatur of quality and prestige (Caves 2000, Anand and Watson 2004, Anand and Jones 2008).

From this purview, the cultural intermediary and her auxiliary in judgement devices exist at the interface of production and consumption in the markets for creative goods. Although the structure of creative production, with creative producer and distributor separated by legal distinctions and different sets of organizational practices, often gives a superficial appearance of consumption as the passive follower of production, production and consumption are dynamically connected. Production is only completed in consumption, as McFall (2014) suggests. Further, she chides (McFall 2014: 46), cultural intermediaries are 'in possession of a unique mix of engineering skills to bridge a gap that only appears through the constant articulation of the necessity of intermediation'.

As is reflected in our empirical material, the distinctions between producer and consumer are less clearly drawn. Production and consumption work in a continual dialectic of valuation, facilitated by intermediation and intermediaries functioning through and across networks, rather than in linear relations. Furthermore, processes of qualification apply as much to the consumer and producer as they do to the artistic production: as Appadurai (1986: 4) reminds us the economy 'consist[s] not only in exchanging value but also in an exchange of values'. Both production and consumption are mechanisms for sending and receiving social messages (Appadurai 1986), rendering the individual a 'practical sociologist, expertly negotiating matters of social ordering via thousands of clues embedded in the everyday actions of others' (Cohen 2012: 37). Cultural products, both their nature and the way they are consumed, position, and allow individuals to position themselves, within a system of social relationships (Smith Maguire 2014).

We understand orders of worth as constructed through the interactions of producers and consumers: the market for creative goods is an 'economy of qualities' (Callon et al. 2002), where buyers and sellers mutually singularize and value goods. Quality is not a given, but established through a process of 'qualification', namely the 'singling out of specific characteristics and the attribution of specific meanings that establish a connection between object and market actors' in an economics of quality that refutes the *de gustibus non disputandum* of formal economics (Beckert and Musselin 2013: 1). Crucially, this process of qualification spills out beyond the symbolic value of the text, and into the market-driven valuation of IPR.

Recognizing the Value of IP

In Chapter 2 we note the expressions of pleasure, pride, and possession that attach to creative production, and the moral rights identified and invested in this. Just as there is no recognition that moral rights have economic effects, so there is little recognition that the skill and knowledge necessary to satisfy the 'aesthete's eye' also incorporate economic worth. Although creative producers understand such skills to have been acquired over a period of time and as a result of much effort it may, as the following comment shows, take some time for a producer to recognize the dual nature of their IP. Here IP stands both as a measure of esteem within the field and a means of generating income:

> I work in an education institution so I am used to explaining things, talking about processes, and giving students ideas. I am a printer. The problem I have had with students is that you show them a technique and you show them a process, and they come and do a work placement with you—I am quite happy to give people advice, in the same way that other people have given me advice—but some people have taken it a step too far. Often they don't realize. They don't see it in terms of how much you give away. You take them to trade shows. They meet your customers. They then go away and set up their own business. When somebody comes into your business to do a work placement, it is then that knowledge transfer... effectively what are you handing over? At what cost? They tap in using the same fabrics and the same processes, and the same combination of those things. They tap into

> the same customers. That is when it gets a bit scary. Sometimes when things happen, you think, 'That is across the line'. Recently I have stopped having placements because I think, how useful are they? [F&T 35]

In this case, the value of the tacit knowledge of techniques and networks that have been built up comprise both the symbolic and economic resources available to the producer, as well as her goodwill based on reputation and authenticity within the sector. Value is embedded in concrete situations such as tradeshows as much as it is in the material expertise of printing. A student 'tapping into the same customers' is exploiting the IP of the instructor both in terms of symbolic capital, and the economic value of seemingly mundane interactions with others in the field. Thus, value need not lie in the direct creation of a product. It may also come from knowledge of a network, as is seen in this example from a music company producing sequences for film, TV, and ads:

> A lot of our guys are multi-instrumentalists. If you came to us with a project that was piano, guitar, strings, voice, etc., anything that was 'bandy', we would do it in-house. Outside of that, if you were wanting a chase sequence for *Spooks* with some really nice da-da-da strings and stuff, we would normally have a select pool of musicians. The ones we use are locally based. We want them to come in and to know them, to like them and to work with them. The guys we work with are normally from the orchestras, or even just session players, and we bring them in-house and record them here. If we were doing anything of a larger scale, like a full orchestra section, say 30 players or larger, then we normally go down to London. We have got a couple of fixers down there that we use, and they know who to book. But again, we have got a fair idea who we would ask for. We would want 'so and so' to lead the session, and we would want 'so and so' for the harp, etc., because you get to know players' skills. [Music 88]

Value here resides in the knowledge of a network in terms of who would be appropriate for what projects: the IP of the arranger stems in part from his ability to work as an intermediary in the field, combining specialist knowledge of musical skills with the much more mundane apparatus of booking and arranging recording sessions. Yet knowledge, in whatever form it takes, may not be automatically acknowledged as having value. Instead, it emerges as valuable through the interactions of producer and consumer, which may not centre on a commercial exchange. As the following example from service design shows, the ability to successfully monetize one's own IP depends on being able to recognize the value that is offered clients, and can become part of the 'billable process':

> When I think of IP and what we do, for instance, even just fleshing out and identifying what the issue might actually be for a client, to me it is a part of the billable process. I think in the past that has been given away and the client says,

> 'Thanks, we are off'. We are now viewing that basically as our intellectual property. Now we will share that and give that to you once you are our clients. When we are using our experience to help somebody frame a problem or a challenge, then that is somebody using our expertise. [Design 17]

The value of IP emerges here through a process of qualification between producers and consumers, as the collaborative framing of a challenge transforms the specialist knowledge of the designer into a source of economic value. Similarly, in this example from the computer games industry, the worth of a project is qualified through iterative market interactions:

> We created a sports game and put it out on the X-Box Live Indie Games channel. It totally failed. I did not make enough money to pay back what I did. But the game came to the attention of an American guy who wanted to make another sports game and was interested in the engine. He licensed the engine. He paid royalties at certain milestones through the development of his game. The game IP is his. The engine remains ours. He had to license the engine again for another game. [Games 52]

A game—a source of value envisaged by its designers—failed, but led to a third party's recognition of value in the underlying mechanics of the games structure. The worth of creative goods emerges through a process of qualification on the part of producers and consumers, an 'economy of qualities' (Callon et al. 2002). Not only this, the intermediary role of qualifying value is clearly distributed, not simply across human agents, but also across the material technologies of game building.

Quality and differentiation, aspects of the symbolic value of IP, also are seen as having a broader economic purchase. IP becomes associated with ethos or identity, which becomes in turn a source of economic value:

> I think a big part of our brand is our openness, honesty, and personality. I don't think that there are many organizations who are as open and as honest and as friendly. I think that is definitely part of our IP. How do you put a value on that? [Design 27]

The designer uses 'brand' in an informal way to signify reputation and worth (the role of formal brands as cultural intermediaries has been discussed by Moor 2008). In doing so, the speaker makes an implicit statement of the economic worth of a good reputation and good working practices, just as she asks the rhetorical question of how one values openness, honesty, and friendliness. Differentiation, creating an identity, involves identifying a particular focus or rationale, as with this statement from theatre:

> The primary driver for this organization is as the home of new playwriting, and the buzz phrase around that is 'from page to stage'. It is not a new phrase but it has become increasingly important that we cling on to that because that very much is a unique selling proposition. In terms of local and indeed international markets,

> our expertise is in terms of taking work 'from page to stage'. That is not about developing writers but it is about developing plays and so there is a distinction and it is very important that we maintain that. [Theatre 102]

Differentiation is here understood as a crucial means of staking out the organization's local and international markets, and with them its revenue streams. Indeed, business vernacular has penetrated this space, with the organization's rationale a 'unique selling proposition' (USP), and its differentiation a 'buzz phrase'; combined with the well-articulated strategic focus of the organization, we gain a sense of clear recognition of the connectedness of specialist expertise, IP, and future revenues.

Cooperative relationships and associations are seen as adding value, as producers enrol further participants into networks of qualification. Association with high-value broadcasters, for example, is a way of enhancing profile and identity. However, producers must tread a careful path, for excessive associations present the danger of diluting a particular identity, as is explained in this example from theatre:

> If you have so many co-producing partners, whose is it? Where is the artistic style? Where is the house style? If we diminish the brand, the hard-won brand in any way, shape, or form, then who is having the conversation with whom? [Theatre 102]

Concern with artistic integrity means that revenue may be forgone, for fear of identity losing its value, as these two statements indicate:

> One theatre company licensed out their production for somebody else to recreate. They are not touring it themselves. We have not done that. No. It is very, very important that our artistic and authentic artistic voice is loud and clear. [Theatre 102]

And:

> Associations through product licensing may be detrimental to brand image. I won't have control over how it is marketed or how it is presented and therefore I want [licensing] to be quite separate from my brand. [Design 14]

It is noticeable in these quotations how the speakers refer to the value of their 'brands'. Brand is being used in an informal manner here rather than the professional practice discussed by Moor (2008). Each speaker uses the term 'brand' to refer to the economically valuable aspect of the organization's IP; brand is part of a business vocabulary including marketing, design, and USPs, and stands alongside a vocabulary of creative work that speaks of artistry, authenticity, and style. Creative producers are able to not only articulate but also manage these dissonances in their own practices, to exploit and produce multiple kinds of value.

The brand clearly belongs to the organization. It is hard-won, and may take years of marketing, reputation-building and related efforts to establish. A necessary stage in translating value into a potential financial reward thus comes with identifying property: economic rents stem from assets. IP/IPR serves as a market device where symbolic worth and economic value may be mutually constituted, whether in relatively informal accounts of 'brand', or through more legalistic approaches to the ownership of IP rights. The necessity of recognizing the value of property is reflected in the journey of one games company, initially intent on supporting nascent designers, but soon realizing that it should secure the IP of its involvement:

> To start with, the whole point of publishing was to make some money, but the biggest thing we wanted to do was to have someone in our community to have a massive hit. We did not want to prevent that by sitting there saying, 'Oh no– we own the IP'. The youngest person's game we have released is 14 years old. You'd have to get his parents to sign the agreement. Now, we have more professional games being made because they have a better chance of being hits. Ideally, that is what we wanted. But our remit now is we own the IP. If we are working on it, we own the IP that is released. [Games 51]

The firm here has developed, or matured, from a zealous community focus to a position embedded in professionalism and legal structures, although the intention remains the same: to invigorate the games design community with a hit.

As has been seen, the recognition of the value of assets and property varies between sectors. In some areas, there is resistance to the concept of property being attached to a creative output, particularly because of the implicit link between property and alienability. This resistance is articulated here by a designer, who sees value as being linked to inalienable personal experience:

> A lot of the value that we generate is not capable of being translated back into that notion of property. In effect the ability to define something as having value in the context of intellectual property is its ability to be alienated. The concept of value that we work towards, and that we generate, is essentially mostly inalienable value. You can buy a cinema ticket, so that is an alienable transaction. But most of what we try to generate here is actually meant to be inalienable. The fact is that you cannot buy or sell the experience of going into the gallery. It is not something that we would value. You might be able to buy a ticket but actually you cannot buy or sell that value. The conventions of intellectual property don't necessarily reflect the values that we are generating, because the notion of intellectual property is effectively, how do you monetize forms of value that exist within the organization? There are forms of value that we have that cannot be monetized. [Design 10]

Nevertheless, the survival of creative producers depends upon their ability to monetize IP; this is, as we have said, the fundamental *business* of creative industry. Having established that a text has symbolic value, the creative producer must set about establishing IPR that may be exploited. IP rights offer the entrepreneurial producer multiple ways of exploiting the symbolic value of a text in economic terms, and they do so by constructing boundaries around different aspects of the market object.

The IPR Object and Boundary Construction

Sociological approaches to valuation focus on the mechanisms by which objects are constituted as valuable: the entanglements of legal form, materiality, and practice that distinguish, to use Kornberger et al.'s (2015) example, between a high-stakes sporting match and a knock-around in the local park. In the creative sector, IPR becomes a crucial mechanism whereby the artefacts of creative labour are constituted as *economically* valuable; as Fourcade (2011: 48) reminds us, law 'is not the context for economic activity, it is a location where a set of economic outcomes is produced'. The ascription of ownership and property rights to creative products is premised on the ability to construct boundaries around objects and claim them as distinct: multiple economic outcomes are often ingenuously sliced from the creative work. Traditional concepts of property, however, map more directly onto the perceived boundaries of things, with law premised on the 'thingyness' of an entity (Cohen 2012: 18). A book, for example, can be understood as a solid, bounded object that can be bought and sold; as soon as it takes another form, it may accrue other kinds of rights, to be licensed, for example, and refusals:

> I have, in my time, worked in the second-hand book trade and that all seems so simple. People buy a new book and when they don't want it anymore they sell it to the second-hand bookshop .... But with the e-book thing? Once you digitize it...and as long as the data doesn't get corrupted, you don't have the right to sell that because [the e-book] is exactly the same. [Publishing 73]

Even though it is often portrayed as something with existence prior to, and separate from, the law, IPR is not a physical object. The IPR object exists only as a result of the legal framing of particular rights. It is a 'non-existent object' (George 2012: 9). Defined by law the boundaries of the IPR object do not necessarily coincide with a physical form, and, as such, are 'redefinable', 'never entirely known' (George 2012: 98–9). IPR is a complicated creature, and may bear little resemblance to the intuitive understandings of rights among creative producers:

> Say you are a young act and you have written a song. You have recorded the song once in your bedroom. You go into a recording studio and the guy who owns the

> recording studio says to you, 'I really like your music and I am going to let you record in our studio for free. No charge. I really like what you are doing'. The [phonograph] recording is created and obviously that particular young person does not understand anything about neighbouring rights and so who owns the recording, who owns the song? The song is owned by the songwriter(s) depending on how that is agreed among those writers. That song will lead to completely separate rights. For simplicity let's just call it the work. The work is owned by the songwriter(s). The phonograph will obviously be owned by the person who paid for it, so that would be owned by the studio. If those young people, or inexperienced people, then decide that they want to release that record out on iTunes, they put it on Spotify, or they release it as a physical CD single, they can be somewhat surprised when that studio owner comes and asks for his share or brings them an awareness that they infringed his copyright as the phonograph owner. [Music 91]

In this example the speaker distinguishes between the various related rights accruing to a song and to the recording—and also between the experienced musician and the young novice. Clearly, the subtleties of IPR have to be learned by those in the field, as different art forms and collaborations raise issues of object and boundary construction that form the basis of claims to ownership:

> In the UK, if you create a piece of music you are always deemed as being the author of that music and you would always be recognized as such. There are rights that come along with the creation of music. The imagining of that music and the recorded hard product are completely separate. Most people think about a recorded piece of music, you know a CD or a flat recording of some description. In that recording there are both the master rights, the rights that relate to the actual recording itself; and then the other rights which are of the song—who wrote the lyrics, who wrote the melody—which is separate to the actual pressing of the music. As a composer you would create music. It would be published in some capacity and you would receive royalties for the broadcast of that, and if it was sold you would receive royalties for the selling of that part. If you are a publisher you get different royalties. The money is always split. [Music 88]

Aspects of a creative object, rather than its whole, thus have a variety of different potential IPR facets. These different facets may be present in a variety of different ways, to different audiences, through different media, in different territories, and at different times. Each of these existences or manifestations has the potential to be labelled IPR and monetized. The IPR process thus extricates an entity in a particular form, bounds it, labels it, and assigns ownership. IPR is performative: it simultaneously recognizes, creates, and formalizes the multiple claims of ownership which may attach to a creative work (Towse 1999). Rights also come with different possibilities in the sense that they might be sold, or licensed for different purposes, such as reproduction, performance, or broadcast.

IPR—as a store of value—may be sold on to raise money for cashflow or investment. Even within sectors where rights are well established, however, understandings of rights may not reflect the technicalities of ownership when it comes to distribution and sales, as for example, this comment from film:

> I think sometimes producers, independent producers, don't understand the ownership issues. They don't understand what they are giving up. People will sign a sales company deal and then a distribution deal and then they celebrate that. But they might not always realize that in fact they are giving almost complete ownership of that away. Producers will do artwork for film and then be horrified when the distributor will dump it and do their own stuff. [Film 65]

Sales and distribution agents invest in films, providing part of the 'slate' of investments that finances the film. In securing investment, producers sign away IPR rights, with the result that the now-alienated 'product' is marketed according to distributors' requirements.

As the label copyright indicates, the primary right is the right to make copies. The rights an author assigns (or does not assign) to his publisher via contract can be hugely important. In publishing, for example, copyrights include film rights, play adaptation rights, merchandising rights, and other licensing opportunities. Other rights include the right to license pieces of a work, such as excerpts, to third parties.[2] These secondary and tertiary rights can be more lucrative than primary rights, as their market potential is much bigger. Thus, for example, as well as owning the IP rights of the book, a publisher also will try to secure rights to e-books, translations, film, radio, TV, or stage optioning; games or any potential apps that might be allied to the book; and merchandising if the brand is strong enough. A book is no longer just a book, but a constellation of primary and subsidiary rights, each having different values and different markets:

> There is the whole cornucopia of subsidiary rights. If you are dealing with the author direct the chances are you can just gather them all together, bundle them, and it is about squeezing the value out of every book. For us, the real challenge is actually getting as many rights as we can possibly to work with. Sometimes an agent will hold back rights. It is hard to get film rights because normally, if there is an agent involved, they want to keep them because it is just more money and they will cut us out as another person. We tend to only get the film rights if the author is not represented by an agent. Even though a film is really good for the book we don't actually get money for it, beyond what might come in increased sales. In the past, for example, some authors were very pleased to be published at all and would sign away world rights for example, and sign away for the period of copyright. That was very nice for the publisher, because the publisher could then go off and

[2] Unlicensed use of excerpts, as per the Google Books project, has proven controversial, as its compatibility with copyright law is contentious (Na 2006).

> sell the other rights and exploit those other bits of rights. But now, a lot more authors are agented than they were, even 10 years ago. There is just far more agent activity. The trend is now to retain more of the rights and to offer limited rights. You would offer, for example, English language rights for certain territories, and then the author and the agent would keep the rest of those rights and be able to sell them separately. But, for the publisher sometimes it makes it slightly less attractive for you to take on that particular book. [Publishing 77]

This example shows the complexity involved in managing IPR objects, and the multiple ways in which a creative work can be sliced up as a source of value; it also shows the skills needed on the part of market participants in maximizing a value that is, in this example at least, understood as a zero-sum game. IPR makes it possible to realize value, but at the same time places the creative producers (writers or songwriters, their agents, publishers, and record labels) in a conflictual economy.

Development of all the potential facets of a product is also an essential aspect of building the brand. Investing in a brand multiplies the value across all of the products derived from that IP:

> We are looking to license the rights to produce toys, books, posters, bedding sheets, all the things that go along with a successful game. We have several of the top manufacturers in different areas all looking at doing that. It is the same with publishing because we have licensed the publishing side of it. For all of these people the first thing they want to see is what have you secured, what are your intellectual property rights? [Games 41]

These rights are highly contested, with purchasers seeking the best deal available to them:

> Once upon a time it used to be TV rights. Now they want video on demand, online, DVD. You could say 'That is the only territory' [e.g. UK, or the Americas], but now they just want worldwide rights. They want this. They want that. [TV 53]

Changes in technology may create the opportunity for new IP rights which may not be captured in existing contracts. Theatre, for example, is responding to the impact of digital with experiments in live-streaming of performances and rehearsals:

> We have put something in the actor's contract that basically agrees that they are happy for that to happen. We obviously have to ask the permission of the writer and sometimes the translator. We have always made it quite clear that we have permission to live-stream, but we don't have permission to put that up on, say, Vimeo, so that anyone can then watch the recording completely. We do use the content to create trailers out of it. But again, it is not exploited. [Theatre 103]

This illustrates the shape-shifting nature of the IP object and the attempts to secure its identity in order to monetize it. Each intervention in the 'journey' from creator to receiver becomes entangled in a rights and potential monetary stream, with different agents in the chain accessing different IPR and from this the ability to generate monetary reward.

Rights have both longevity and value—Caves' (2000) *ars longa*—which can itself be the object of further market transactions. Over time rights ownership becomes complicated, and the habit of large firms strategically buying up rights can impact upon the plans of smaller producers.

> We have actually got an intellectual property query going on at the moment over an app. The point of it is to geolocate Scottish books, Scottish authors, Scottish settings and so on .... I think it is fine to put up a book jacket and to geolocate it, but any further use of that character in any way would start contravening trademarks. Rebus is trademarked, also Long John Silver, and Peter Pan and Tinkerbell are all trademarked by Disney, even although they came from books, and they are out of copyright. The whole aim is to sell more books. It would be free to download. It is a publicly funded app. We are not making any money out of it. We are simply producing it and the whole aim will be to get people to discover new titles when they are out and about, and they will hopefully buy them. For us it is a non-commercial app for publishers and for the authors, so we hope that it will generate some revenue. We have engaged a lawyer to help us on that whole area of how far can we go in using those characters. [Publishing 74]

Or again, with a firm seeking to base a computer game on an old British TV programme:

> We did a trace of who owns the rights. It turns out that Dreamworks own the rights. You think, 'They have got more lawyers than we have got staff, so can we really approach them?' The programme probably only resonates in the UK, so is that actually worth it? [Games 50]

The process of settling outstanding IPR claims on existing or future projects is known as secondary rights clearance. It can sometimes work out as too expensive to continue the project, and can be seen as adding additional risk:

> I have just signed a deal with a distributor to take on quite a few of our shows, but one or two of them we have found couldn't be sold because the revenue did not justify what we would have to spend to clear the rights. If we continue making history [programmes] and use a lot of secondary material, and we cannot afford to clear a lot of it up front at a better package level because we don't know if it is going to sell, it is quite prohibitive in terms of actually making lots of sales. [TV 53]

The costs of clearing rights are not only in terms of expense but also in terms of time:

> As a smaller company it all comes down to yourself to check the rights clearance, which can be a burden on resources and very difficult unless you have got in-house teams. [TV 63]

In selling a programme, there is more than one bundle of IP involved, with, more often than not, music rights to be cleared:

> The music all used to be composed and the composer used to keep more or less all the rights. Then we went to audio networks because we were fed up with the composers taking all that income and charging us for it up-front, so audio net was very cheap. But they had all the PRS [Performing Rights Society (now PRS for Music) licences] and they made all the income. But now we have realized that there is money to be made from PRS and MCPS [Mechanical-Copyright Protection Society] licences, and the composers have realized that they cannot play us as they used to. We now have a 50:50 split, so that means that now I can count on not hundreds of thousands of pounds worth of income, but tens of thousands of pounds worth of income from music on certain shows. Actually, the shows we make are really well-suited to it because there are beds of music running all the way through—it is not just the titles and the end credits. That is an area where we kind of have a secondary line or a secondary layer of IP which is a secondary line of income. [TV 61]

There is clearly a great deal of sophistication involved in managing the rights to creative products, and the subsidiary rights that they invoke. Creative producers must learn the skills and at the same time must learn to manage the associated symbolic value of the product. For example, leveraging the symbolic value of accessing something requiring secondary rights clearance in a broadcast may be unwise unless the rights can be guaranteed:

> You should never let an editor to get hold of material that you have not cleared the copyright of. Because as soon as it has gone into the edit and it works, and then the series producer and the executive producer of the programme, both within the company and at the broadcaster, have seen the programme, and think it is fantastic, and really love it, then it is very, very difficult, if you have not cleared a piece of material for use. There is a tendency because clearance takes so long and the edit time is so limited, to say, 'We will use it, I am sure we will be able to clear it'. Then you can get yourself into difficulties, sometimes only internally with your bosses saying, 'I am really sorry, but we could not clear it' and they think that the film does not look as good as it did. [TV 63]

Conversely, the productive 'dissonance' between different media and the associated rights may form the spark for an entrepreneurial reworking of a product in a different format (Stark 2011), as is illustrated by this example of a creative product originating in theatre:

> I went to see a theatre production of a play and I just thought that it was brilliant. I could see that people might think that it would be good for TV and there was a TV company sniffing around. I thought, 'It's not very easily done on TV but for radio it would be brilliant'. We just pitched that. We got accepted by a broadcaster before I had been able to have a conversation with the theatre director. That was

> quite difficult. It was embarrassing for the broadcaster because they loved the script. But we had not actually got the rights to do it. The theatre could not see why we were interested in pitching it because there is not much money in radio—the budget for that was something like £20,000; you have got to pay the actors, everybody involved; there was not a writer to pay. So I just said, '50:50' which seemed a fair way to do it. The thing is there is not a huge market so they can be fairly relaxed. It was not like me saying, 'In doing this we own the TV rights and the film rights'. It was just radio we were talking about. Something like that has its moment and that was its moment. [Film 68]

IP/IPR as the Business of Creative Work

The previous sections have shown how IP/IPR allows creative producers to slice their work into multiple revenue streams, simultaneously performing an object of economic value and recognizing claims of ownership to it. This value is made manifest in economic exchange and through mechanisms of capitalization such as business plans or accounting (Muniesa et al. 2017). Yet awareness of rights ownership issues relies heavily on the practices of the sector under consideration. In some areas, knowledge of, and concern with, rights are not well-established because the financial reward emanating from them may be limited: 'Intellectual property rights. We cannot even deal with that because we have an impoverished sector' [Dance 121]. Nor does theatre usually generate heated issues of ownership:

> It is quite standardized and everyone knows how it works. We don't make a profit. Although we might kind of co-create work, because no-one is making any money out of it there have never been any issues of anyone saying, 'It is at that script development stage, actually I am responsible for that piece of the play'. I think actors and a lot of creative teams are not actually aware of copyright around collaboration and we just ignore it because no one makes any money out of it.
> [Theatre 102]

In other words, recognition that the development and sale of IP/IPR is the business of creative production depends very much upon there being an effective market for creative works. The demands of originality also may conflict with opportunities for further monetizing some aspects of creative products. For example, although set designers would own the IPR in the design, it is unlikely they would find markets for it beyond the re-staging or touring of the original work, and even reproductions are not guaranteed to recycle the design:

> It is always stated that any reproduction of the show has to be agreed and in writing. Obviously somebody who has designed the show, they own the rights....

> It is theirs to own as they wish. But it is unlikely that they would recreate or re-use work. It is not really likely. A new director would say, 'I am sorry I have just seen that in [x] and I don't want it again. [Theatre 107]

Nonetheless, creative producers expressed concern about the lack of skills in dealing with IP and its role as a crucial device in terms of monetizing and exploiting creative works: 'Very few people really get their heads around intellectual property anyway and seem to misread where the potential exploitation is' [Design 10].

Failing to understand the multifaceted nature of IP exploitation can lead to missed opportunities and revenues:

> When I first started, we were selling designs to companies and they would then use the prints in whatever garments they made. You would be paid for your design and they can do whatever they want with it and you lose all copyright completely... you just got your fee. [Design 23]

'Selling a design' is a rough and ready mechanism used by an inexperienced designer. It shows a lack of awareness of rights and, more important, of the different types of payment systems that might accrue from these rights. A more experienced designer would specify that her designs relate to specific products, thus maintaining control over the use of her designs in different product streams, via different forms of sales: design fees and the sale of copyright, design fees and the sale of licences, or arrangements involving fees plus royalties. Others, however, have deeper understanding of the issue:

> I would never sell my ownership rights to a design. I would sell the licence [to specified reproduction]. In that sense it makes it quite clean, if I want to reproduce a piece then I can. [Design 14]

Although IP/IPR serves to organize and firmly establish music, publishing, broadcasting, and film, it still works through industry norms and practice. In UK broadcasting, the focus on IPR was given an extra fillip by the Communications Act 2003, which gave more control over secondary rights such as foreign and ancillary sales and repeat showings (Faulkner et al. 2008), which meant companies, rather than broadcasters, owned their IP:

> For most Indies, the Act totally transformed the business because it let companies own their IP and therefore they had a value. Because otherwise independent production companies have no value. They only have the value of the people in them. The Broadcasting Act changed the ownership in the IP to us. We would say quite rightly so, because we spend bloody ages working these things up and they [only] pay us for the process of manufacturing it? I don't think so. But that was what was happening before. Also, a small private industry has grown up in distribution. We don't just put it back to the main broadcasters, we put it with other people as well. [TV 56]

Here a legal distinction over ownership has mobilized an entire sector, giving independent producers a 'value'. Once again, the value is performed by the IP/IPR nexus and the socio-material practices—here in distribution—that spill out of it: the 'indies' have moved from an abstract understanding of worth as 'the people in them' to a concrete value embedded in organizational routines, accounting, and contracts or 'rights'.

While the value of IP lies in its carefully qualified symbolic worth, economic rents are extracted from the variety of IP rights that can circulate in the market. As we have noted, IPR offers a fecundity of facets: portable, reproducible, and sliceable in multiple ways. Within certain sectors, we can also identify a further distinction within IPR, as the following illustrates, where 'rights' refers to the ownership rights to a specific programme, and 'IP' relates to a programme format which may then be sold on a franchise basis to other broadcasters:

> 'Intellectual property' is not a term that we use. We tend to deal in rights rather than in the IP. When thinking about television, IP tends to belong to formats. IP is associated with format, rather than 'one-off' productions. *Bake Off* would be one. They are now doing their own range of cake tins and stuff like that. It is brands and rights rather than IP in our world, although it is the IP. [TV 60]

Rights, as this and other examples show, permit the original IP to be spun into all manner of alienable goods: the television show's cake tins, the toy merchandise that follows a successful game, even the gallery's logo and images on posters. In music, where the language of rights informs the sector, creative producers understand that IPR is much broader than the music alone. IPR permeates all aspects of activity: 'mastheads, labels, imprints, logos and so on become literally part of the company's assets' (Ryan 1992: 168), as this example from a festival promoter illustrates:

> Intellectual property and property rights come into everything, every facet in every project, whether it be the branding that we use for our particular projects, the copyright of the things we buy—we pay a graphic designer, we will buy the copyright. We own the copyright for our logo. Intellectual property can be the brand, it can be the music that we commission, it can be the box-office information that we have, customer details, it can be the artist details that we have, the bank information that we have, our website address. There is quite a lot actually. [Music 95]

Legal frameworks establish proof of ownership and simultaneously construct the IP as a tradable asset and source of future revenues; and there may be an extraordinary return on relatively small investment in terms of securing rights for a project. Here a games design was licensed by international entertainment and hotel chains:

> We have only spent a matter of a few hundred pounds protecting what we had, to theoretically go on to negotiations for a price of upwards of £50 million, all based on making sure we had the rights from the start. We did not spend a lot of money to do it and we just took good advice. [Games 41]

Although most creative producers recognize IPR as a means of making their products valuable, fewer recognize the underlying business of creative production is the development of IP and property rights. Only a small number of companies in game and film seem to recognize this, invoking a highly financialized understanding of creative work:

> We will acquire more intellectual properties to grow. Because each time you get one it generates revenue and then you can build into it or re-invest into it and increase the revenue that it generates. We are starting with that in mind so everything we do, we are trying to inflate the value of the intellectual property, either through regeneration or as an asset to sell later down the line. Most games studios that are technically capable of building games don't necessarily understand the underlying value behind the thing they have just built. I think that brand and intellectual property are horrendously undervalued. [Games 49]

To conclude, this chapter has shown that the business of creative work is the construction and exploitation of value through IP/IPR. Its core is symbolic production and it is this symbolic worth that is traded in markets for cultural goods. The construction of symbolic value is distributed across heterogeneous, socio-technical networks of producers, consumers, 'prosumers', commentators, and devices, with processes of qualification applying as much to the consumer as they do to the idea itself or the artistic production in which it is staged. The symbolic judgement of worth, therefore, becomes yet another aspect of value coordinated in the IP/IPR nexus. Crucially, the symbolic valuation of worth is contingent upon the slicing of IP/IPR facets into works of all kinds that can circulate in the market and be valued. The process of qualification is the interplay between economic value, property rights, and symbolic capital embedded in the IP/IPR nexus. Our empirical material shows creative producers continually working to articulate these simultaneous orders of worth, managing their frictions and exploiting their dissonance (Stark 2011), all in the pursuit of creating value. In the next chapter we shall seek to explore how that value can be exploited by market participants.

6

Realizing Value

For all its Romantic inheritance and connotations of art and creativity, 'cultural work is still work' (Banks 2007: 8). As such it demands compensation; creative producers must eat. In the last chapter we argue that the IP/IPR nexus is the mechanism through which creative products are constructed as valuable: that it orders and settles the multiple evaluative principles at play in creative production, and bounds and singularizes goods. The present chapter follows these goods into the marketplace as creative producers seek to realize value from their work by moving it through the commercial distribution system essential to the continued production of art (Becker 2008).

The previous chapter concluded that IP/IPR brings creative producers to the realization that the business of creative industry is the exploitation of IPR. It is not creative labour that produces value, but capital, here in the form of IPR. As one musician notes: 'You have to understand that musicians and writers are manufacturers of copyrights. Copyright is where all the money comes from. It is not the most glamorous aspect of the music industry, but it is absolutely the most important' [Music 92]. Creative goods, even once sold, continue to generate returns: the *ars longa* property (Caves 2000): 'It is a product but unlike other things. You continue to make money from it if you own it, you continue to make money out of it' [TV 59]. This enables the IP holder to pursue the rents from creative goods through time and space (Caves 2000), and in the last chapter we saw how the slicing of IP into IPR gives rise to multiple economic contracts for future revenues.

Market situations represent contests over value. The present chapter seeks to describe the struggles and mediations that encircle IP/IPR as it becomes the site for these confrontations. As a fulcrum of the market for creative goods and services, IP/IPR allows us to draw links between the structural forces identified earlier in the book, especially debates over creative labour and entrepreneurship—casualization, precarious labour, the oligopoly of corporations—and the day-to-day activities of creative producers as they seek to realize substantial enough returns to allow them to continue in the business of creative work.

We begin by considering simple kinds of exchange, such as the provision of a service or the sale of goods. We show how IP, understood as reputation, brand, and technical skill, allows creative producers to strengthen niche market positions and support prices. The discussion then moves to the role of market intermediaries, whether digital gatekeepers or specialist distributors with a knowledge of particular markets, and their positive and negative aspects. IP/IPR offers a means of transacting with intermediaries as it circulates through the market, generating revenues from a wider range of sources, seeking to turn the proliferation of media to the advantage of the producer. IP/IPR also forms the legal basis for the licensing agreements that allow producers to generate revenues while holding onto ownership of their works, often brokered by large-scale collecting organizations. At the same time, economic pressure may dictate that creative producers give up their rights: money talks and economics trumps law. In sum, following IP/IPR through the market allows us to trace the conflicting opportunities for, and pressures on, creative workers as they seek to realize value from their products.

Industry Structures and Standards

We have already seen how the creative industries are bound up in discourses of entrepreneurship and self-governance, and are a microcosm of broader labour relations in the twenty-first century. This is compounded by the 'full torrent of Romantic thought' (Ross 2000: 14) with continuing implications for the artistic wage. The joy of making 'art for art's sake' implies that creative workers are more likely to settle for 'psychic income' (Throsby 2001). Indeed, Caves (2000: 231) refers to a 'pact' among creative personnel that 'sustains the pursuit of shared artistic goals despite paltry pecuniary reward'. With the exception of the few stars, creative labour has a capacity for self-exploitation through low wages, insecurity, long working hours, not recognizing 'work', and the general precariousness that characterizes the field (Butt 2007, Oakley 2009).

Such structural relations are played out through the mechanisms of payment for creative work. In the most simple arrangement, IP—the creative work—is commissioned or exchanged for a fee. Practices vary widely across sectors. In theatre, for example, the writer earns a fee, or a writer and a translator will split the fee and may receive a percentage of the box office. Contracts with artists and designers involved in production, such as set designers, lighting designers, or dramaturges, are usually fee-based. Professional associations such as the Writers Guild and the Society of Authors may set rates or negotiate scales for their members. Other sectors are less well-organized:

> Dance is very, very different. I think dance as an industry is so far behind theatre. It is less formalized. There are fewer practitioners operating at that professional level. We may employ a choreographer who might be equally as inexperienced [about fees] and then you are in this place where you are trying to suss each other out. It is about haggling, you are haggling here. [Dance 115]

TV and radio—once characterized by national collective bargaining which regulated wage rates, and now by freelance labour and individual contracts following 'debureaucratisation' (Saundry et al. 2006)—pay workers by the job rather than the hour (Ursell 2000, 2003). Overall, there is limited labour organization in the creative industries: 'With a vast population of new entrants wishing to join this labour market, union organization along traditional lines is seen as either irrelevant or simply bypassed' (McRobbie 2004: 133).

This example from the games sector illustrates the oversupply of potential talent and the dangers of continual undercutting of rates in order to secure exposure:

> Graduates will normally just go around and say, 'We cannot find a job. I tell you what, maybe we should strike up on our own and start our own company'. So, they form their own little company. They will get some money from somewhere, from their parents or whatever, and they will cobble together and spend six months trying to work and build a game. They will then quickly realize that you cannot actually make money from self-publishing games because it is very difficult to do. They then start going out and getting contract work and then they are starving students that are used to the student lifestyle and are more than happy to take fairly low wages. [Games 46]

In the absence of any form of collective negotiation, creative producers may be valued solely by 'the marketplace', however poorly understood. This leads to a lack of parity in the distribution of rewards in a given sector:

> We caught [X choreographer] at the very beginning of his career and so we got the original work for a really, really cheap amount. When we extended the right, it became much more expensive. We were paying double, for a year, than we had paid for the original for three [years]. But that was because he went global at that point. I always felt bad because we were paying him so much more than we were paying for the other choreographer's work that we were re-buying. But it is just the marketplace, isn't it, and the fees that a certain choreographer can command. [Dance 122]

Market rates, prompting scruples about differentials in pay, are dependent upon fashion, interest, and competition. A further complication comes from previous 'greats', the big names whose works are now out of copyright, and drag market rates downwards. Caves (2000: 359) puts it in the language of the economist: '[a]mong creative workers, the serious composer faces a particularly adverse situation. Besides the art-for-art's-sake oversupply common to all creative workers, she faces Beethoven as a formidable and un-depreciating competitor who benefits from lower performance preparation costs and asks no royalties.'

In certain sectors, the unions still provide some protection, specifying pay rates for different types of activity (see Caves 2000, Hesmondhalgh and Baker 2011, Saundry et al. 2006). Theatre, for example, has well-established standards on payment:

> Theatres are more consistent. They would get caught out if they are not following the industry standards. Because actors move from one house to another, they are going to say, 'Hold on'. [Dance 115]

Union regulation stipulates actors' payments for a minimum number of weeks on a film or at the theatre (Caves 2000). Music also has established practices with performers' rates, covering a range of activities, set by the Musicians' Union. Pay rates are firmly established by agreements, as in the case of music being recorded for a film track:

> When we hire musicians for sessions there are very set rules, which is great for us because it means that there are no grey areas and there are no problems. If I am booking a session, I will say, 'We are looking for a three-hour session,'—which is your standard—'here is your set rate, this is what we will be recording on to'. We have got very strict rules of how long you can record them; what breaks they have got to have and how much overtime they can have, how much of the recorded music from that three hours you can then use on screen, if they are dubbing an instrument, and what payment they have to have. We basically get them to sign off to say that you can use this music for this project and this is it. [Music 88]

Union rules are necessarily territory-based and influence hiring decisions:

> We are able to use a lot of Scottish, English and UK-based musicians because they are not under the American union system, so for the American clients that is very highly prized. If we had a musician here we would have to pay him a session fee, and we would also have to pay them a porterage, a payment to bring their music or musical instrument. It is just a nominal amount depending on how big or small the instrument is. In the American system they have to pay their players a session fee, porterage, health and welfare, dental insurance—all sorts of additional fees that we just don't have here. For the American market they see us as a cheap option essentially, much as we would see the European players because they don't have the same union rules as us and so they are much cheaper. [Music 88]

Music is characterized by numerous forms of payment, for example, residuals (royalties) for master recordings, performing, and rehearsals (see Ryan

1992, Toynbee 2013). Royalties accrue to the mechanical reproduction of music. 'Mechanical royalties (the name harks back to the mechanical reproduction of sound) are paid by record companies for each copy of a song that they record' (Caves 2000: 299). Performance royalties are paid for a public performance, either at a concert, on TV or radio, or as background music (Caves 2000). A synchronization licence is paid when copyrighted music becomes a soundtrack to a film or TV. Rates are often high, however, as, once used, it is usually difficult to re-use such music in other contexts. Neighbouring rights (i.e. related copyrights) distinguish between composers' and performers' rights for music (Towse 2007), the latter now having rights in their performances. There is a distinction between named performer or principal, and chorus, with the former paid fees or percentages, the latter paid wages. Featured artists have royalty contracts, while backing musicians are paid a flat fee.

One of the main challenges for creative producers is the increase in the number of platforms, media, and payment methods through which creative content may be accessed. Ironically, as access has increased, the ability to secure meaningful income from these various outlets is reduced:

> Access has devalued what a piece of music is. People don't expect to pay for music now. HMV is closing down. Record shops are struggling. People will pay for some music online. But free service funded by advertising does not get much for the songwriter. A debate for the next generation in the music industry is how we make it still worthwhile to record music commercially. We all go to see bands. We all love live music and so live music has got an assured future. But with recorded music, it gets to the point where if you cannot make something from the weeks that you spend in the studio and the effort you put into songwriting, then what is the point of doing it? The Internet has been a wonderful thing in terms of people being able to get their music out there and reach the public. The days when they had to have record deals, that is gone. It is fabulous. It has never been easier to get your music out there. But it has never been more difficult to make money from it. [Music 92]

Changing distribution channels, alongside changing technologies and listening habits, affect the cultural art form that is dependent on them. The first half of the following quotation makes this point, alluding also to the changing structural relationships in the market. The second half raises another point, not dissimilar to the problem of *ars longa* raised by Caves: the market—in this case for recordings of major classical works—is saturated and there is little justification for adding further:

> Increasingly in the classical arena, orchestras now have to raise funds for their own recordings. They get a more generous royalty percentage after the record company has gotten rid of their costs, which in most cases they don't do. The time when

> orchestras made sensible income from CD recordings, I would say, are gone. I don't know if an orchestra would make significant income through these. If you look at the longest established labels like the London Symphony Orchestra's Live label, I think the income that has generated through those recordings is not by any means what it used to be when they actually were paid by the recording industry to do that. Because all the record shops have closed, and specialist record shops tend to be closing. I would not go into a relationship with a label that would not have an online distribution. I think physical sales tend to happen at concerts. One place where you can still shift reasonable amounts of CDs is when you have the repertoire on CD that has been performed that night. But the market has changed. With the classical area there are 20–30 recordings of all the major pieces and at a very high level and they are available, so you have to have justification for doing it. [Music 89]

Musicians have seen other profitable markets shrink, for much the same reason as a vast expansion in broadcasting exposure led to a decline in the worth of its content:

> As an industry, television has really taken the same kind of hit as music. The budgets for programmes are much smaller. There is some good television music out there and there is some dreadful stuff too. [Music 93]

A proliferation in outlets also has affected fees:

> Now, there are about 300 channels on television so the value for music on an advert that is going to be shown for a very short time on one channel, is going to be far less than what an ad in a world that only has four channels is going to be worth. [Music 91]

Publishing also has well-established norms, with standardized contracts between author and publisher reflecting the conventions of the sector. Up to the nineteenth century, authors received either a fixed fee or shared net profits, not royalties. Sales-dependent, open-ended deals only became possible with advances in technology, with George Eliot one of the first to receive royalties in 1860. By 1900, royalties had become standard in both the UK and the US (Caves 2000), with differences between hardback and paperback; books in translation paid less due to translation costs. Because of the higher risk, first-time authors may get a contract based on net receipts, which may, after time, become a percentage of recommended retail price. A publisher explains the basis of calculations:

> Recommended retail price was the traditional method. Now, increasingly, people are using the percentage of net revenue, which is a percentage of the money that actually comes back to the publisher. This allows publishers to do deals that otherwise they would not be able to do, and which are in the author's interest. If you are selling to book fairs, some will look for something like an 80 per cent

> discount. It is a whacking big discount and the margin is very thin. Percentage of net revenue allows you to do those deals. [Publishing 78]

Industry standards are dictated by the leading publishers in the field with others looking to them to set rates:

> The royalty rate for e-books is generally, not always, 25 per cent of net receipts. Agents are looking at this again and many are asking for higher rates, which we don't give. Because we feel that it is not something which should be decided on in a piece-meal fashion from contract to contract. It should be decided across the industry, the Penguin and Random Houses, by them and the big agencies. It might go to a straight higher percentage. But I have had an agent with a very established London agency suggesting that it will go in with 25 per cent, but if the books sell more than a certain number of copies then the royalty rate would go up and that would mirror, if you like, the hard copy arrangements. [Publishing 78]

New entrants to the industry and changing structures trickle through to the payments made to authors:

> In 2005–06 and even 2007 there was a panic in the publishing world. Sales were going down. Digital was coming in big time. Amazon was dictating prices to all of the publishing houses, pushing them down to below the point where they could make any profit. The big publishers were seeing the digital world was dictating the terms and conditions and their profit margin. It had to tighten the strings. So across the board amongst the mid-listers, there was about an 80–90 per cent cut in advances. Mine went down from £30,000 to £3,000. I think some small publishers don't give any advances at all. [Publishing 81]

In sum, work across the creative industries is subject to greater pressures of fragmentation, competition, and insecurity. Workers in sectors with well-developed protocols may fare better than those in the most unorganized or casual labour markets, but the overall trajectory is the same: changing distribution channels, a proliferation of access, and increasingly powerful gatekeeper corporations making it harder for the majority of creative workers to receive adequate recompense, while concentrating rewards in the hands of a few at the top of the market. If they are not to be exposed to the marketplace without protection, creative workers must develop means of justifying their prices for products and services. We now move to an analysis of those practices.

Pricing and Selling

For goods to circulate in the marketplace, creative producers must price their work. Price mechanisms are symbolic systems, all the more so in a field based on symbolic production and consumption. They convey meanings about the object, and those who make, distribute, and acquire objects, including their views of a just or fair value of the good (Beckert and Aspers 2011). Thus, a price is not just economic, but also a social, cultural, and moral entity: 'There are social worlds behind the world of prices' (Fourcade 2011: 42). Although prices are suspended in a web of meanings, of which the 'impersonal business-like meaning is only one' (Velthuis 2005: 159), prices help to organize the market, offering 'standardised ways of constructing proxies for uncertain and elusive qualities' (Velthuis 2005: 160; Espeland and Stevens 2008).

Pricing in the creative industries, as our discussion will show, is complex, embedded in social norms and market structures. Creative producers often struggle to attach prices to their work through conventional means (such as the marginal cost, or cost of materials) and may experiment with different formats. Our interviewees articulate a labour theory of value, stressing the uniqueness of the producer's IP as a basis for maintaining a reasonable standard of pricing. Their IP, understood as an instantiation of technical ability and tacit knowledge (itself understood in terms of the historic labour involved in gaining skills) and reputation, acts as a market device capable of stabilizing prices in the face of market fragmentation and competitive pressure.

Pricing an object moves it into a realm of market circulation. On this basis, the search for an equivalence might seem an appropriate means of arriving at a price. Yet equivalence is thwarted by the uniqueness of creative objects—not necessarily in terms of seeing them as commodities that are singular yet still exchangeable and need to be evaluated by skilled intermediaries (Karpik 2010), but simply in terms of things that are *incommensurable* and often *unable* to circulate. Here is one such example, a company asked to provide the music for a public art installation:

> A concept artist created a 3D piece of sculpture in Germany called 'The Singing Mountain', that you moved 'round and it sung to you. A group were asked to make the music for it, which they did. We had to do strings on the track they used for this. But how do I contract for this because it is a mountain in Germany? When I say mountain, it is a big hill. I thought it was like a papier mâché mountain, but no, it is an actual big hill with hidden speakers. It is open for three months, six months. I don't know what the footfall is and how do I even quantify this? There is going to be an album so that is fine. We can deal with that. We know how that works. But a big fat mountain? I said, 'Can we agree on some kind of percentage as an uplift fee that they are happy is reasonable enough and that we are not taking the piss?' Essentially we both know that there is no way to quantify the amount of people that will come round and actually hear this mountain sing. It was a really weird one. [Music 88]

The search for equivalence often can appear ridiculous, a device for justifying figures pulled 'from the air':

> We were asked to go and contact a label for a very famous old Rat Pack track. We said, 'Look, it is for a Scottish advert—television only—for a kitchen company, for one year'. We got asked by them, 'How many folk are in Scotland? How big are you? What should we charge you?' We thought, 'You just pull these figures from the air. Blatantly.' [Music 88]

Future revenues, another possible source of price, remain frustratingly uncertain, leading to comparisons with gambling:

> It is quite hard to make money in fiction. It is a bit like gambling in terms of you might win big, once in a while. But it is very once in a while. If you win, you win really big. But the rest of the time you are bumping along. We have just bought two books from the same author and I have effectively paid an extra £1,000–£1,200 for the theatrical rights because I think that the second book lends itself to film in a major way. I am taking a punt. A total punt. That is why publishing isn't for people who need to feed their kids. Because it is gambling. It really is. From that £1,200 we would get back, say, £6,000 or £8,000 for a first option [to develop it into a film]. Now with the vast majority of books, they will only ever go to first option. [Publishing 77]

Pricing raises the contentious issue of the relation between market prices and other forms of worth. There are etymological links between price, prize, and praise, and pricing is necessarily linked to appraising and prizing (Stark 2011). Creative producers tend to think in these terms. For many, pricing denotes 'value', a composite term conveying uniqueness and quality:

> The uniqueness of a lot of the products we have in the retail space, I have to explain time and time again: 'This piece is a one-off' or 'it is a small-batch production piece so there will never be hundreds of them'. The price point reflects that.
>
> [F&T 27]

Value is linked here to scarcity, but it may equally reflect quality, including the 'thought' that goes into a piece:

> The more expensive pieces I sell are valued for their design as well as the materials and things that are used. I think they are much more thoughtful pieces. Quite a lot of research and time has gone into creating them. It is hard to explain it without almost making the cheaper things not sound as good, because they are. The value, I think, is in the thought behind them. [Design 3]

Another simple solution to pricing goods might be at cost plus a mark-up, as if they were standard, manufactured commodities. Yet this analogy does not work well in a sector where material costs are unpredictable and where they are only part of the canvas of creating work. Producers struggle to articulate the cost of their own skills and imagination, which undermines any cost and margin-based approach:

> I have just done a new body of work which is more about trying to explore the preciousness of silver, by trying to not have as much silver in it. I was working in base metals and industrial enamels to lower the overall material costs. But then you get to that point where it still has to have some value, because if you look at it like, 'It took me three hours to make, £60 worth of materials', and use that to come up with a cost, is that really the cost? I don't know. [Design 15]

As noted in the previous chapter consumers must possess sufficient expertise to decode the value of the 'thought' hidden in these creative goods. The responsibility for communicating such value may be delegated to cultural intermediaries or may be, as seen in the earlier examples, part of the routine interactions of the creative producer. In previous chapters we have noted how the links continue between producer, or author, and the product, even as it becomes detached to circulate in the market. Creative pieces, like art, are thus only partly dissociated and detached from their maker (Slater 2002b, Velthuis 2005). The product becomes attached to the consumer via the IP of a creative producer and following a process of qualification between sophisticated producers and consumers. These are the active processes through which the product becomes valuable. They re-establish the social relations that money obscures, recording the strength of the attachment in the price.

These quotations from producers point to some kind of labour theory of value, where economic worth is created by the transformation of raw materials through labour (Beckert and Aspers 2011: 9). Velthuis (2005) identified such a discourse in his study of pricing in the art world:

> Whereas a labour theory of value has by and large disappeared from academic discourse since the late 19th Century, it still figures prominently in everyday models of the market. Invariably the argument is that an artist deserves a certain price level either because of the skills he masters, the training he received, and the experience he accumulated or because of the amount of labour he spent on making the work. (Velthuis 2005: 137)

The labour value does not, Velthuis (2005) points out, correspond to the actual labour time employed by the artist but instead is a broader reflection of the skill and reputation reflected in the IP of the creative producer. In the following example, a designer reflects critically on her early failure to price in her historical labour, the time that has been invested to get knowledge and skills to a certain level. It is only with experience that this producer learned to incorporate this historic labour into the pricing of a product:

> The first time I did the Chelsea Craft Fair at the King's Road, I was exhibiting next to a ceramicist. She was producing these huge big conical pots with very thin bases

> and they were £400 each. They were flying out the door. People were buying them up. She was doing really, really well. I said, 'How long does it take you to make one of those?' She said, '25 minutes'. I said, '25 minutes and you are charging £400?', and she said, 'Yes, but it has taken me 25 years to get to the point where it takes me 25 minutes to make it'. Now I also understand what happens with kilns and ceramics and how much they explode, and I thought 'You are absolutely right'. I was a bit green then because that was the first time that I had ever done a show like that and I am sure my price points were not that brilliant. But people will come into the shop, pick things up and say, 'How much? Oh god, I could do that!' I say, 'Go and do it then and do it to that level of skill'. Part of my job is to educate these people and to tell people about it. [F&T 27]

Once again, a producer stresses the role of education in terms of opening the eyes of consumers to the real worth of a product, as embedded in her own IP. Consumers do not necessarily see this. Association with 'craft' or 'hobbies', for example, may be pernicious in limiting perceived value, resonating with deeply held prejudices regarding cultural production as a 'pleasurable vocation' rather than 'real' work' (Banks 2007: 8).

> Because it might be related quite closely to a hobbyist market, some people see the fact that you do it as being a real privilege for you. It is, and we do have to remind ourselves that it is a privilege that we can do something that we enjoy. But it is not a hobby. I think that does affect their perception in the sense of, 'You do that for fun, so you should not be charging too much, should you?' I think with jewellery because it can become quite a hobbyist, evening-class thing, sometimes it is not until you have tried it that you realize how long it takes and how difficult it is. [Design 22]

In some cases, the materials being used undermine their perceived 'value' or worth:

> Because I work in plastics, there is a pre-conception of what plastic is: 'I can buy that for just £5'. You are constantly fighting against that. There has to be the value and you almost have to design pieces that portray a value, to portray something that is distinctive in order for people to want to part with money. Because unless you charge about 1p an hour for your time you are never going to be able to justify it. [Design 14]

In Chapter 5 we saw creative producers speaking informally about brands as a means of capturing the economically exploitable value of their IP. Here we see producers reflecting in a sophisticated manner on the power of an individual brand to secure prices and generate economic worth. Following are two producers' understandings of the economic possibility of the brand in terms of organizing prices. The first sees a recognizable brand as a strategy for supporting high prices and understands this as a longer term aspiration:

> I don't think I am in a position yet to put my prices up massively because of my brand, because I don't think it is established enough yet. But at some point

I might, especially if I start using a part of my logo on everything, then that will become the pivotal point. [Design 9]

The second reflects on the recognition and development of a brand as a collective ordering of worth, to be invested in and developed through prices that reflect value but are understood as reasonable:

I try to keep it as reasonably priced as possible but still maintaining that this is worth money. Not just the product, but the brand as well. I want people to buy into the brand and buy into everything that the brand represents and be part of that as well. I think that there is value in that, so that is how I price things. [F&T 27]

This IP-driven theory of labour value is often illustrated by the counterfactual:

We learned very rapidly that you could not just put anything out on an IOS [Apple operating system] market and it would make money. You would think that there are millions and millions of users out there who buy this many apps that surely selling 10 units per day is doable. But the point is, that if you are putting rubbish up there, no one is interested in it and that is it. [Games 51]

Unsurprisingly, in view of the more general structural trends in the creative industries and the continued downward pressure on remuneration for creative work interviewees made much of changes in quality which result when there is a focus on reducing costs:

The DVD revolution came in round about 2003–04 where it was possible to self-shoot a lot of stuff. If you were doing a difficult documentary subject you don't want a crew crashing about, so one person with a camera who was also trained to do sound was often the best way to do it. That has been misused because what tended to happen was that production companies who wanted to maximize their profits realized that they could send out a lot of cheap, young people to wave a camera around and it does not cost as much. But all that meant was that you ended up with a lot of rushes that often are not very good because there is nobody there telling you that you do need to direct your shoot. [TV 53]

IP may support a variety of strategies for the realization of value. In games, for example, there are a number of different revenue models including monetization through advertising; add-ons or micropayments for items in the game; freemium, in which some content is given away for free or premium content is available for purchase. In freemium, the free content is fundamental to attracting and building up a customer base, yet, as it does not directly generate revenue, is loss-making. The gamble by creators is that the loss-making will be more than compensated for by the large customer base, of which a portion will pay for content. This strategy requires large numbers, and benefits from the low marginal costs of reproduction of digital content.

Additionally, such a strategy benefits from the network effect, where the value of the content for each user increases with the number of users. In practice, the strategy is challenging:

> [Freemium] requires a much larger user base. If you look at the free-to-play conversion rates and all the metrics that surround that model, you're lucky if you convert 2 per cent. So, if you want 60,000 paying customers with an average of $20 then you need 3 million users. To acquire that many users is very expensive—or you have to make something that everyone is talking about, but then you're relying on every game being a hit. [Games 49]

Freemium distribution requires specialist expertise and enormous reach in terms of distribution. Moreover, it seems to be far more corrosive to the internal goods of this particular branch of creative production, as the strong language of this quotation shows:

> We don't do any free stuff for a number of different reasons. It is a specialist market, freemium, and we would not know what we were doing if we were doing that. It is also a terrifying, scary and soul-crushing world. So, we sell our games. The mobile, especially the iPhone and iPad store, is really brutal and prices are very low. We try to put our heads above that. For our last game we did not put it at the lowest price possible. We put it at one level higher. We have not lowered the price at all. I think it was a game that lent itself to that. I think it is a game that had some extra value in it that people were willing to pay a bit more for. But compared to some other studios that we admire we are still pricing a bit lower. But I think if we were established in the same way they were, we could charge more. [Games 47]

In response to the alienation and helplessness of the freemium model, small-scale creative producers pursue higher added value, higher price strategies, and once again refer to the reputation of their IP as a means of securing higher prices. It is interesting that in this case, as with those earlier, the producer alludes to the future possibilities of reputation, brand, or IP as a means of leveraging revenues: in each case the future remains frustratingly out of reach as market forces squeeze prices and sales.

There are complex conventions around the ascription of economic value to IP, and prices therefore 'only become operational once some form of market order including status hierarchies, identities of agents and standards of value are (temporarily) stabilized' (Velthuis 2011: 195). Understandings of pricing vary by region and by sector, understandings that are often most visible at times of contest or breakdown, for example disagreement between London-based and regional agents over the value of an advance: 'London agents often have very different expectations of the level of everything that we should be offering just because they are used to dealing with big London publishers' [Publishing 78]; or excessively cheap pricing for e-books: 'Publishers are trying to stick to under £5 for an e-book. Some people price them very, very cheaply. It does seem to be the mark of a beginner' [Publishing 80]. Prices are intimately related to the kinds of social relations, prevailing institutional rules, networks, and conventions that underlie specific markets (Mears 2011). Prices may be shaped by social context, for example, in areas of high deprivation: 'People have no money, so you really notice audiences. We have very accessible pricing here. We have £2 for unemployed and [X (a high deprivation area)] residents. The top price is £19.50, which is significantly lower than venues of our size and the quality of the production' [Theatre 107]. But for many there is real difficulty in trying to articulate any mechanism of pricing. Here, the speaker struggles and eventually just laughs:

> Basically, my strategy—you are talking about value-added things—it is like . . . well, not really. I don't have a strategy for it. There is no percentage. Sometimes I just look at what is the going rate and try to balance it with that. There is no structure to it. (laughing) [Design 5]

Market Intermediaries

The previous section explored how creative producers seek to organize simple exchanges of goods and services in return for revenue. These firms or individuals use the knowledge, reputation, or brand embedded in their IP to support prices in the face of potentially overwhelming competition and fragmentation in the market. Nonetheless, there remains a great deal of uncertainty as to appropriate prices and for many creative producers, the effort of understanding distribution mechanisms in the market, or of educating consumers, may simply be prohibitive. As a consequence they rely on market intermediaries to take on this role (Bielby and Bielby 1999). In publishing this role is taken by the agent:

> Some authors feel uncomfortable talking about the money themselves. Or they are first-time authors and they have no clue of what they should expect, and they have no idea if a publishing company is trying to screw them or not. If they want an agent then fine. But that agent then takes 10–15 per cent of what they earn. They could probably have done without. But that is my perspective as a publisher and if it makes them feel safer or happier, then fine. [Publishing 83]

Agents, once seen as 'collectors of rents that an inexperienced author might leave on the table' (Caves 2000: 54), are now understood as serving an important filtering or 'recruitment' role, matching author with publisher (Gulledge et al. 2015):

> We are very conscious that we have to keep the agent and the author happy, because if they are not happy then they will just stop selling us books. We are quite

> wedded to them really. The editors have really good relationships with the agents because they want the next big book. Some are excellent, but certain agents are very self-serving and don't have the author's long-term benefit in mind. They have got their own short-term need to put food on the table, which is a wee bit frustrating. [Publishing 77]

Agents function in areas the creative producer does not have access to. In some creative areas, the agents' role as gatekeepers may raise tensions between the immediate interests of those involved and the wider interest of the creative form. For example, artistic directors, who have a necessary interest in the future of music, commission new compositions. But agent negotiations can complicate the financial risk already posed by such work, which, as unknown products,

> do not bring in audiences, in fact they turn audiences off a lot of the time. Agents can be a disadvantage in trying to negotiate large fees for composers or singers . . . sometimes composers don't get commissions, because agents want to charge so much. [Music 86]

While agents are common in certain sectors they are not in others: 'We don't have agents. We don't work in that way very normally. Dancers, choreographers don't use agents typically' [Dance 119].

Creative production entails the mobilization, coordination, and management of a number of professionals (Hirsch 1972), many of whom act as filterers (gatekeepers), promoters, and distributors, whose function is not only to maintain value, implicitly grading and ranking talents, but to match production to suitable distribution (Caves 2000). As market professionals, intermediaries are an essential part of production and distribution systems and decisions (Khaire 2017). Their role comprises brokerage activities and expertise around the geographical and sector-based specialization of contracts and remuneration. In fashion and textiles, for example, retail is handled by both agents, usually commission based, and distributors:

> The distributor controls everything including the price, the retail price. They control our press. They control the whole market. I think that certainly with markets where there are big language barriers it is really helpful. Russia is an area that I would look for a distributor. But in Europe, agents work well for us. [F&T 33]

Specialist knowledge is important, for example, for realizing value from broadcast territories:

> All television has overspill. British television is, for instance, captured by Irish Cable and Dutch Cable companies and relayed there. There is a small amount of royalty that comes back to us and we have now signed up with a distribution company. The distribution company approached us and said, 'We think we could maybe make some money for you'. The first quarter there was nothing. The next quarter it was £100. Four quarters on and it was £25,000, a staggering amount of money. [TV 56]

The use of agents and distributors is sector-specific. In the case of films, agents vary in experience of movie genre, arts versus horror for example, and how these will sell in various territories:

> To self-distribute... you know, life is too short for me to begin to imagine how to do that, not just the energy it would require, but it is the knowledge and the experience to make that quite effective. It is the sales agents whose role it is to ensure distribution. I hand it all over to the distributors and sales agents and everything goes off to my collecting agent. [Film 66]

Agents' knowledge of the 'long tail' is useful to companies: 'A little series we made for BBC4 a few years ago is with a small distributor and they sell to airlines. I like the long tail' [TV 60]. A skilled agent is able to transform the proliferation of media outlets into a revenue opportunity:

> There are just so many stations and even if you make a crappy series, it makes its money in the end. It will find its audience in some area of the global market. If you go to Argentina and you turn on the TV there are channels and channels of obscure American TV series, movies, and things. If you have got something then you will find a market for it. There is a big hunger for content. [TV 59]

However, by funding new films, distributors are influential in what gets made: 'Art works come to be what the art world's distribution system can handle because for the most part, work that doesn't fit doesn't get distributed' (Becker 2008: 94). The influence of distributors often runs against artistic experimentation. Distributors play an influential role in areas that might be considered the producer's purview, dictating marketing, for example:

> I know a lot of new producers will do a lot of artwork with designers etc., for the film and then be horrified when the distributor will dump it and do their own stuff. Then they will say, 'I don't want my film presented with that', and then they will suddenly realize 'tough'. They [Distributors] will put a helicopter and zombies in. 'But it is not about having a helicopter and zombies'. 'It does not matter, that will sell it'. [Film 65]

In other words, agents can radically transform the commercial proposition of a creative product. At the same time there is unease over the size of rents collected by such intermediaries. High street retail has traditionally filled a distribution role for many producers, as is still the case where the tangible element of the product is important: 'It is hard to work online with jewellery. People really want to touch it and try it on. They quite often have to see it' [Design 22]. Retail outlets, however, may charge high mark-ups on goods, which are then in danger of becoming too expensive:

> Prices are never going to be able to be cost driven because you always have a whacking mark-up wherever you are selling your pieces. We have done pop-up

> shops and all that kind of stuff and I understand why that mark-up has to be there. Retailers and galleries are a business too. But it means that in order for new pieces to sit within any feasible range, your price has to be so low that you are constantly competing against how long it takes you to make, versus how good the quality of the actual piece is. Their IP is, 'We have created the brand. We have selected you. We are bringing customers in. People know us for quality and we are going to add that on to it'. Their mark-up then goes on to your mark-up, your IP. Then you have this product which does not make any sense, because there is no way that something that is £250 becomes, what, £600 or something. I have sold work that has cost me a lot of money and the gallery has got double the amount that I get. You take my amount and my materials and hours, and they have got that times two. [Design 5]

Another detraction of retailing through intermediaries such as galleries is that typically, they show producers' work on a sale-or-return basis: 'What you are doing is putting a lot of work out there that is decorating other people's spaces and making them look quite good, but you are not getting any money for that' [Design 22].

As French et al. (2004) note, there has been much discussion on the impact via the Web from disintermediation or 'reintermediation' of production networks and value chains, 'short-circuiting' existing links with different networks. The Internet offers

> considerable potential for the reduction of both entry and fixed costs, and can thus disintermediate existing retailers whilst also offering access to a much larger customer base. In addition, [it] . . . offers the potential to circumvent, re-order or even remove what were hitherto key nodes within prevailing value chains, and to directly connect consumers with producers and designers/creatives and even with each other. Customers in turn have access to far greater information about commodities, their value, and their supply chains (French et al. 2004: 54).

As the designer quoted above continues:

> I guess with the growth of the Internet and people being able to Google names and trying to get to people directly . . . that has happened quite suddenly for the galleries. It took them by surprise. A lot of the customers did not realize how little we get for the price that they are paying [through galleries]. [Design 22]

The unprecedented opportunity to reach consumers directly has disrupted reliable and established distribution channels (Hirsch 2000). Many freelancers and SMEs use popular websites/e-stores (e.g. ASOS and Not on the High Street) to reach larger audiences and to sell directly. For example, crafters and fashion designers often use platforms such as Etsy, an online retailer specializing in vintage and handmade, to set up online boutiques rather than bricks-and-mortar retail spaces. As with the impact of digital on media, these changes have resulted in market turmoil, with the growth of new distribution channels at the expense of existing, offline retailers. Online shops may grant increased contact with customers, although in a more crowded marketplace. These new channels come with their own difficulties. E-commerce websites have become highly saturated marketplaces, and only provide front-end sales infrastructure with physical distribution left to the producer. There are restrictions too on how designers can package and brand their products and how they can collect customer data—opportunities that, elsewhere, a producer could exploit to build reputation. This designer describes such disadvantages of one website:

> They would not let you put in any of your marketing materials. Now obviously my products have my name on the swing tag and on the label so at least people would know that it is from me as a designer, but it limited your opportunities to build a customer base. That is actually something that I have moved away from. If I was continuing with the business just now, I would definitely look towards retailing myself just because of that. And you can keep the customers' details. [On the website,] there is data protection. They will give you the customer's details to send them the product, but you are not allowed to use their email address for your mailing list. There is missed IP in that you cannot build a customer database, you cannot build a mailing list. A huge amount of sales was going through Not on the High Street, but I was not able to connect with those customers afterwards. [F&T 32]

Such disintermediation turns out to be another form of gatekeeping, with producers and customers separated by the intermediary's own regulations.

The music industry has perhaps received the most attention as to the impact of the Web, with the decline in the power of record labels and the rise of new intermediaries such as iTunes and Spotify, large tech companies that have pioneered and benefited from the market for downloaded music. As Toynbee (2001: 18) notes, 'the music industries have for a long time puzzled with the question of how to maximize music's circulation and yet restrict access to maintain exchange value'. Publishers or distributors have an important role in the intermediation of exchange due to their access to a customer base. In music:

> You have to use a distributor. If you are going into the shops you have to go through a well-oiled organization that can hit all the stores. With the digital sales the downloads are organized through the distributor—CD Baby, iTunes, Napster, Rhapsody, e-Music. If it is iTunes it is usually paid well but if it is e-Music, Rhapsody or Napster, you need lots to stack up. [Music 87]

Many decide to forego more traditional forms of intermediary and publish themselves through the new distribution channels provided by the technology giants. A games designer talks of getting a new game to market in minutes:

> On IOS . . . once you have got your developer account set up, you can submit a game, once it is tested and ready and you have got your assets ready. You know,

> your marketing material, your screen shots, copy, key words and everything else that is required for IOS. Once you have that information ready to put up on the store you can get your game submitted within 15–20 minutes. [Games 51]

It is equally easy for an author to self-publish:

> I was very impatient with sitting around waiting for agents and then publishers to make up their mind. But I did have readers and I did know that the work I was putting out there was okay, and I was quite interested in the business side of it. I use Amazon and I will probably move on to other platforms in due course. Amazon make it so easy. You format the book, you upload it and there it is. I think it is a misapprehension to think that Amazon is a publisher. They are not. They are a distributor. They give you 70 per cent on anything over I think it is £1.99 in the UK. Once your book is uploaded into the Kindle store then it is available worldwide. [Publishing 80]

Again, the accessibility of these distribution channels leads to a chronic problem of visibility and the difficulty for self-published works to be discovered among the 'cacophony of stimuli available to consumers' (Khaire 2017: 196). Self-publishing through the App Store faces the task of surmounting onerous competition. Getting the product known, particularly in markets where there are a lot of small-scale players, is a particular trial. A games maker laments: 'That is the challenge of being discovered. You have got great content but how do you get discovered?' [Games 42]. There are similar issues in fashion, as this maker explains:

> Initially all I wanted to do was to produce on my own. I would make every piece and sell it online. That was the plan. Make one-off pieces and sell them online. But it has proven to be extremely difficult to do that. The difficulty is getting the website seen by enough people and getting it seen by the right people. [F&T 28]

Equally, the technical ease of self-publishing neglects the reality of this competition, as this author illustrates:

> There is no point bringing out books and self-publishing them unless you are willing to spend time and money promoting them. I don't have six months to spend promoting that book. The problem is that many people think that because they have got a Word document they have got a book, or a book that will sell on the Internet. There are 3 million new books on the Internet in the last year, which are all just self-published. [Publishing 81]

Producers can employ social media or seek to generate positive reviews online, but are not optimistic that either strategy can grow the audience in the face of powerful gatekeepers:

> I see people just developing on iPhone. They think there is no gatekeeper. There is, and it is called Apple. Either it is called Apple, or it is called having a huge amount

of money to throw at adverts to get people into your game. There is no other way to do it. We have seen first-hand that reviews of games—there are a lot on review sites—make no difference to the number of downloads. [Games 50]

And,

We have been doing more on social media although I am not convinced that actually widens your audience. I think that it makes your audience more loyal potentially. [Music 94]

For this reason, creatives still sign contracts with distributors for production and promotion, ceding a percentage of sales to publishers and marketing specialists:

Frankly it is no good having a great product if you don't market it just as well, if not better. I think, generally, for some in the games industry, they don't have a clue. Just not a clue. It is a mentality of production and not sales. They can make great content, but they are terrible at selling it and I don't see that changing. [Games 42]

They also recognize that the skills needed to successfully generate revenues from creative products are discrete and separate from those involved in creative production itself:

We are really good at making games. We are really good at making really cool stuff. But actually, making cool stuff does not make money. What we really need to do is to partner up with the people who can actually go to market in those places. At the moment we are trying to find a partner, a marketing-branding partner for our games to help them go to market. [Games 46]

Those who deal with digital intermediaries, particularly small firms, also need skills to survive bargaining interactions with industry titans:

Amazon are really scary. This one big dominant force who are completely driving the prices and who are very, very difficult to negotiate with. I don't think it can be healthy in the long run. But they are really important to us because Amazon is one of our, in fact it is our biggest customer now. It is probably about 20 per cent of my total business. But their attitudes and their behaviour are rapacious and frankly unethical. If you don't pay them marketing spend they will promote nothing. They will make life very difficult for you. They are extremely aggressive. We have been very lucky. We keep a very tight discount with them. Because it is such a ghastly place to work, the staff move on so quickly. With the staff it is always 'We must talk about discount', which we then manage to prolong until the next member of staff comes in. There is no real continuity. But the Amazon pricing model is one that is market predatory. Basically, we are looking at a more concentrated monopoly industry now than we have ever had. Penguin Random House is the biggest publishing house that has ever existed. It has totally swayed the entire industry and it is precisely to fight the impact of the digital economy. [Publishing 79]

In sum, digital distribution reinforces Garnham's (1987: 37) comment, that 'it is cultural distribution not cultural production that is the key locus of power and profit'. Access to distribution determines returns on production. Ross (2013) predicts a bleak prospect for small producers, with self-publishing and digital distribution just two further aspects of the broader picture emerging throughout this chapter: it is progressively harder to make a living as a creative producer.

Licensing

In lieu of the outright sale of IPR, firms may choose to retain ownership but license their work, usually based on a percentage of royalty (Towse 1999, 2003). Where the estimation of future sales, the foundation of a lump-sum payment, is difficult to gauge, licensing is a key strategy for turning assets into revenues, assisting risk management, and creating flexibility. Smaller creators licensing to players with different capacities or roles may be strategically clever; for example, merchandising through licensing agreements given the inefficiencies of expanding into manufacturing and retail. In the previous chapter we saw how IP can be translated into multiple partitions to create IPR. Licensing is a strategy to support such slicing, allowing creators to separate content into different markets, such as licensing a film option on a book, or geographical areas, where jurisdictional copyright law also dictates licence limits. Digitalization of cultural goods and their distribution via the Internet mean that 'licences to use creative work are becoming far more important in economic transactions' (Towse 2006b: 83). The music business, for example, has changed to handling rights. Publishing, film, TV, and radio may also follow suit. Digitalization also allows for more market segmentation reflected in price discrimination.

Rights to the use of work may be granted on a time basis, and are especially the norm in the performing arts. In dance, the choreographer is paid a fee, or royalty for use, with rights reverting after a period. In theatre, copyright remains with the individual playwright or the individual creative team. Elsewhere:

> If a broadcaster wants to broadcast what we do, they have to pay us a fee that goes to our players, based on Musicians' Union rates. Rights are attached to the performance of the music. If a recording is sold, we own the performance. The composer retains the rights to the piece. The recording company also owns some rights there. It is quite a complex, tripartite agreement. [Music 86]

The musician(s) will be offered the rights to the recording created as part of the live broadcast, with the broadcaster having a restricted number of transmissions. Those commissioning music usually hold rights for a certain length of time, including its first performance or the first recording rights:

> When a non-profit entity decides to commission a composer, they pay for the commission. For that they get the right to perform the premiere. They would normally be expected to also pay for the production of the performing material, i.e. the scores and the parts. Then they pay higher for the privilege of actually performing the music. We have started to say that we want it for at least the first run. It depends entirely on whom you are dealing with and how famous the composers are. The more famous the composer, the less leverage you have. We would like to do even more new music. But when you look at particularly more established composers, we are having to pay lots more for the project. We could play Beethoven until the cows come home and we would not have to pay a single pound for that. IP, whilst it guards the artists, in our context, actually it restricts. The commissioning body does not own anything of the piece bizarrely, when it actually pays for it. We don't get paid if that piece is performed by somebody else, even although we commissioned it. It is a very, very generous process on behalf of the commissioner, actually, because you are commissioning for a lot of other people as well as yourself. [Music 86]

Licensing also is a useful strategy where creators are anxious to maintain control of their designs. Because ownership resides with the rights holder, licensees can use the work only as stipulated:

> The design always remains with ourselves. We are producing a piece of artwork and the requirements, the functions, the budget, are all laid out in the contracts. Clients never own the copyright or the design; the ownership of that is always retained. They can reproduce the designs in terms of advertising and photographs. But they cannot specifically go and get the same thing done somewhere else. IP is retained within the company. We will never re-do the design for anyone else. But by the same token they cannot use it to then start spraying it on to all sorts of materials. [Design 26]

IPR provides the fundamental legal mechanism for licensing: 'One could license and expect the licensing model to work only if one had strong IP rights: without them the licensee might well be the one who captures value, at the expense of the innovator [creator]' (Teece 2010: 184). Control over IPR secures not only revenue streams from existing products but also potential new revenue streams. Changes in technology, for example, make possible new ways of exploiting existing products and at the same time cause problems for conventional contracts:

> The main problem is that for a company with a long history such as ours, the old publishing contracts do not specify e-rights. E-books just kicked off really about five years ago. A lot of publishers have embarked upon a retro-fit of their contracts with electronic rights, in other words, they are coming up with a clause and going

> back to each of their authors and asking them to agree to it. Suddenly we were trying to clear e-rights in every single book in our catalogue. It is just difficult because you don't always know who the copyright holder is, and it is hard to get in touch with people and clear it with them. It has been a huge issue with trying to get authors to sign up for e-rights, which is not just an issue of wrangling about control, it is an issue of good housekeeping because they are not protected otherwise. [Publishing 79]

However, as is the case in other areas of IPR, smaller, less experienced firms may lack knowledge and struggle to negotiate appropriate licences:

> I don't know if artists and designers are particularly well-equipped with this knowledge and I would certainly include myself here. We have very little knowledge or experience of exactly what goes in to a licensing agreement or even how to go about attracting that kind of relationship. [Design 26]

The main obstacle to retaining and controlling IPR lies in the access to finance. In film, for example, distribution deals, often required before filming has begun, usually stipulate ownership of IPR (Coe and Johns 2004). In the games sector, most companies aim to move from being a contractor, where the hiring firm owns the IP, to developing products and retaining IP ownership that may then generate revenue from licensing or sales. This in turn necessitates engaging an intermediary to facilitate exchange, a process often conditional upon rescinding part ownership:

> For those that are aware of the need for marketing, they probably don't have the financial resources to do it effectively, which puts them back working in partnership with a publisher or someone who can fund that and all the rest of it. Which means that we will share the success and won't generate all the benefit. [Games 42]

Licensing may offer a means of spreading risk, but again trims the upside available to producers. In this example from the games sector, where the changing nature of games development and production causes considerable uncertainty for developers, a licensing deal and a longer term relationship with publishers spreads risk, but results in loss of IP:

> With games moving more towards the service model where they are updated and they are maintained on a daily basis, you are tweaking the game economy, you have essentially a retained team. You have got a game to launch, but then you have a post-launch team as well who are retained. Because it is now a much longer period, we find it easier to negotiate a back-end royalty share—80–90 per cent of all of the deals we do now are long-term relationships that we are getting into, with a royalty share on the back end. Original IP is high risk, high reward. But there is also the potential of medium reward from the partnership. The partner will recoup the development costs first, 100 per cent, and then once they have recouped them we

> will be cut in for a revenue share of some sort at the back end. We are now into double figures, somewhere between 10 and 25 per cent, depending on the type of project. Obviously, we want to push for 25 per cent but it depends on the partner and where they see the risk. For us, it is a quite conservative approach that allows us to take risk in a managed way, so that the risk would never kill the entire business. [Games 42]

As this shows, licensing is essentially a cautious, risk averse strategy, but one that limits the potential gains available in the case of a great success.

In view of the structure of the creative industries with their large-scale distributors and small-scale producers, licensing deals are inevitably subject to market pressure and legislative protection of IP ownership makes little difference. In the UK, independent producers are granted copyright of their productions for terrestrial broadcasters, even where these have been fully funded by the broadcaster. Producers were therefore free to exploit their IPR aboard, cooperating with international distributors (Zoellner 2009). The pattern of competition and ownership simply changed to reflect this and further changes in legislation:

> It suddenly became a very valuable thing to have a production company. Bigger companies—News International, for example—bought all of the smaller production companies. I think we went through a period where the networks thought they had to play with these big 'super indies'. But actually, it does not work out well for the writers. The networks have been doing very bad deals with writers. I think the networks are now returning to smaller and more creative companies. [TV 59]

Takeovers are just one form of market pressure. Cable TV networks usually demand the signing away of rights, particularly residual rights—payments for each transmission made to actors, directors and writers, and important sources of income to sustain 'talent' during 'dry' periods (Christopherson 2008). Changes in broadcasting finance also impact on IPR control:

> There is a company called Group M which is a huge, huge advertising conglomerate which will do deals with broadcasters where Group M takes the slot. They take a substantial part of the advertising revenue from the slot, so they take the risk and they fund the programme. In return for that they swipe just about all our rights and there is nothing left. It has certainly happened with Channel 5 and with some of Channel 4, some of ITV. Channel 4 has just announced a big-time partnership with this one single company. So we have replaced one vertically integrated, dominant partner who has far too big an interest in it, with another one. What do you do? Money talks. [TV 56]

Licensing may provide opportunities for greater revenues, particularly in the case of 'hits' where merchandising and cross-media deals become possible. It may also provide a means for financing new projects and managing risk but, in doing so, often reduces the upside available to producers themselves. While IP may provide the legal structure to enable the realization of value through licensing, the translation from IPR to cash is not straightforward.[1] Licensing agreements reflect bargaining power, and the ownership of IPR itself does not necessarily translate into a favourable outcome for the licensor. As Towse (2002: 11) notes, 'the value of copyright royalty rates is decided in the market place'. Money talks: economics trumps law.

Collecting Societies

In the face of pressure from distributors and intermediaries, collective management organizations (CMOs), or collecting societies, are an important institutional structure across the creative industries. Their role is to safeguard the protection of rights and access income from these, thus ensuring artists' work is recompensed. This is especially the case in the music industry where, if there were no CMOs, the rights holders of a song would have to individually agree a licence with every shop, radio, or pub that played it (Street et al. 2016). The transaction costs associated with the collection of many small amounts of money would be prohibitively high. Music users would have to deal with individual writers and publishers and negotiate deals. Instead, users go to collecting societies, with whom writers and publishers register their works. These agencies act as intermediaries between music consumers, such as public venues, broadcasters, and streaming sites, and the people who create and own the music, the publishers, and songwriters. Their role is largely to negotiate and issue licences, monitor use, and collect and distribute royalties to the IPR owners, publishers, and writers (Towse 2007, 2013a). They also serve as copyright enforcers and take a percentage of revenues. Although limited jurisdictionally, well-established reciprocal arrangements ensure remuneration for artists through an equivalent collecting organization in most countries (Towse 1999, 2012). Their role, effectively as authors' trade unions, combined with their financial heft, make CMOs a powerful lobbying force in copyright and cultural policy (Handke and Towse 2007).

Collecting societies also work to preserve the reputation and IP of the artists they represent:

[1] IPR can be also directly used for other financial mechanisms, especially where the artist is known and where previous work may impact on future benefits. For example, the photographer Annie Leibovitz used her assets—including the IPR on her work—as collateral in a bank loan, allowing her, theoretically, to better manage her cash flow. In the 1990s, David Bowie issued ten-year 'Bowie Bonds' which paid the bondholders an interest rate from royalty payments (based on IPR licensing contracts) from his albums.

> There are also moral rights involved, as for example, a vegetarian having written a piece of music does not want it used for a McDonalds advert. Or something might be felt disrespectful, a toothpaste commercial might be thought derogatory by someone serious about their music. MCPS would also ensure that moral rights were respected. [Music 92]

More important, perhaps, these societies help to return some revenues to producers in an increasingly fragmented and opaque market, as changing distribution and listening habits impact more traditional ways of earning income from music:

> My PRS cheques are bigger than they used to be but my MCPS cheques are literally pennies.[2] Or pounds. But they are not even one hundred pounds. But my PRS cheques are pretty healthy every quarter so that does form a fairly substantial part of my income. That is from commissioned work. God knows what it would be like if I actually owned the rights to my stuff. That would be keeping me. But it doesn't. [Music 93]

Again, an artist identifies ownership of rights as the basis for a satisfactory income stream, and again this ownership is elsewhere. The artist does receive royalties from collecting societies, but the amount paid reflects broader structural trends within the market for creative goods (Towse 2013):

> Royalties will come back. But it is a question of the amount of royalties, because even if you are getting millions of streams it is negligible. From the artist's point of view, the biggest value in a download is from the sound recording right. If you are an artist and you had a track on iTunes and I downloaded it for 79 pence, probably 55–60 pence of that goes to the sound recording. Now if an artist has made their own sound recording they will get the lot. If they are signed to a record company that goes to the record company, which pays the artist according to their contractual agreement. But the songwriting side of things comes through MCPS/PRS and it is by far the smaller part of it. [Music 92]

In addition, there are practical barriers to the realization of value:

> If you are not a member, the record company will hold on to your share until you join and MCPS will have a back claim on it. There is a lot of money lying in

[2] In music, the main UK collecting societies are the MCPS and PRS who operate collectively under the banner of PRS for Music. The relationship between the two is hugely complex: 'MCPS income comes from the royalties collected on the declining market of physical product e.g., CD, DVD, and vinyl. Downloads, a PRS right, is a reproduction right because the music comes through the ether and is delivered to phone, tablet, or computer. When the music is stored on a computer or a copy is made, it becomes an MCPS right. Streaming is primarily a PRS issue, but when it goes from server to server just for a nanosecond it makes a copy on the server so there is an MCPS involvement in streaming. Using iTunes as an example, to download a track and pay 79p, 8 per cent of that is a joint PRS and MCPS royalty. Two-thirds of it is MCPS and one-third of it is PRS. With streaming it is the other way around. Streaming is performance heavy, so PRS gets the lion share of a very, very, very small royalty, about .085p' [music 92].

> copyright control accounts which are unclaimed because the writer has never joined MCPS and never had a publishing deal. They have had a publishing deal or are members, but they have never registered their songs. Every now and then you get quite amazing things happening where somebody hasn't claimed something for a few years, and the next thing they discover there is £20,000 waiting on them. [Music 92]

It is unclear, in some cases, where unpaid royalties go. Another concern is the level of accuracy in royalty payments. Collecting societies have long been accused of a lack of transparency and more recently policymakers in the UK,[3] Australia,[4] and EU[5] have sought to improve the situation.[6] While a good licensing agreement grants the licensor auditing privileges, these may not be exercised and the process of auditing may not be straightforward. Music, for example, has had a number of high-profile disputes. Complaints range from miscoding of data leading to mismatched or unpaid royalties, to royalties from back catalogues not reaching the artists. In 2004, for example, the New York Attorney General, after finding record labels had not maintained good records or contact with artists, ordered major American record labels to pay out USD $50 million (Billboard 2004) in unclaimed publishing and recording royalties to artists. More recently, a private audit accused Spotify of underpaying songwriters by 30 per cent, resulting in a public dispute and the temporary removal of some content (Sisario 2015). Auditing royalties, which may be interpreted as an IPR enforcement cost, may be prohibitively expensive for the individual artist.

The Economic Value of Value

The definition of the cultural industries is those 'whose primary economic value is derived from their cultural value' (O'Connor 2000: 27). The relationship between cultural capital and economic capital and the conversion of the former into the latter, is most certainly ambiguous. Our final aspect of IP/IPR to be considered, is the capitalization of the entity itself. As capitalization is an essential part of the contemporary economy (Muniesa et al. 2017), we might ask if creative producers are able to capitalize their own IP/IPR and, if so, how. Producers often do not seem aware of this aspect of their IP/IPR beyond a most basic 'common sense' understanding of IP/IPR as products and designs: 'The

[3] See Intellectual Property Office (UK) (2012).

[4] See Australian Government Department of Communications and the Arts (2018).

[5] See European Commission (2012).

[6] Licensing and collecting societies have been the subject of recent policy attention. A number of countries, including the UK and Australia, also have encouraged the development of collecting societies' codes of conduct. Such codes of conduct are self-regulatory agreements, based on principles of transparency and fairness.

monetary value? It must be massive. It must be huge. Because if you take those products away my business would fail' [Design 15].

And:

> The value of our IP? It is valueless really. Actually, for the business plan, we have put a commercial value on existing designs. It is based on their resale value at the lowest end, if they were to be replicated in a pattern book or through a magazine. We have taken a basic figure and applied it to the designs that are on paper so that gives us a figure. But that figure is always questionable and would not be brought into any accounts for the bank or for the company accounts. It is more an intangible amount that is there. Tomorrow we could pull out 100 garment designs and they would actually be sat here on the table, so they exist. [F&T 34]

Others, however, see value as, first, firmly established in IPR ownership and second, associated with brand, where brand and brand awareness are seen as lying at the heart of value:

> Within certain business documents, if I am actually sat with someone who is interested in what the actual value of the company is, or if I am actually pitching for some sort of funding, I will make sure that they are aware that I have made every effort to protect my IP, which obviously goes against company assets and it is something else for them to take on board. I think the measure of your value, of your IP, is very much in both what you have created to date, and in customer base, loyalty, sales to date. I think also if there is a way of measuring it, it is . . . your market's brand perception of your company—where does that position you in terms of the market? Who would people say your competitors were? But then also moving forward, it is your future potential earnings and market growth. That is the main part, isn't it? [Design 25]

Games is another sector where there is huge variation in understanding, ranging from the very basic: 'It is worth what you can get for it. It is not worth jack shit until somebody buys it and so it is hard to value it' [Games 52]; to a distinction between game value and brand value: 'the value of the game would be its revenue and potential revenue over xx number of years' [Games 45]; to a more considered appreciation of the various dimensions of IP, in particular differentiating between games and underlying technology:

> The game IP probably is not worth anything really because there has not been that breakout hit. The one or two successes we had are now quite a long time ago and have faded a little bit. It is probably the technology that is the big thing now. That has had an impact definitely. We had an investment offer and we did get an evaluation of the business. We have got a rough idea of how that IP has improved the valuation of the business to a potential acquirer and it is quite substantial. It has probably increased the valuation of the company by maybe three- or four-fold in the last couple of years. Quite a tangible figure. But it is not down to any one piece of IP. It is down to a collection of IP. [Games 42]

Creative producers only begin to articulate IP/IPR as having economic value in and of, itself when they grapple with the techniques of valuation necessary for, and interaction with, the financial world, an investment, or an incorporation.[7] In each case, as the following example shows, accounting technologies offer different ways of seeing and understanding value (Miller and O'Leary 2007):

> We are about to reincorporate as a company and our accountants are going to be doing up our final balance sheet as a partnership. For the first time we are actually going to have to put goodwill on to it—the value that the company has, the reputation it has, the IP it has and whatnot. Until now, we have never actually formally valued our IP, or the reputation of the company, so that is going to be the first experience. Informally it is just sitting down and trying to figure out what is this piece of technology going to be worth. How can we reuse it in the future?
>
> [Games 43]

Once again, concrete practices of valuation are shaped by the market, and broader understandings of how one might realize value as a creative producer. It is as Faulkner et al. (2008, citing Cox 2004: 61) write: 'the definition of personal success in television now is as much financial as creative.... One of the most powerful role models is the independent producer who builds a company to the point where it can be sold for millions of pounds to a broadcaster or a major international media company, or whose formats are bought by the big American networks.'

To conclude, we have begun to see IP/IPR as a site where struggles over valuation are played out. IP/IPR provides opportunities for smaller firms to strengthen niche market positions through developing their IP in the form of reputation and brand and building up a loyal customer base. It offers a means of transacting with intermediaries, whether digital gatekeepers or specialist distributors with a knowledge of particular markets: IP/IPR can circulate through the market and generate revenues from a wider range of sources, turning the proliferation of media to an opportunity for the producer. IP/IPR

[7] There are three standard approaches to the valuation of IP: cost, income, and market methods, each with their own challenges. Cost methods value copyright on the costs incurred in the creation of the IPR, typically research and development. In the case of a song, this could include studio hire costs, session musician fees, songwriter fees, and estimates of the artist's time etc. Yet these costs may not have bearing on the ultimate value of the IPR; blockbuster movies may fail and amateur videos may go viral. Income methods value IPR on future potential earnings, which typically involve projecting future income streams and discounting them to present-day, a well-established financial valuation method. The more established the artist, and more stable the market, the easier this valuation method is. However, given inherent unpredictability, there is an element of crystal-ball gazing, relying on a degree of 'hope': 'For brand new titles, a lot of the estimation comes down to past experience and looking at what comparable competitor products are generating' [Games 49]. A market valuation method is an estimate of how much the market would be willing to pay for the IPR. In tangible assets, similar transactions provide insight. The market value of IPR is often challenging as goods are, by definition, unique and market transactions often confidential.

also forms the legal basis for the licensing agreements that allow producers to generate revenues while holding onto ownership of their works, and these can be brokered by large-scale collecting organizations. However, reflecting broader trends in the marketplace for creative goods, structural forces in the market lead to growing casualization and precarity, concentrating revenues in the hands of a few increasingly powerful, and usually technology-based, gatekeepers. Economic pressure may force creative producers to give up their rights, undermining the scant regulatory protection available. We return to the matter of legal protection in the next chapter.

7

Protecting Value

The previous chapter explored strategies for realizing financial reward from creative work via IP/IPR. If artists are to realize value from their work, it follows that they must be able to protect that work, which means excluding others from generating rents from the same materials, here and elsewhere, now and in the future. This, of course, is the stated purpose of IPR (Towse 2010). In particular, the incentive-to-innovate theory depends upon the availability of future revenues to encourage production. As we have shown throughout this book, however, protection is just one of IP/IPR's many functions.

In this chapter we conclude our journey with IP/IPR as it travels in the market, examining how it operates as a means of protecting value. We find that its role in providing protection is—at least from the perspective of the small-scale producers we have studied—highly limited. First of all, in a sector that depends upon the construction of symbolic goods, the nature of copying itself is far from clear. As is the case for intangible investments (ideas, knowledge, aesthetic content, software, brand relationships, and networks) more generally, creative products create overflows, where 'non-rival, nonexcludable investments are likely to spill over beyond the companies that make them' (Haskel and Westlake 2018: 72). Secondly, as we have seen, the weak market power and financial resources of small-scale creative producers erode their ability to go to law. Instead, creative producers use mechanisms embedded in the social and material relations of their community in order to protect the value of their work. Again, it transpires that the picture is more complex than legal theory might suppose; we use the IP/IPR nexus to navigate the creatives' experience of protecting their work, and their subtle and varied responses to the act of copying itself.

The current context for creative producers—notably digitization and the Internet—presents a number of challenges in terms of protecting work. Digital technology allows easy and unlimited copying of digital material with no loss of quality: '[u]nlawful producers can copy, at zero cost, any sign of creativity seen, perceived or detected in a creativity-based object' (Santagata 2004: 83).

This copying is not limited to digital media; the ubiquitous nature of the Internet means that the creativity of industries, such as performance and fashion & design, is also widely distributed online through videos and images.

Consumer perceptions of copyright are also problematic: consumers do not see illegal downloading as unethical, with a favourable attitude towards piracy (copyright infringement) negatively correlated with adoption of subscription services (Lysonski and Durvasula 2008, Cesareo and Pastore 2014, Watson et al. 2015, Fleming et al. 2017). Lines are particularly blurred when consumers feel some ownership over the content as in the case of 'modding' (consumer-generated modifications of existing computer games) and 'fan-fic' (consumer-authored fiction based on existing literature). Both display an ambiguous relationship to copyright, combining 'both resistance and cultural reproduction' (Cohen 2012: 69). As Cohen (2012: 55) notes, '[t]he person who contributes to mass-media fandom participates in a community organized around resistance to copyright rules that give copyright owners most of the control of most adaptations, but also around appreciation for the mass commercial culture that copyright plays a central role in enabling'. Blurred lines may be exploited by producers, as, for example, when games publishers see modding as a source of free labour (Dyer-Witheford and de Peuter 2009).

Yet it is not just unlicensed—pirated, modified, or borrowed—content that poses a challenge to commercial success. Many creators have chosen to release works online for free at the point of consumption. Access to different channels gives creative producers increased visibility in the hope that exposure will lead to sales or commissions. While consumers may be paying for these works in kind, via advertising targets or personal data, the price point of free can serve as an anchor—creating a heuristic in the minds of consumers by which all subsequent prices are judged. Unsurprisingly, small-scale creative producers contest the expectation of free content: 'There is no such thing as "free" content. In the real world, things do cost money to make' [Music 87]. Such producers see themselves as under threat from global economic trends, suggesting that the demand for free access to creative products is a reflection of the modern economy, stemming from the experience of globalization and access to cheaper products:

> It is something that annoys me in that so much stuff now is manufactured and made in China, where materials and processed labour [are] much cheaper, so people here expect stuff cheaper. People will come up to me and say, 'It is too expensive'. [Design 8]

And:

> Consumers think that they have a right to get stuff for next to nothing and this is a problem. It is not sustainable. It is not sustainable in lots of industries over and above the arts. It is not sustainable that people will be able to get trousers in New

Look for £3.99 or designer trainers for £15 in TK Maxx. We have engendered this in consumers through ideology, through changing market conditions and through under-cutting, through race-to-the-bottom pricing. It is a hard one to fix. They are not thinking of the overall consequences of this. The consumer who wants things for free has to be disallowed to do that, has to be told, 'No that is wrong'. [Publishing 81]

The demand for free content also represents a misplaced sense of politics:

It is all symptomatic of the decay of respect for IP. There is a fundamental misunderstanding as to what IP is. I think also that the Left is hugely responsible for this as well, because there are so many people, specifically in the arts, who see there being something radical in fucking with IP and in music as well. This was the alibi for so long: 'We are taking down the big corporations'. It is your duty to like ripping off music. You are being radical and you are rebelling if you are doing that. [Publishing 81]

Many creative producers respond to these structural and political pressures with an argument based on fairness, good pricing, and appropriate rewards—an echo of the natural rights theory that underpins notions of IP. Customers will pay if the price is right (Santagata 2004, Towse 2006b), suggests one television executive:

I think if you can make compelling content, overall you will be paid for it. It is just a question then of how you release it to the audience. The big thing is always access. If you restrict access then people will find a way around it. If you give access for a reasonable price then people will pay it. [TV 61]

The speaker echoes Chiou et al.'s (2005: 170) conclusions on music production, that:

[Producers] should always try to market music products at reasonable prices and improve the quality of their music products continuously. They have to let their consumers think that they really get their money's worth. Excessive publicity regarding the exorbitant income of pop singers can only direct consumers to think that the company and the musicians enjoy unreasonable profits and that minor infringement of copyright is acceptable to this wealthy group.

But producers may not be swayed by these value-for-money arguments. They also seek to articulate their value as inimitable, embedded in the quality of the IP, just as they justify prices in the face of market forces. As this musician says, 'you cannot steal live music':

Students love Spotify. They will pay their monthly whatever it is and they will get to hear 128 kilobits per second of really low-quality music. Hopefully they have got good ears to hear that it is low quality. Because there is a big difference between streamed and studio-master quality. There is a real difference. Although going to real concerts obviously is where music is at its strongest. Because you cannot really

> create that on a CD. You cannot steal live music. You cannot take away the live event. You have got to make that as special as possible and you also have to make it sound as good as possible. [Music 87]

These examples, while setting the stage for a discussion of IP protection with the assertion that work must be paid for—and as the last chapter made clear, creative producers must eat—do not begin to do justice to the complex issue of copying in the creative world. Not all copying is bad, nor is it all theft. In the next section we delve into the attitudes held by our interviewees when discussing the ownership of work, copying, and protection.

Attitudes to Copying

Chapter 2 argued that creative production takes place within communities of practice and employs shared symbolic resources. Producers learn by imitation, practising techniques and coming to understand what constitutes artistic work within a given field. We saw that the notion of original work produced by a single maker, to whom legal rights of ownership can be attached, is a fiction derived in part from legal necessity and in part from the Romantic notion of solitary artistic endeavour. Individual authorship of creative texts is performed by the legal framing of IP.[1] In view of this, it is unsurprising that creative producers expressed nuanced attitudes to copying.

First of all, while the protection of original work hints at a point of origin for an idea or creative product, a social world replete with potential sources of inspiration makes it difficult to identify that point:

> Social media drives so much visual now. On a daily basis we are absorbing so many pictures, images, and flashpoints. Look at Pinterest. It is just hundreds and hundreds of pretty pictures. At what point am I unconsciously going to then translate that into something which could be classed as copyright infringement?
>
> [Design 25]

It is the same in the case of dance:

> I think that we all absorb the things that we see as we go along. It is impossible to unsee things. Your unconscious absorbs things and then you regurgitate it as something slightly changed and I think that is what creativity is also about.
>
> [Dance 116]

[1] Specifically, by the black letter legal framing, because the courts and case law often provide a much more nuanced understanding. Black letter law approaches law via its core principles rather than in context.

As a consequence, there are often many similar creative products, as similar ideas are drawn independently from a common cultural context:

> We have just been informed by a large company in London that we are potentially infringing on their design. But we had no knowledge that this actually existed. I can genuinely sit here as a designer and say, 'I was not aware that this other piece existed'. [Design 25]

Second, it is hard to separate copying from the creative act (Negus et al. 2018). For many, copying is implicit in creativity: 'Creativity is centrally dependent on the freedom to appropriate and experiment with artefacts and techniques encountered within the cultural landscape' (Cohen 2012: 31). In jazz, for example, collaboration takes the form of engaging with past music and through improvisation, subtly changing or developing it:

> You would have to have some serious plagiarism police, because jazz musicians play lines—if they are not improvising truly, they play lines stolen from other musicians. They will play a line from Charlie Parker, or that is from Miles Davies. [Music 87]

Such imitative collaboration is part of the mechanisms of music: 'Listening to sounds and copying them, abducting rules and breaking them: such practices are absolutely central to the mode of social authorship in popular music' (Toynbee 2001: 17). Because of this, copying is important in the process of learning a craft or tradition, where pedagogy takes the form of a 'dialogue between the past and the present' (George 2012: 228, Negus et al. 2017). Copying is endemic to fashion, part of how designers and makers learn their craft (McRobbie 2016). As copying is such an ambiguous concept, the boundary between originality and plagiarism is drawn through social norms:

> If you are making your way up the ladder, there is the learning experience where you may be drawing from different choreographers' styles. You essentially want to develop your style because it will be frowned upon otherwise. Other people will notice if you're too reliant on others for inspiration, and that cannot be good if you are trying to make your name. [Dance 116]

In the games industry, too, copying forms part of the production process:

> The games industry is extremely self-referential. Games studios look at other games. Every game we make is a copy of five or six other games. I have a process, when I am prototyping a game, to steal stuff from other places, putting things together—this is how it is going to sound, this is what I want it to look like—enough to get something playable together. Then you have to be careful to go back and do another pass that says, 'We need to get rid of all these graphics which are not ours, or these sounds which are not ours'. [Games 50]

Copying offers a strategy for managing the uncertainties of the 'nobody knows' aspect of the creative industries. One means of approaching the difficulty of predicting whether a product will be successful is to base products or ideas on previous successes (Erickson et al. 2015):

> They [a production company] just take movies, movie titles, when they are doing brainstorms and throw them up. Then they say, 'If you have loved this movie then . . . ' It is a good starting point. [TV 54]

So copying becomes a central part of the creative process: of learning, reproducing, even of innovating. The reliance on existing work during the making of creative products means that work practices have to guard against falling into inadvertent plagiarism:

> I think to protect yourself against falling into the trap of copying somebody else, you might say, 'Does this look like something else that somebody else has made?' I try to be aware of what else is being produced by fellow contemporary makers as much as possible, following the industry and looking at what is out there already, seeing what other people are making and being aware of it so that I don't fall into that trap. [Design 14]

An awareness of the field is necessary, not only for drawing inspiration from existing work, but also preventing oneself from drawing on it too heavily. For some, developing these practices begins in the early stages of developing as a producer.

> You have to be careful. Students might have listened to something about fifty times and it is in their sub-conscious. Then they write a piece of music and they think that it is their own. But it isn't. You have got to be careful not to listen too much. [Music 87]

The risk of being copied is inherent in the 'nature of business', with products 'open for copy' [Games 44] by the act of being made. As Pasquinelli (2007: 74) remarks, 'creative ideas that are not imitated have no value'. Copying can drive innovation in the field, leading to what Arthur (2009) terms 'combinatory innovation', as this maker somewhat romantically explains:

> Innovation comes from the fact that there will be someone looking at an idea. They will say, 'That is a really cool idea and I want to copy that idea. Actually, I don't have either the skills, or I don't have the money, or I don't have the resources, or I don't have whatever to be able to build that. What I am going to do is to build a pared-down version of that'. They build it and everyone says, 'Wow, this is amazing', when it is just basically a constrained version of some other thing. Then someone else copies them and if you have got enough copies of that thing, what does that become? It becomes a genre and actually you could be the first person that started that genre of games. [Games 46]

There is, therefore, a spectrum of imitative behaviour, rather than the law's necessary binary differentiation between an original and copying. As we saw in Chapter 2, originality lies in the pitch, the variation, or the slant:

> When you have done something it sparks people to think about what they are going to do. For example, we made a film about jute in Dundee, about a commodity and its relationship to Scotland. Then, obviously, the BBC had a brainstorm and came up with an idea about Scotland's relationship with four commodities: sugar, alcohol, cigarettes, and opium, and I could see how they had worked up the thing. They had seen our thing and they brainstormed it. I have just kicked myself for not coming up with that idea. That, I would not say, was plagiarism in any way. [Film 68]

Creative producers agree that there is 'a fine line between inspiration and copying... a very grey area' [Design 23], with subtle gradations of activity: 'What is homage and what is plagiarism?' [TV 54]. In some art forms, being able to discern direct copying is very difficult, as, for example, in dance:

> There are moves that are used by everyone. Copyright infringement needs to take a substantial part, a significant part of the work. Knowing what is infringing and what is just inspiration is a very grey area. For a lot of people working creatively, it is often hard to discern if somebody is actually infringing your work. Somewhere there is a line between being influenced by something and copying something and who knows where that line actually is? [Dance 120]

Producers determine copying by the intention as much as the result. Despite the subtleties displayed in the quotations above, creative producers see deliberate copying as anathema. It is prevented—or at least rendered futile—by the social relations of the creative field. Interests and rights attached to IP, and the interest in its protection, stem from a sense of identity and reputation (O'Mahony 2003). From this view, copying as a conscious act is difficult to comprehend: 'It would have to be a complete [decision], "I am going to copy this work". I don't know, maybe I am just naïve, do a lot of people do that?' [Design 19]. Implicitly informed by a personality theory of property, copying is seen as a betrayal of one's artistic truthfulness or integrity: 'I actually don't see the point in me slavishly copying an object that somebody else has spent time making. I would not be being true to myself' [F&T 27].

As the theft of 'reputation as well as property' (Becker 2008: 23), plagiarism engenders strong reactions: 'I would be absolutely mortified if someone were to say, "Yes, you have copied that person"' [Design 25]. From this perspective, copying or stealing reflects a deficiency in the copier rather than a theft of property. In keeping with the importance of moral rights in production, it implies a moral failing, a lack of integrity, and a lack of technical and artistic ability: 'The people who do that, they have a lack of integrity in general, in their style, in the sense that you can see they jump about a lot. Other makers can see it' [Design 22].

The lack of integrity that makes someone copy is part of a broader failing visible to those who can see—who have imbibed the understandings of symbolic worth circulating within the field—and that will limit the future possibilities open to this individual. A natural justice is at work:

> To literally copy something—they don't get far with it. They might put up one piece but then what is next? Where do they go from there? It is obvious: You have to come up with the ideas for them to be developed. [F&T 36]

The same understandings of individual style and development provide reassurance that there will be no lasting damage:

> People quite often plagiarize me. You can see it. Or people tell me. But they don't do it as well... it is not done to the same quality and they don't have that thing, whatever it is. So yes, it is not really an issue. But I have to keep continuously moving on in my work. [Design 2]

In other words, the reputation and technical skill developed by a producer—reflected in their IP—provide protection against instrumental and malicious plagiarism, while at the same time being flexible enough to accommodate the imitation endemic to the functioning of the field. Copied products will not be produced to as high a quality and, more importantly, will not have the authenticity that ensures genuine value. The lack of integrity attached to plagiarism infuses both moral ethos and aesthetic ability; the moral element of creation and its intricate links to identity prevent copying, or at least ensure moral opprobrium, should it occur.

The distinction between influence and direct copying is determined within a community or tradition. Thus, norms of practice vary between sectors. Fashion flourishes despite—or perhaps because of—very weak IP protection. This is fashion's 'piracy paradox' (Howard 2008; Raustiala and Sprigman 2006, 2009, Blakley 2010; Marshall 2013), where copying is endemic to the industry. Searle (2011) classifies copying in three directions. In 'copying down', high-street brands copy high-end luxury brands—a model common to the fast-fashion industry; 'copying across' occurs both in collusion within the industry in determining annual trends and colours, and copying from the past; while 'copying up' occurs as large designers copy small designers, co-opt street style, or appropriate culture for commercial gain. Copying down and copying across generally benefit the industry, speeding up the fashion cycle as designs go out of fashion more quickly, thus generating demand for new ones. In the absence of strong IPR protection, however, the imbalance between the market power of large brands and small means that copying up can be problematic for small designers. Interviewees frequently complained about being copied by high-street brands, and displayed a high degree of scepticism about the practices of some of the large high-street retailers:

> I have seen, time and time again, established makers who are very famous and have an established style, the essence of their design being pulled out and brought into the high street. There is nothing you can do about it because there is a little bit of change [in each product]. It is frustrating enough to see makers ripping off other makers, but when you do see the likes of Top Shop doing it, the irony is that it is normally so much more obvious when it is the bigger company, that it is a direct rip off. [Design 11]

The lack of clearly defined property rights poses a problem for the sector. Proof of infringement, for example, is difficult. 'People don't enforce their rights, because the results are very unpredictable' [F&T 27]. Small changes might render legal challenges invalid: '[i]f a proportion of the design is seemingly altered, it becomes another design, so you can't do anything' [F&T 29]. Such action is seen as deliberate: '[y]ou do get companies that copy work. They know the law well enough to change the piece just enough, and they know that they can get away with it' [Design 14]. Instead, producers learn to be smarter in their practices:

> Once we sent some samples to a nice, big retailer. Then we got a call back from somebody who worked there who said, 'Don't send samples. It is stupid. They will get copied. I am sending them back to you today. If you have got ideas get in touch with us, yes, but don't show us until the end of our talks'. That was a good bit of advice. Then we saw some products really similar to ours in their shops, and we said, 'Yes, they were right'. [Design 13]

Creative producers who have been copied, especially by industrial firms, are unlikely to gain legal redress. Instead they are forced to find ways of reinterpreting or talking away their losses. If copying is understood in terms of theft of reputation it can be restated as a form of emulation or flattery, as this games maker illustrates:

> Actually, I think it is quite flattering if someone clones your game. We have some anecdotal evidence of people looking at some of our projects and making versions of them. It is actually kind of cool. [Games 47]

An understanding of copying as flattery, at least in the case of design, fashion and textiles, and games, becomes the default:

> My attitude generally is that if you are developing your design work and you are the maker, you know the provenance of it. You know exactly where it has come from. To a degree it is a form of flattery if somebody is copying your work. [F&T 34]

The following quotation, from a designer who finds work copied on a large scale in Japan—a situation which would be very difficult to redress—shows how the community advises the wronged individual to deal with the infringement as an act of flattery. It is certainly a post-hoc rationalization on a difficult discovery:

> I was selling quite a lot in Japan at the time and there was an organization there who had bought quite a lot of my work. I went back to Japan the following year and there were bolts of fabric that were identical to my work and I thought, 'Whoa. That is mine'. It was a distinct copy of a weave structure that I was using at that time. I was with a number of other makers, a lot higher profile than I am. I spoke to them about it and they were saying, 'It could go two ways. You could be really pissed off and do something about it. Or you could do nothing about it and feel flattered'. That is what I did—I just thought, 'I could feel flattered'. There were very strong elements of my work which were in this work. They were able to produce it. The only difference was that they were able to produce it industrially and I cannot do that. Because it is in Japan, they had access to different processes over there. I chose to be flattered as opposed to being pissed off. This organization is international. But it is enough for me to think, 'Yes, they have bought my work. They have looked at the work. They have obviously taken influence and they have done something with it and that is fine'. If I were so precious about it, I would never want to sell a piece of work again. [F&T 27]

As this quotation shows, the copying can be normalized as something that happens in a different industry or market: 'If a bigger brand takes on a design and slightly changes it, they have moved it up into their market' [F&T 28]. Producers seek to maintain their own worth by differentiating works both horizontally based on characteristics, e.g. stressing small-scale production, artisanal techniques, or vertically based on quality using high-quality materials. Copies that are mass-produced can be seen as different, and less important (as opposed to lucrative missed opportunities):

> We use high-quality materials that would last an awfully long time and therefore are really expensive. I don't think that using expensive materials stops people copying you. They will just copy you using cheaper materials, and use the same ideas. We saw examples of products really similar to ours where we had used leather and they were using plastic. If there is a design that is quite good but really expensive and somebody else produces something that is slightly different and it is way cheaper and it is accessible to others, is it really that terrible? [Design 13]

In this narration, the copying is less a direct challenge to the individual and their artistic integrity, or their market, and more a response of growing a market. In this it is distinct from direct copying, as seen in the following example, when one choreographer seeks to openly borrow from another, ignoring the norms of the practice:

> Someone came up and he just blatantly said, 'I want to do that in my new work. How did you do it?' They were very blatantly honest about it. I could not say what I thought, so I said, 'I would rather you did not do that'. I just thought I would never do that. [Dance 120]

Similar reinterpretation narratives come from those exposed to the problems of piracy. In the face of potentially lost revenues, producers insist upon the quality of the original, or recast piracy as a mechanism for spreading word about the quality of work, of building reputation, and developing revenues elsewhere. This may have overtones of special pleading, but shows the producers emphasizing their own IP—understood not in legal terms but as social relations, and sets of skills and practices—as the source of worth underpinning their work. For example, a film producer claims that a pirated copy will not be as good a quality as the original and will push people into accessing an authorized version:

> There is a YouTube version of the film that we have made quite a lot of money with. It is a very bad version and it has had 49,000 hits. Which is 49,000 DVDs or VODs [that could have been bought]. But also I noticed people saying that it is an amazing film, but the quality is so bad. Then I know that they will go and find where they can buy it. I'm sure that some of the people who watch it on YouTube would not have bought one anyway. My audience would not want to watch it on that. They want to own it. They want to download it properly. [Film 66]

As with copying, piracy is also given a positive gloss of increased visibility:

> You want loads of people reading your book and a proportion of them will do so for free. It has always been the case that people can go to the library or whatever. You want them to talk about your book and make it more widely known.
> [Publishing 84]

In music, the discourse is similar to that heard from designers. Infringement is seen as inevitable, with its only advantage being attracting more individuals to the art form:

> Once it is out there it is virtually impossible to do anything to prevent people from putting it elsewhere. I think a lot of the classical music industry has resigned itself to the fact that actually it being out there, and it being seen, is more important. People seeing it, that will drive them to attend concerts or maybe to go and purchase it. If they see something, they will maybe purchase the whole CD or the full download. That is where we are at, at the moment. Of course, ideally we would like to have more protection and try to find ways of creating income streams from it. That has not really been cracked, and I cannot see a way round that.
> [Music 89]

The benefits of increased visibility tend to be clearer in those cases where economic returns are less developed, and where there is a sense of contributing to cultural output:

> I am not that worried about piracy. I have certainly had radio plays pirated. There is nothing I would do about it or really want to do about it. If they think that it is worth pirating and want to listen to it, then well and good. There is a lot of angst

> out there about piracy. I am not at all sure that you can do very much about it. I don't think a pirated copy equates to a lost sale because I don't think they are willing to pay anyway. They are not going to be buying it. The people who are set up to buy legitimately for a Kindle or a Nook or whatever, they are going to be doing that anyway. [Publishing 80]

Interviewees seem to assume that the audience is already segregated between those who purchase and those who pirate. In this sense, piracy may not represent a lost sale so much as a loss-leader, evaluated in terms of a cost-benefit trade-off between word-of-mouth conversions following piracy and the costs of pursuing legal infraction:

> The way I view someone who pirates our game is, he is free advertising. I did not have to capture that user through any of my marketing channels, but he is going to tell his friends. If he tells enough people and we can convert enough of the people he tells into paying customers, then we will always make more money than if we try to enforce protection, with the costs of that. I do know that we have been infringed. There are a lot of arguments to say that piracy actually helps some brands because it makes it ubiquitous and that is what the driving force is. But then, a large proportion of those players will think, 'Do I really want the hassle of trying to pirate it, or shall I just buy it?' Again, if it is reasonably priced .... Like if I saw a game and it was, say it was £10, £12, £15. If I wanted it, I would rather pay that than go through the hassle of trying to pirate something. There was a chap who pirated our game. He sent us an email and then said, 'You guys, the game is amazing. I want you to carry on making games'. So he went and bought the game. He has gone and infringed the copyright, but we could not care less as that is the best email we have got. He pirated it, emailed us, and told us that he loved it, and then went out and bought it. [Games 49]

Where concerns are expressed, they are with the impact of piracy on the sector or industry as a whole (Yar 2005, Danaher and Waldfogel 2012):

> [X film] was downloaded, before we were aware of it happening. The UK distributor had already done the small theatrical release and the DVDs and television sales had all taken place, so it did not have a major impact on that particular film. With the next film, the producers have quite a substantial investment in this film, so are reliant on income to make any money. I suspect it is more to do with indifference in the people who are pirating the material, because I would guess they assume that film-makers are all leading, if not wealthy, at least comfortable lives, and that it is a victimless theft. But it is not a victimless theft. One of the effects it has, of course, has been to drive down the budgets and the quality of what you are producing. [Film 69]

It is a position that is felt strongly in publishing:

> What is troubling is not the impact on the author. We have got to get away from thinking about authors as individual entities. I like the idea of houses. A house is

> impacted by piracy massively. I can go online and I can pick up all of the Raymond Chandlers, all of the George Orwells, people within the 70-year duration who are still protected by copyright. All of this stuff is just available for free. There is no more revenue stream coming in from these books, whereas there would have been before. That damages the house. You damage the house's ability to take risks on new talent. [Publishing 81]

Copying, therefore, is a complex and subtle matter within the creative world. To an extent, it is a necessary part of creative production, not only for learning but also for generating new ideas or simply getting things made. Creative producers distinguish between this kind of innocent, and necessary, imitation, and malicious plagiarism, with a theory of copying that points at a deficient artistic personality and invokes natural justice to ensure that the copier will not be successful in the longer term. The community's discernment will provide sufficient protection against small-scale imitation, but cannot do so against industrial copying by predatory high-street chains or overseas manufacturers. Where producers have no redress, they seek to rationalize the copying as a form of flattery; a new, irrelevant market; or as a threat, not to the individual, but to the whole sector. Legal protection is nowhere on this list.

Recourse to Law

Economic theories of innovation and creative production require that the law offers protection through copyright and design rights,[2] and mechanisms of redress if claims need to be enforced. Despite the existence of, and theoretical necessity for, such rights, many creative producers, especially sole traders and SMEs, do not see legal protection of IP as a priority. It is perceived as a distraction from day-to-day business, prohibitively expensive, and worst of all, ineffective (Hargreaves 2011): 'We don't think about that too much, because we are too busy preparing for the next order' [F&T 30]. Or:

[2] Design rights protect the shape and configuration of objects. Both the UK and EU have two forms of design rights: registered and unregistered. Unregistered rights are automatic, and require no formal process on the part of the rights holder. However, this low threshold is matched with a relatively low level of protection as they may be difficult to establish in the case of conflict, and have a relatively short term of protection (three years in the case of the EU right, 10 to 15 in the UK). In contrast, registered rights require a legal process of registering the design with the appropriate government authority, involving a more precise description of the design, registration fees, and legal costs. Registered rights last roughly 25 years, and have a more robust legal standing. In the UK, most designers prefer to register their designs with the professional association, Anti Copying in Design (ACID) (Hargreaves 2011).

> We should trademark our products but we don't even do that. There is not really a reason behind that. It is just because we are a small start-up and we have not been focused on our legal side. [Games 52]

Even in broadcasting, where IP is an established part of sector practice, it is not necessarily the priority:

> The IP side of it is important. But the day-to-day for a company our size and what we do is about getting enough hours through the door to fund ourselves. The focus has to be for us to get enough commissions. [TV 58]

Sometimes producers see their small size as protection: 'I just always assume that I am so wee, so I have never actually thought of protecting anything' [Design 4]. But the main obstacle is cost:

> With IP it is not just that we have a lack of financial resource, staff resource, but there are so many shadows and grey areas around IP. Couple that lack of understanding with the lack of resource and I think that it often does get ignored. It is something to be done another day. When we are bigger. When we have more time. When we have more staff. When we have a marketing manager. It never actually gets done. I think some things are forgotten about. Pushed aside. Ignored. It does not really matter. [Design 11]

Our findings here chime with existing literature, which recognizes that the SMEs and micro-enterprises of the creative industries make little use of IP (see for example Hargreaves 2011, Hynynen 2013, Sukarmijan and Sapong 2014). Greenhalgh et al. (2010) identify a number of barriers to effective use of IP by SMEs, including financial costs, incidental costs (e.g. time), difficulties enforcing rights abroad, and the general assumption that small firms stand little chance in conflicts with larger firms.

Yet our interviews suggest that creative producers are strategically calculating, trading the merits of legal protection against the protection offered by the IP embedded in their own work. The law is costly and ineffective, while technical skills and reputation—the symbolic IP they possess within the community—are efficacious and free:

> I am a sole trader. I just think that I cannot afford it. I have not, to be honest, looked into it very much, just because I instantly think that it is just going to cost me money and you need to weigh that up against what it is. If I was doing things that would be easier to produce, then that would really worry me and I would need to get much more involved in IP protection. [Design 4]

Legal rights take second place to the expert eye and a detailed knowledge of the field, in the face of which they are not necessarily a guarantee of protection:

> I was just about to go to a show at a big trade fair with a range of textiles. Maybe one month before I was due to show there, I got a lawyer's letter through the post,

> saying that their client was claiming that I was copying their design. They were sending me a letter saying 'cease and desist'; that the design was not mine, and that she wanted damages. She wanted me not to go to the trade fair. She wanted me to take it down off my site. If I took it to the trade fair, they would contact the show organizers and they would pull down my stand and all this stuff. There were absolutely no grounds to this, but it was a serious threat nonetheless. Interestingly she had a European Design Right for her design. It was a style of pleat she had registered. She had paid, I guess several thousand euros, to be registered as a European Design Right for a wall covering. First of all, my use of this pleat predated hers by about six years and I could prove that. I had press, media, I had images in the degree show catalogue, and in a college of art prospectus when I developed those designs. There was all this evidence to show that this was my design. Second, I was in a different market, I was doing textiles for indoor design. Not paper. Mine were colourful and hers were black. There were these little differences between it. Then there was also the fact that this was a generic pleat. This is an origami structure that dates back hundreds of years and if you look up any origami books or online resources, there are instructions out there on how to make those pleats. It is not something you can copyright. She did not have any rights to it, and basically, no leg to stand on .... Lawyers and the people out there who are supposed to be there to protect you, are maybe making the wrong calls. They have expertise in law, but they have no idea about design. But if they don't know, if they have never seen that pleat before, they think that it is a brand-new thing. They don't realize it has been around. They just don't know. I suppose you could say that of any design; is anything really new? [F&T 32]

For those who do attempt enforcement, the first step is writing a 'cease and desist' letter, as seen in this example. Letters are usually issued with the intention of encouraging compliance, rather than pursuing the more expensive route to secure damages. This is easier in some sectors, for example, publishing:

> We have got a Google thing that is set up for all our titles, so when something pops up, we contact a site and invariably they take it down in a day or two. The sites have always been responsive and we are quite used to issuing a cease and desist notice saying, 'Take this down' and they do. [Publishing 82]

Cease and desist letters, however, depend upon community adherence to legal norms rather than the force of the law itself, and there is no easy follow-up for many (O'Mahony 2003); as the example shows, letters are not necessarily effective, especially if the recipient feels there are no grounds for compliance. The next step would be to sue, if a maker wishes; from a policy perspective, IPR offers an entitlement (an option) to pursue copyright infringers. But small-scale producers assume that in David-and-Goliath IP disputes, Goliath always wins:

> It is very scary when you are talking to large companies. Especially at the start, where you are giving away all your ideas, even under a non-disclosure agreement, because you would not have the money to sue them. One of the things about IP, if

> somebody did copy you or design around something that you are doing, which is very possible, you are probably not going to be able to do much about it. That is still not a reason not to secure it, because you just never know what is 'round the corner'. [Games 41]

Many, particularly in games, design, fashion, and textiles, consider that the legal enforcement of rights is simply not an option. Here, a designer compares the prohibitive cost and effort of seeking legal redress with the protection offered by brand identity and specialist technique:

> I have no problem proving my IP. Everything that I do is recorded. The techniques are very specific. We have our own brand identity. The problem is actually in taking it to court. It is not the uncertainty of the outcome. It is the cost. It is purely cost. Taking on a lawyer. If there is infringement, for a lot of companies this is a real headache because they cannot afford the amount of work it takes to actually take the case forward. You can put as much in place and pay as much money as you wanted to protect yourself but that will do nothing if you cannot afford to then enforce it. [F&T 32]

In sum, law and policy may be focused on IPR as a mechanism of exclusion and protection, but smaller scale creative producers are sceptical of the real value of these rights (Hargreaves 2011, Schlesinger and Waelde 2012). The cost of enforcement renders the whole enterprise of legal property rights invalid, for IPR is only as strong as its enforcement (Towse 2010). The boundaries of copying in art worlds are blurred (Becker 2008), and copying may be seen as inevitable, even flattering. Nevertheless, creative producers may use other strategies to protect themselves from copying.

Other Strategies of Protection

In the absence of effective legal redress, creative producers must seek other ways of avoiding being copied. Good practice—good housekeeping, not sending samples to high-street buyers—is one means of avoiding imitation. Not giving too much information away online is another, but as the market often dictates that goods for sale are displayed, this is limited in its effectiveness. Instead, creative producers believe the best means of protecting oneself from plagiarism is through innovation, craft knowledge, and superior technique. Designers, for example, may display their goods but be protected by a complex, hard-to-copy design:

> We do have our product [displayed online] with zoom and so people can see quite clearly what we are doing. You just have to accept that people might try to copy. But it is not the easiest thing in the world to copy. Our designs are hand-knitted. Sometimes our designs have twelve colours in them. I think we have gone up to

> eighteen colours at times and most machines can only do eight. We use yarns that are very difficult to get a hold of. You have got certain built-in advantages of uniqueness. That tends to be our protection. [F&T 33]

Here, the producers have intuitively built what Haskel and Westlake (2018) refer to as 'synergistic clusters of intangible investments', developing marketing, networks and customers in ways that potential competitors find difficult to replicate. Where design information is only usable in combination with distinct technologies and techniques it may provide better protection than the law. Trade secrets and know-how—intimate knowledge of the production process, sourcing unusual materials and using traditional production methods, and the knowledge, skills, and the ability to make complex designs and to innovate quickly—are seen as more effective than protecting designs through copyright and design rights:

> We know it is hard to copy because a company that tried to not pay us, tried to get a designer in London to replicate one of the pieces that was proving incredibly popular—and he couldn't do it. He did not understand at all how it had been knitted. It makes us smile each time we think about it. When I design I am thinking that everything I do, it would be impossible to knit on a machine. [F&T 34]

Building complexity into design can prevent copying. Complexity, like the use of trade secrets, provides protection by *not* disclosing (Cohen et al. 2000), in contrast to the publication and disclosure associated with copyright, design rights, trademarks, and patents. Standard practices for the protection of trade secrets include clauses in contracts, non-disclosure agreements, and simply not disclosing the relevant information. Loshin (2007), for example, identifies the unique set of IP norms amongst magicians, including secrecy, employed to protect magic tricks.

Alternatively, continuous innovation may serve as a means of protection:

> We have always found the whole area of IP . . . a densely complicated and difficult thing. We are very much a small design business. We depend on our design to keep it going and we depend on being able to keep it fresh and unusual and different. If conditions do change and people start mass-producing what we make, then our next response would be to completely redesign the production and make things that are no longer usual and normal. [F&T 30]

Just as the willingness to plagiarize was recast as a personality deficiency on the part of the copier, so creative producers articulate the necessity of constantly evolving the artistic form as a moral imperative. If one is copied, it is not just the fault of the copier:

> If you get ripped off, you are not advancing your own career with new ideas. There is a part of me that really feels that you deserve to be ripped off to an extent. You must always change and make the product or the art or whatever it is impossible to

> recreate by another company. I know people who have made a career of making the same thing for decades. It is not a practice I could tolerate, for myself. If I am not moving on, then let them copy it. You have to keep a step ahead. That is what a good, healthy designer will be doing most of the time. I suppose in a way I have protection. Although I have key pieces in my range, I am always updating them and always changing them. Actually, even if my work was to be reproduced or copied, I am always going to be evolving anyway. I am not somebody whose work has really stayed the same over the years. It has moved quite dramatically so I don't really ever worry about that. [Design 14]

There is an almost Darwinian motif to this designer's comment: the slow-moving artist falls prey—deservedly—to the predatory copier, while the fittest survive through continuous evolution. As Qian (2008) and Cho et al. (2015) note, differentiation through product innovation and quality enhancement often arise in response to copying and counterfeiters.

It may be possible to build products that contain the mechanisms of preventing plagiarism. In television, where, as we have seen, ideas may very quickly be appropriated, a producer builds protection from copying into the basic ideas for a new programme:

> I would say that protecting IP on the factual area of TV is tough, at times semi-impossible, unless you are a very big beast. It is all to do with scale. Frankly are we going to sue people who steal? No. Is somebody big going to sue them? Yes. It is very hard. I spend a lot of time with ideas, actually saying to myself, what is it about this idea that (a) I can protect and (b) they are going to come to us for? What is it that I can do to make this idea even makeable, let alone protectable? All of these things have to be built into it. It is a tricky world out there. It is a real fact of life... the IP in its initial stages is not protectable. It is very stealable. [TV 53]

The very idea of the programme, so easy to steal, must fasten itself to its creator. Games designers can use strategies such as freemium to achieve a similar effect. Freemium games allow players to become involved with the game before they part with any money; there is simply nothing to steal:

> You mostly lose your IP because people just pirate your game and then they sell it on. To get around that you use a free-to-play model where there is no reason to pirate it, because it is free. That is actually our biggest protection of IP. The way the industry is dealing with piracy is by moving more to free-to-play. The standard business model for our type of game historically would have been a box purchase at £30, £29, and then a multi-subscription to play. I was in China last year, where obviously piracy is rife on everything from physical assets to IP or whatever. When I was asking them what their business model was for the games we were looking to publish on their behalf, they said, 'What do you mean?' I said, 'What is your business model? Is it purchase price or box?' He said, 'Why would you do that?' Because they only have free-to-play models—that is the only way for them to get around the piracy issues. [Games 45]

Constant innovation is structured into some sectors. Fashion, for example, is 'lucky because it keeps moving. If somebody takes a chunk out of you one year then they have to try all over again the next year' [F&T 30]. The continual process of innovation and the search for new fashion ensure that copying, although quite pervasive, is seen as a temporary problem:

> Our techniques never live longer than a season. You have to build on them every single time. You have to come up with tweaks and new materials. Someone can copy it over for a short stretch of time, perhaps a year. But by that time we are somewhere else. [F&T 36]

The nature of the industry, with the fast cycles of designs and constant innovation, makes legal property rights less important than the search for next season's new idea:

> I think in the fashion industry you just have to be constantly looking at new ideas. We spend a lot of time looking at the trends, making sure that our collection is going to be innovative and different but also in demand. I think fashion is quite a unique industry in that sense. [F&T 33]

Time-to-market, or 'early mover advantage' in business parlance (Cohen et al. 2000) is important for staying ahead of imitators: 'A lot of it is first-to-market and just getting it out there' [Games 44]. Being first to market also provides proof, if challenged; for this games designer the best means of protection is visibly associating oneself with one's most innovative products:

> Ultimately if you release something good you are going to get copied. Part of it is actually getting to market first and talking about your product first online and just getting it out there. It is doing it in such a way that you are known for that innovation or that mechanic or whatever first. My attitude with IP stuff has always been it is way too expensive and impractical to actually legally protect anything and the only practical way of protecting what you make is to just be really public about it. It is just to make sure that every product you do is 100 per cent associated with you and so if anybody else was to come out with a music sequencing, side-scrolling game then they would say, 'Hey, that came out before and it was made by [X]'. That is the only way really. [Games 44]

IP protection comes in the form of developing the 'aesthete's eye'. Indeed, being overly concerned with legal protection is likely to detract from the overall purpose of the production:

> I think games in general, unless you have a really clever bit of tech then you cannot really protect it. If you have a really good, clever bit of tech, generally your game sucks, because you spend more time worrying about the tech than you do worrying about the game. [Games 46]

These games designers stress that the softer aspects of IP—innovation, gameplay, particular styles of game—are more effective means of safeguarding value than legal protection. The same can be said of brand development, in this case for a publisher:

> It would be great to tie everything up in lovely ribbons of IP protection, but you need pots of gold to do it. Our strategy is focusing on brand building and using that as protection to some degree. It does leave us exposed to a point but again it is risk versus reward. [Publishing 77]

Small-scale designers can achieve reputational protection by developing signature pieces with distinctive characteristics, a strategy similar to that outlined by the games designers above:

> Our things are very recognizable. People say that we have a signature. Years ago, when we started, there were quite a lot of designers around but we all established our own signature. It was very clear exactly who had designed what. You could tell by somebody's design, their colour choices, by the shapes of garments that they made, what sort of textured fabric they were working with and what sort of finish and production methods they used. All of those combined to create a signature in design which was very, very distinctive and very, very obvious—not just to those of us who were in the know, but to the public. [F&T 30]

Crucially, this means of protection is effective for the public as well as those imbued with specialist symbolic knowledge of the field. Creative producers stress the intimate relationship between producer and product, the sense of the object as integral to the self, thus ensuring uniqueness as an essential guard against copying. For producers, the creative ideas and the act of creation are seen as inherent protections. The inalienability of individual creativity becomes the basis for securing IP:

> I do weave classes. There is no way in this god's earth that any of the students are going to copy me. Weaving is very much process-based. You have to prepare your work; thread your loom, and get weaving. Amongst all of that there are 101 different ways that it could turn out. You have to plan all that out. So, I am not going to get pissed off if somebody comes to one of my workshops and then becomes a very successful weaver. I will say, 'Bring it on, that is fantastic'. [F&T 27]

Creative producers also benefit from protection within their community. The existing literature shows that social norms are key to protection in areas of the creative industries not well-served by conventional IP rights (O'Mahony 2003). The restaurant industry (not a creative industry but having similar characteristics) does not have protection for recipes and cooking techniques. Chefs are willing to share knowledge when the recipient is expected to adhere to particular norms (Di Stefano et al. 2013). In stand-up comedy, Dotan and Sprigman (2008) similarly find that social norms serve to fill the gap left by the absence of legal IP; a sophisticated social code dictates the ownership and performance of jokes:

> More often than not . . . norms deviate from copyright law's defaults: for example, whereas copyright protects expression but not ideas, comedians' norms protect expression as well as ideas. Or take the issue of authorship: under copyright law, two individuals who cooperate in creating a work are considered joint authors and owners of the work. In contrast, if one comedian comes up with a joke's premise and another thinks up the punchline, under comedians' norms of ownership, the first owns the joke and the latter has nothing. (Dotan and Sprigman 2008: 1790)

Likewise, Iljadica (2016) describes an equally sophisticated system of attribution and ownership amongst street artists. Here, social norms dictate when artists find it appropriate to tag, what conditions lead to one artist being entitled to paint over another's work, what constitutes acceptable types of copying, and the re-use of images. Given that the very act of street art may be illegal, social norms act as an effective substitute for the legal protection of IPR. In communities where creative producers are well known to each other, the possibility of social sanctions can be very effective:

> You would not really want to be known for copying. So maybe that is a form of protection because other people would instantly know that you have copied someone else's work. [Design 5]

Community surveillance means that copying is unlikely to go unnoticed.

> It is a very small world and word gets round very, very quickly once it is known that so and so has pinched an idea or done something to somebody else. People talk. People are aware. I would be completely pissed off if people were speaking like that behind my back. [F&T 27]

Online public forums are important avenues for highlighting transgressions (O'Mahony 2003). Social media alert those in the community and beyond to perceived infractions:

> Something got Tweeted around recently. It was a jeweller and a little design she had come up with a few years ago. All of a sudden it appears for £2.50 in [X a high-street retailer]. Hers were in silver and these were done in a cheaper material, but almost identical visually. [Design 1]

Social media can also provide an effective enforcement mechanism, and are seen as a legitimate resort in the case of infringement. Saundry et al. (2007) illustrate how the Internet has facilitated the formation of informal groups sharing information and trying to mobilize interests, especially important in an increasingly fragmented workforce. The games sector, for example, benefits from a vocal community base committed to the creative form, which at times becomes a source of protection.

> The indie games scene is quite a thing, a movement worldwide. If anything the indie games scene is a little too vociferous. There have been several instances in the past year of games being perceived as rip-offs and then blogs or Twitter just go insane on these people, and just rip them apart until their games have to be pulled from the store because they are worried about it. Sometimes I think it is maybe a little bit too much a herd mentality. At the same time it is quite good that exists, because it means it is a very, very, very strong community. A small community. There are maybe, 10,000 people. It is a very, very strong community still.
>
> [Games 47]

To conclude, the innovation-based economic justification for IPR is not a position that finds much resonance in the practical world of 'Me & Co', where the demands of running a small business overwhelm other concerns (Hargreaves 2011). The discussion on infringement by consumers (piracy) revolves around the media industries, where it is largely seen as an insolvable problem but one to which creators are resigned. Most of the discussion of copying by other creatives has centred around two sectors: design, including fashion; and games. Both are characterized by a large number of small players and a smaller number of large players. Protection here is seen as coming from innovation, being known in a community, building a reputation and brand—in short, IP development.

Creative producers have an intuitive awareness of positioning and differentiation that arises out of creative practice. Awareness of difference also comes from the experienced or 'aesthete's eye', the development of an awareness of, and a language to describe, differences in style between creative producers. Producers also are aware of the overflows and complexities of copying within their field and display nuanced understandings of the nature of imitation among symbolic producers. Across all creative sectors, however, the recourse to legal protection and enforcement is seen as entirely the province of the large corporations: 'I think designers like us feel that the IP industry is broken' [Design 7]. For micro-organizations and SMEs, IP law is something of an irrelevance: too complicated, too costly, and ultimately unenforceable.

This is not to say, however, that IP is irrelevant to the protection of creative work. Personality theories of IP reinforce a sense of attachment between producer and product. Rather than goods being alienable and pacified, they are seen as inalienable. These two characteristics are, respectively, closely aligned with the novelty requirement for IPR protection and the social-contract expectation of continued innovation, but viewed by creators as beyond the IP framework. These qualities provide a distinct concept of protection, ensuring that goods have a unique signature and ensuring future creativity. Protection also comes from being entangled within a knowledgeable community, for knowledgeable producers and consumers recognize ownership, constituting the collective mechanisms that both ascribe and protect ownership.

8

Conclusion

The Ambiguities of IP/IPR

Our journey through the creative economy, accompanying IP/IPR as it transforms symbolic value into economic worth, has proven insightful.

Economic claims to creativity, its contribution to entrepreneurship, innovation, productivity, and economic growth, highlight the role of the creative industries, and in particular the role of IP as its core (Bazalgette 2017).[1] Our analysis of the functioning of IP within the freelance, micros, and SMEs that comprise the vast majority of creative production[2] emphasizes the subtle interplay of creators, texts, and communities that together combine in an understanding of legal and economic constructs. Within this context, the entrepreneurial tag applied to creators is ambiguous. The tag itself attaches to a number of debates. One strand links to *homo oeconomicus*, the calculating actor, rationally motivated by the advancement of personal interests, acting in the light of preferences and incentives (Karpik 2011, Espeland 2013). As a quasi-caricature of parsimonious economic models, such a depiction bears little resemblance to the lived experiences of our interviewees. Rather, for our creative producers, entrepreneurship reflects a desire to pursue their artistic *métier* within the economic realities of uncertainty and insecurity, the latter brought about by factors such as casualization, a rebalancing between public and private enterprise, withdrawal of public support for cultural activity, and new technologies and their impact on production and distribution (Beck 2003, McRobbie 2016). An economic necessity, self-employment offers a

[1] We took the definition of the creative industries as 'those activities that have their origin in individual creativity, skill and talent, and which have the potential for wealth and job creation through the generation and exploitation of intellectual property [IP]' (DCMS 1998: 3).

[2] As noted in Chapter 1, the creative industries have a higher than average number of self-employed, micros, and SMEs. Recent analysis by Bazalgette (2017) indicates that 90 per cent of creative businesses have no more than five employees; 80 per cent no more than two; and 60 per cent just one.

degree of freedom in what, and how, work is done; 'having' as opposed to 'being' a business, and a way of preserving individual autonomy, however precarious (Baines and Robson 2001).

Property is the distinguishing feature of entrepreneurial cultural creation; we focus specifically on intellectual property, which we see as an independent unit of capital. We argue this redirects the focus from creative labour as human capital, and thus the entrepreneurial self, to the authorial self. In doing so, it provides a particular means of addressing the aesthetic/commerce relation characterizing debates on the creative industries. Our actors come to their activities steeped in meaning from their creative field and remain connected and engaged with networks 'outside the economic frame' (Slater 2002b: 242). This informs their understandings of economic and legal forms, and the 'rules of the game' for their interpretation. Our focus is thus the construction of legal and economic categories and how they are acted upon within their forms of creative practice (Slater 2002b), in order to see how those 'without the possession of the relevant code of competence' (Toynbee 2001: 15) develop their own codes based on what is familiar and what works, discovered largely through trial and error.

In making our argument we stress several factors. We take neither the law nor the economy, perspectives normally associated with studies of IP, as our starting points; instead, we focus on the activities and practices that surround our object. In this, we parallel Çalışkan and Callon's (2009, 2010) concept of 'economization', and follow their injunction to study the work of qualifying behaviours, organizations, and institutions as economic. We show that for the creative economy to function, a multitude and diversity of actors and objects must be in play. Things are rendered economic through the actions of producers, governments, media, consumers, and socio-material objects; the process of economization is partial and unstable, and things move in and out of 'the economic' though their life cycle (McFall 2014). We therefore do not subscribe to the view that copyright law 'provides the institutional framework for markets' (Towse 1999: 370). As Fourcade (2011: 48) notes, law is not the context of economic activity, 'it is a location where a set of outcomes is produced'. IP is one such economic object: but, as the empirical material soon showed, IP is not an easily identifiable pre-existing thing. IP was variously identified as ideas, identity, the physical manifestation of ideas, symbolic output, as well as a performative legal formulation for the exchange of goods. Hence our focus on IP/IPR that combines IP as symbolic text and IPR as propertized object.

Our analysis starts by following the metamorphoses of the creative object as it moves from production to final exchange (Appadurai 1986, Kuipers 2014, McFall 2014). In doing so, our object, IP/IPR, is mediated as IP or IPR. Its qualities are in flux, changing over time, depending on its position in social space. It is able to act in this liminal fashion as the one form (IPR) is inherent in the other (IP). Chapter 2 illustrates how IP/IPR structures conterminously the commercial, artistic, and moral object (Velthuis 2005). The realities of creative production of IP contrast with the constructions of the legal regime of IPR, and its performative identification of an individualized 'authorship' and 'originality'. We identify, too, a strong concept of 'authorship', not understood in some narrow legal sense, nor as a form of 'human capital', but in Cohen's (1992) sense of self-directed production.

In Chapter 3, we explore how IP/IPR contributes to the assembly of the market agent, and becomes a vital market device, contributing to the market's functioning not only as an allocative but also as a definitional mechanism (Velthuis 2005). IP/IPR also configures a calculative economic agency, introducing a temporal dimension to their productive activities, helping agents distinguish tradable assets and disentangle themselves.

With the relationship between cause and effect in cultural production essentially unknown, the complexity of cultural work requires producers to work within an inherent uncertainty, necessarily relying on the producer's professional judgement to limit harm and to generate opportunity. Chapter 4 shows how the IP/IPR nexus mediates the inherent uncertainty of symbolic IP production, mitigating its risk by rendering it more knowable and concomitantly manageable. Chapter 5 explores how IP/IPR acts as a mechanism through which things are rendered valuable, ordering and settling the multiple evaluative principles at play in creative production, while Chapter 6 concentrates on their economic realization, illustrating how economic valuations are contingent on the social relations entangled in the creative object (Fourcade 2011). Chapter 7 illustrates the intricate interrelation within the IP/IPR composite as it becomes involved in the process of protecting value.

Through tracing this journey, we show that IP/IPR is performative: it is a crucial device in ensuring that creative industries function *as industries*. We mean here that it functions to produce creative products and configure a form of economic agency among participants. We show how IP/IPR becomes a vital market device in the assembly of an economic market for creative products. In its transition from commodity production to final consumption, IP/IPR also acts as an object that circulates in different regimes of value. Artistic meanings and values may become temporarily subordinated once a work is in the commodity phase, and thus involved in the exchange of rights, but these meanings and values are not erased (Velthuis 2005). We describe some of the realities of the functioning of the creative industries; and if the result seems at times familiar we are reassured by Becker (2008: xxiv): 'good sociology does not discover what no one ever knew before (unlike science), but produces a deeper understanding of things that many people are pretty much aware of.'

Our argument is informed by several streams of literature, some more prominent than others, and some of which might be thought of as oppositional. We take from Bourdieu (2005), Foucault (2008), and Callon (1998) their spirited critiques of *homo oeconomicus*, and from the first two their criticisms of human capital. From Bourdieu, we find the concepts of field, habitus, and symbolic capital useful, but deny the 'economic' reading of Bourdieu's work (Gulledge et al. 2015, Townley 2014, 2015). From Foucault, we take his insight that practices (and disciplinary regimes) produce rationalities and rationalities produce subjectivities, here the calculating approach of economic agency (Townley 2008). From Callon, we take the ontological power of economics: 'the power to economise the material world through language and calculative agencies' (Fourcade 2011: 44). Economics performs a world in which calculability becomes a 'cultural competence'. This 'back and forth' between practices and economics constitutes over time stable economic objects of markets or prices (Fourcade 2011: 44).

Several things follow from our argument.

First, nomenclature. The coherence of the creative industries as a sector is questionable (Matthews and Smith Maguire 2014). Although the term 'made creatives more conscious of themselves' (Ross 2013: 180)—especially with regard to their political leverage—as O'Connor (2004) notes, the 'sector' itself fails to recognize the term. There are different 'creative industries', each constructed according to different conventions, communicative practices, economic and legal practices. Splitting the creative industries into different 'classes' on a 'creative/commercial' continuum, however, obscures similarities that our focus on IP/IPR makes clear. There are, for example, similarities between games developers and craft designers in terms of their response to protecting value through a reliance on the aesthete's eye and community-based action. More importantly, the catch-all 'creative industries' obscures important differences, especially between large, often conglomerate production and micros and SMEs. This is seen, for example, in games design, with the former demanding a 'rationalisation of creativity', the predictability of franchises, established genres and corporate management of risks. In turn, such demands lead to a lament of frustrated creativity among micro and SME designers and a well-developed pattern of 'exodus and entrepreneurialism', often clustered in one location (Dyer-Witheford and de Peuter 2009). Indeed, several creative sectors display, and perhaps depend on, this symbiotic dynamic.

Second, the analytical purchase of IP/IPR allows us to show that the radical separation of artistic and economic is untenable. We have noted a binary art/commerce relation that characterizes debates in the creative industries (Espeland 2013), although some of its demarcations, such as cultural and utilitarian, are becoming more blurred (Rantisi 2004, Lash and Urry 1994).

This relation is variously described as 'at odds', 'conflicting', 'contradictory', or 'antagonistic',[3] in part exacerbated by an often-institutionalized divorce between the production process and distribution. We noted earlier that Velthuis (2005: 23) refers to 'one market, two logics', with various sociological and anthropological terms such as logics, spheres, or domains capturing the divide. On this basis, there is a tendency to consider the creative, with its attendant associations of spontaneity and socially embedded relations, as being without calculation, 'sui generis and set apart from the context of economic institutions that construct incentives in market economies' (Christopherson 2008: 92). Likewise, exchange is often depicted as object-centred, relatively impersonal, and of an asocial nature, 'free of moral and cultural constraints' (Appadurai 1986: 11).

Such sharp distinctions often reflect scholastic fallacies, denying 'the tensions inherent between explanatory accounts and experienced reality' (Smith 2011: 277). Those trying to make a living through cultural production negotiate a lived process rather than formal categories: 'Practice is larger, more complex, more messy than can be grasped within any particular logic' (Law 2002: 34). IP/IPR allows us to identify 'the practical social knowledges that economic actors necessarily employ in order to *be* economic actors' (Slater 2002a: 74 emphasis in original). From the standpoint of specific social actors, 'economic and cultural categories are logically and practically interdependent' and cannot be meaningfully separated out (Slater 2002a: 59).

Our analysis shows that independent and micro cultural and creative production consistently displays market-based rationalities recognizable as 'calculation' (Callon and Muniesa 2005; Stark 2011). As Hutter and Teubner (1994, quoted in Bröckling 2016: 11) state, 'the medium "money" and the medium "legal norms" create their own appropriate forms of reason'. Actors necessarily act as interpretive bearers of socially structured rationalities (Ryan 1992), and processes of production, distribution, and exchange 'construct certain ways for people to conceive of and conduct themselves' (du Gay 1997: 4, quoted in Hesmondhalgh and Baker 2011: 54). For creatives to function easily in a business environment, for it to become 'human nature', requires 'a particular form of subjectivity' (Read 2009: 26), and appropriately configured socio-material apparatus. We see that, as its journey continues, IP/IPR functions performatively to encourage a form of behaviour that might be recognized as being indicative of 'calculation' (Stark 2011). In fleshing this out, we are informed by Swedberg (2010), who identifies several aspects of what might be involved in developing an economic habitus able to function

[3] It is however important not to exaggerate this. Several commentaries note that culture, creativity, and aesthetics intertwine with commerce in the 'aesthetic economy' (Aspers 2005, Entwistle 2009, Mears 2011, du Gay and Pryke 2002).

within a field of cultural production, including: recognizing the importance of work as a means of securing money, and not solely as an obligation 'to one's art'; the development of a specific attitude to time, in terms of a relationship to the present that recognizes 'opportunity cost' and also a control over the future; action underpinned with some knowledge of economic and technical issues, rather than being wholly guided solely by the social milieu of one's fellow creatives and collective cultural habits. Whilst not using the term 'good business model', content creators come to understand how value is created and captured (Neff 2012).

Our findings play into what Smith (2011: 279) identifies as learning how to 'act sensibly'. Acting sensibly is a process, not a 'state of being'. And it is a matter of survival; naïveté and lack of knowledge should not be mistaken for not wishing to make a success of a business venture. Aspects of 'acting sensibly' include identifying and prioritizing objectives; monitoring manifest and potential markets; identifying and juggling rules of thumb; adjusting and correcting one's course; and maintaining an escape route (Smith 2011: 280). 'The way in which people construct themselves as economic subjects is deeply social', highly influenced by the circumstances of particular sectors, companies, and projects (Neff 2012: 142). There is a 'business repertoire' informing the way a product is marketed or prices set (Velthuis 2005: 18). Circuits of creative commerce are distinguished by their business rituals and repertoires, organizing economic activity with specific understandings of practices in terms of how to measure success, what is good taste, and deciding upon appropriate payment (Mears 2011).

As one of our interviewees puts it:

> Unfortunately, a lot of musicians, artists and writers still have this idea that it is somehow distasteful to create music and money. It is not about greed. It is about survival, and it is about making a basic, average wage from music. I just think that you have to respond to the world that is around you, and you have to be able to see where you really are. [Music 93]

This business repertoire must be learned, or rather absorbed. In some cases it becomes part of a habitus, a set of predispositions informing the behaviour of actors in the field, a necessary adjunct of the artistic competence of the craft. In others, it may be encountered through classificatory structures and material architectures of the field which work to shape the actions of market participants in a suitably economized manner: attending a craft fair, for example, provokes comparison, positionality, and an extension of the maker's economic rationality. By the necessity of functioning in a field, agents will be guided towards a degree of self-interested and calculative forms of agency (Fourcade 2011: 44). They learn how to act sensibly: 'the rationale of the market is not the effect but rather the cause of human reason' (Bröckling 2016: 55).

Informed by a practical logic, 'economic behaviour' is necessarily reflective of its collective genesis (Bourdieu 2005). We have seen the performance of 'calculations, monetary interchanges, transactions and relations of all kinds' (Law 2002: 25). Artistic culture production contains multiple markets; it is far from being *a* market. Centring on IP/IPR, our analysis illustrates the 'cultural' and 'economic' are entangled and interdependent within 'the social practice of making markets' (du Gay and Pryke 2002: 13, Slater 2002a). As Negus (2002: 119) remarks,

> it is misleading to view practices within entertainment and arts institutions as primarily economic or governed by an organizational logic or structure. Instead, work and activities involved in cultural production should be thought of as meaningful practices which are interpreted and understood in different ways... and given various meanings in various social situations.

We do not argue that the 'economy' is culturally embedded, but rather stress with Law (2002: 35) the importance, when talking of economically relevant activity, to do so in terms of 'the complexity of practices and the heterogeneous materials that produce and are produced within those practices'. Different regimes of value play multiple roles simultaneously, in an 'overflowing of domains' (Velthuis 2005: 189).

Callon (1998) argues that the disentanglement of products from their makers and owners is an essential first step in the exchange of goods. Products rely on a process of abstraction, disentanglement, or reframing, such that they become alienable. An entity abstracted from its context may then be labelled property and transferred through exchange. Law plays a necessary role in this abstraction, constructing a legal entity and attaching to it property rights. This is the foundation of economic and legal theory. Like others writing about cultural production, however, we find only a partial disentanglement (Slater 2002b; Velthuis 2005). We show that objects remain necessarily entangled with the symbolic field in which they are produced. Their entanglement is the source of value, originality, and protection; their disentanglement the source of transferability and economic return. The creative industries depend on this unique linkage of symbolic and economic, and we have shown how it is mediated by IP/IPR.

Implications for IP Policies

Towse (1999: 369) argued for an understanding of law 'at the ground level' in order to understand 'the loftier issue of the principle of law'. Although focused on providing a nuanced analysis of this 'ground level', we should say something about the implications our findings have for IP policy.

Copyright in Context

The copyright regime has been described as a 'clever system for financing the creation of works of art... by granting statuary property rights to creators'. In this sense IP functions as a 'type of "enclosure", creating rights that privatise the use of works' (Towse 2006b: 85). This provides a financial incentive, as well as moral rights and the recognition of artistic status (Towse 2002: 11). Stemming from a market failure argument, the copyright regime seeks to promote the supply of creative content through the balance between protection and circulation or access. The 'general welfare' argument ensures that the ease of 'making copies' does not undermine their original creation, and in this sense, it is argued, legal doctrines act as a sort of 'modern invisible hand that overcomes market failure and promotes private economic efficiency and social welfare' (Towse 1999: 371). However, statements for copyright law often go further than this, for example, arguing that 'copyright law provides the framework for transactions in the cultural industries and enables artists and firms to appropriate returns to their investment, thereby increasing the incentive to supply' (Towse 1999: 388). This not only assumes that publishers' interests in dissemination or distribution, and authors' interests in creation are convergent, but that there is an 'underlying behavioural relationship between creativity and the incentives copyright offers' (Towse 2010: 461). The problem with the dominant economic argument for copyright is the assumptions it makes for incentives, that it provides an incentive to creativity; the model is assumed and then applied as part of the explanation. As Waelde and Schlesinger (2011) note, there is little support for the 'incentive theory' of legal policy. 'Monopoly revenues', secured through copyright, do not encourage the creation of art. It does however serve the 'industry' side of the creative industries (Towse 2006a).

Changes in the current context, in particular, the impact of digital, present issues for the copyright regime: 'in this context cultural industries need to find means of establishing boundaries around, and legitimate, claims to "their" products' (Toynbee 2001: 5). These changes have prompted calls for changes in IP law: 'The profitability of cultural products is more and more dependent upon the establishment of an effective international regime of intellectual property rights ensuring the protection of particular artists, firms and localities from product piracy and imitation' (Power and Scott 2004: 12).[4] Bazalgette

[4] In the UK, concerns about reduced royalty collection stemming from copyright infringement have prompted lobbying from the licensing sector to pressure government into increasing copyright enforcement. However, the 2011 Hargreaves Review of IP recommended, and government subsequently implemented, a number of provisions to expand the use of copyrighted works without traditional licensing; this includes exceptions such as Orphan Works (the ability to license works without identifiable rights holders) and Text and Data Mining (the ability to access

(2017: 31), for example, states that IP is 'at the core of the creative industries and protection is paramount'. An effective IP regime is frequently interpreted by policymakers as strengthening copyright, often an argument for increasing the length or duration and scope of copyright, for the benefit of rights holders, in the hope that technological innovation will make catalogues more exploitable through new delivery techniques (Towse 2003). It is an argument that finds resistance from others: 'copyright attaches to a bewildering variety of human creations . . . the rights conferred by copyright have become inexorably broader, encompassing nearly all secondary uses and adaptations of copyrighted content' (Cohen 2012: 61). Although digital reproduction and the Internet present issues with the copyright regime in that material is easily used or appropriated by others (Watson et al. 2015, Watson et al. 2016, Fleming et al. 2017), the impact of digital has blurred the lines between user and producer, as well as extending the opportunities and possibilities for creation. Indeed, strategies of monopoly become questioned when value is increasingly based on time and speed, and the network of alliances and modalities of usage within a circuit of sharing (Pasquinelli 2007).

IP in Context

Given the disproportionate bargaining power between creators and intermediaries, the question arises as to whether IP policy, and changes to IP policy, realize their objectives to incentivize creativity. The rise of the digital technologies and the omnipresence of digital media have further enhanced the power of intermediaries, now taking the form of giant technology corporations. In this new era, IPR becomes a tool more useful for intermediaries than creators. Yet we are starting to see intermediaries themselves become commissioners and producers of content; Netflix, Amazon Video, and Apple are looking to the creation of original content, rather than serving predominantly as resellers of existing content.[5] The lines between intermediary and creator may blur, and therefore the incentive premise of IP may become less straightforward.

We argue that any evidence-based policy should be based on an understanding of the role of copyright within the valorization process as a whole. IP/IPR encapsulates a mix of motivations, providing the nebulous bridge between artistic endeavours and commercialization. While IP conventions vary

copyrighted works for the purposes of text and data mining). As technology changes, it is likely that the laws and policies which govern IPR will also change.

[5] A 2018 European Union audio-visual services directive specifies a 30 per cent European production requirement for TV shows and films, a 'Netflix' quota. In addition, streaming services will have to directly commission and fund European TV series or films or contribute to national film funds (Rankin 2018).

between sectors, there are key themes that cut across practices. These include the creators' need for acknowledgement, the limitations of IP, and the use of IP as a strategic tool. Collectively, this suggests that IP policy, and changes to IP policy, may not have its intended effects. A key function of IPR, noted by many of our interviewees, is its role in providing formalized acknowledgement and attribution of creative outputs. Here, IPR satisfies some of the core motivations of creators in creating symbolic capital in the form of legal rights. The creative industries often work in a collaborative context, and IPR translates practices into recognized assets both in terms of intangible property and in acknowledgement of individuals' contributions to the creation of works. Similarly, IPR can assist with establishing where the line of copying exists—an important function in trend-driven sectors in the creative industries such as fashion.

The strategic use of IPR, as a means to realize value or as a bargaining tool, again serves a key function in the creative industries. However, the use of IPR as a stick is only as strong as the ability to enforce these rights. While IPR may provide a rights holder with intangible property, these rights do not necessarily overcome the weak bargaining power of smaller players when faced with stronger, larger players. In addition, social norms may provide stronger incentives to respect IP than the IPR themselves. While IPR have a place in the creative industries, and certainly with creators who have enjoyed success, their role may be more aspirational than functional.

Given the constraints of establishing a business, often with limited resources, SMEs and micros frequently neglect IP, thus making it difficult for businesses to capture value. As we have seen, there is a recognized lack of knowledge and legal expertise (Phillips and Street 2015, Street and Phillips 2017). In recognition of the low level of IP awareness amongst SMEs, government innovation support policies often include IP support and training.[6] This training can be couched in a panacea-like language, where IP can 'enhance the market value of your SME', 'turn inventions into profit-making assets', and is a 'vital component of business strategy' (WIPO 2017). This does not, of course, address the issue of the lack of financial resources to pursue legal action (Helmers et al. 2015).[7] The impact of this SME support is yet unproven, and it remains unclear as to the level of IP sophistication required for best practices by SME and creators.

[6] See for example the Finnish case detailed by Hynynen (2013) and the UK case as evidenced by the government's ongoing SME agenda; WIPO has a dedicated SME and Entrepreneurship Support Division.

[7] In the UK, there is the Intellectual Property Enterprise Court (IPEC), an IP small-claims track for copyright, design, and trademark issues of under £10,000, designed to aid holders of low-value copyright, such as micros and SMEs (see Cornwell 2018, Brown 2018).

Creative Business in Context

We must raise the important issue of the financial returns to the freelance, micros, and SMEs we portray. The emphasis on IP is criticized for the perceived iniquities of its functioning, as rewards flow to publishers and distributors rather than creators (Toynbee 2001, 2013). 'IP is most commonly exploited not at the individual level, where it is comparatively rare that individuals will own their own IP in a form that can be used for "wealth creation" but rather by larger corporate structures with the music industry as the paradigmatic example' (O'Brien 2014: 77). Although we have broadened our analysis from the paradigmatic case of music, there is nothing in our analysis to suggest that primary content providers, individual creative producers, and microbusinesses will benefit vis-à-vis distribution companies. Indeed, we must conclude with Towse (2006b: 83) that 'the power of copyright law to reward artists and other creators seems to be limited, while on the other hand it apparently provides disproportionate benefits to the large corporations that dominate the creative industries'. As Bazalgette (2017: 6) concludes, 'significant challenges exist for ensuring creative content creators are fairly remunerated for their IP.'

While the legal framework of IP appears to offer little to the individual practitioner, however, this is not to argue that an 'anything goes' framework would be more appropriate. On the contrary, the impact of the legal framework is immediately apparent to creative producers:

> France bought [X] for TV and DVD and they paid $200,000 for it. China, with a much bigger population, bought it and it was $15,000. Then somebody posted a picture on Facebook at the weekend of a pirated DVD of [X] in China. [Film 68]

Market prices reflect the potential audience for a product, and the lack of IP protection in one (much larger) jurisdiction means that prices are necessarily much lower than in another, as audiences cannot be secured. An IPR framework, and the norms and practices that sustain this, may therefore provide 'knock on' benefits to individual creators.

Indeed, the nature of IP protection has a large impact on the nature of creative production, as Power and Hallencreutz (2004: 226) note: 'Copyright and IPRs are the constitutive institutions upon which the music industry's present configurations rest.' As their study of the Jamaican and Swedish music industries illustrates, different IP regimes influence music industry structure. The lack of an enforceable or effective IPR regime and protection for investment in 'product development' results in a fragmented industry of 'cut-throat' competition and rapid innovation and turnover, in contrast to longer term investments and support for smaller producers with a stronger IPR regime (Power and Hallencreutz 2004).

Is it the impact of law or access to capital that is the defining factor in the relative balance of real rights between agents? Our analysis suggests the latter. Bazalgette (2017: 6) recognizes that access to finance is 'particularly acute', and that micros and SMEs are 'disadvantaged in relation to "growth capital"'. For many, it is a lack of finance necessary for the time and space to develop that is limited and where rights are ceded for investment support. Other suggestions have focused on the importance of valuing IP, arguing that 'transactions such as raising finance, negotiating license agreements, structuring collaborations and buying and selling IP assets rely on being able to value IP in question' (Bazalgette 2017: 33).

The 'bi-polar' nature of the creative industries informs the debate on IP. Ross (2013: 175) argues that US cultural and creative industries view themselves as 'global market leaders' having benefited from government agencies which 'strong-arm efforts to protect IP and enforce IP licensing overseas', with the result that a wave of policymaking in other countries in the 2000s was often presented as 'a catch-up initiative, especially in a bid to grab a chunk of the fast-moving economic landscape around IP'. He predicts that as mergers and acquisitions continue among multinational corporations, 'concentrating more and more ownership of culture in fewer hands, we will also see a steady move towards the "commons" among younger folks involved in arts and culture' (Ross 2013: 182).

More recent, 'open' theories of IP (perhaps overhyped as full-fledged theories), provide nuance to existing approaches. The Creative Commons (CC) or 'open innovation' approach facilitates openness through the licensing and sharing of the innovations protected by IPR. CC provides a series of ready-made licences, based on licensing IPR, that allow for freer usage of works in a system without royalties. Licences range from complete freedom of use with no need for attribution, to free usage only by non-commercial entities with attribution, with variations in between and on the sharing of related works. (The 'commons' is sometimes conflated with 'public domain' works, but differ as public domain works are not protected by copyright). Both public domain and CC expand the availability of royalty-free works, which may be more freely used in the creation of new works.

Making work publicly available, however, does not forfeit the rights to work, nor is it equivalent to disregarding intellectual property rights (O'Mahony 2003). Rather, it refers to licensing terms, which prohibit its use for commercial or privatized use or other forms of proprietary appropriation and exploitation. Protection is secured through a combination of legal (and normative) tactics, including copyright, trademark, and software licensing, allowing the intellectual property to be 'publicly and freely available and yet, governable' (O'Mahony 2003: 1179). Thus, a legal framework is equally as important for maintaining the open source nature of the work as it would be for an appropriation strategy. Law is used to manage rights to digital intellectual property, but decouples its management from possession. While property rights are respected, transport rights (the right to copy), rendering rights (playing and printing), and derivative works rights (extracting, editing, and embedding in other works) may be disaggregated and managed independently (O'Mahony 2003: 1196). Although digital rights management is usually associated with restriction, the open source field illustrates how the legal framework might be used to manage, exercise, and defend rights (O'Mahony 2003). As a licensing system resting entirely on existing copyright laws,[8] open access and CC is more a cluster of emerging thought and action on how to best optimize the existing IP systems, rather than fundamentally question or justify IP itself.

IP and Wider Policy

These debates highlight the importance, as O'Brien (2014: 78) notes, of the interdependence of 'large organizations, smaller organizations, state funded art institutions and government'—the political economy within which the creative industries functions. McRobbie (2002, 2010), for example, identifies three waves of entrepreneurs: 'sub-cultural entrepreneurs' identified as fashion industry microbusinesses of the 1980s; 'despecialization', involving multiple jobs, tasks, and hybrid work; and work as the site 'for generating economic value by the process of managing and creating the individual him or herself' (O'Brien 2014: 82), exemplified by Gill's (2010) 'life is a pitch'. While there is debate as to who might, or might not, be included in the term creative 'worker' and creative 'entrepreneur', more centrally here, these developments are not natural, or given, but reflect the gradual depletion of employment protection and overt support for casualized employment.

More broadly, our study has implications both for education, higher education policy, and cultural policy. Education policy must entail access to and awareness of the arts and the opportunity to become involved in its various forms. McRobbie (2016) has indicated the impact of higher education (HE) policies on the nature of skills for those in the creative area (see Ashton and Noonan 2013). The expansion of HE has seen the move from resource-intensive and therefore expensive craft-based skills from which the ability to produce IP is generated, to more generalist 'product marketing'-based courses, as universities protect a depleting resource base. The tangible foundations of a potentially vibrant entrepreneurial cohort are thus undermined. Equally,

[8] Similar interpretations are found behind organizations such as the Electronic Freedom Foundation, which campaigns for civil liberties in the digital world, and others advocating balanced approaches to current IP regimes (Drahos and Braithwaite 2003).

the rebalancing of cultural policy agenda from the social democratic arts, education, and training threatens cultural institutions that provide the source of 'creative work' providing the basis for future growth (McRobbie 2016).

These concerns prompt concerns with 'the health of the industry', as for example in TV production, where increased outsourcing of production has led to a situation where 'valuable skills which can only be learned through hands-on experience are getting progressively lost while those who do have the skills are becoming progressively more expensive to employ as they have come to represent a rare breed' (Berkeley 2003: 111). The number of publishers, for example, publishing poetry or some forms of classical music as part of their social responsibilities is becoming more limited. Although, like the publisher of *Waiting for Godot,* they may hope for future profitability, the opportunities 'to take a punt' are decreasing, as global providers such as Amazon threaten the profitability base of smaller publishers. Competition policy is at issue here.

Finally, we note that national cultural policy also has implications for the skill base and nature of future creative production. Awareness of, and access to, cultural opportunities entails a vibrant cultural policy, properly supported and sufficiently independent to experiment. Within specific sectors, public funds can be used, partly for promoting culture, but also to promote a production community, help businesses grow, and augment a skill base. Canada, Germany, Australia, and Ireland, for example, have a policy of substantial financial incentives to be put towards making programmes. Such policies are also designed to support indigenous cultural production especially where this is in danger of being dominated by larger cultural producers: 'Canada was one of the pioneers of this because they sleep with the elephant. If you are working with them it means that you have to hire a lot of Canadian personnel to get the tax credits to boost budget. Ireland have a similar model. Companies are able to make and publish all over the world' [TV 53].

In conclusion, we contend our construction of IP/IPR crystalizes an important analytical object for the scholarly interrogation of the creative industries and the construction of economic agency in the creative economy. The evolving nature of the creative industries implies that our understanding of IP/IPR will continue to change as creative producers navigate new economic conditions and market realities. Its political importance will not diminish, as IPR remains a key topic in national policymaking and international trade agreements, pitting large against small. This wider context is reflected in the narrative our interviewees construct as a font of insights into the subtleties of IP/IPR in configuring economic agency, as a tool for managing uncertainty and the means by which creators use IP/IPR to construct, realize, and protect value. Generating and developing the IP/IPR of creative content is a process—it is creating economy.

Appendix

Interview Participants

Participant[a]	Creative Activity	Years' experience (organization)[b]	# Employed[c]	Organization Type[d]
Design 1	Furniture	20–30	4	Ltd
Design 2	Interior Products	15–20	1	Sole Trader
Design 3	Interior Products	< 15	1	Sole Trader
Design 4	Interior Design	< 10	1	Sole Trader
Design 5	Silver and metal work	15–20	1	Sole Trader
Design 6	Design Education	15–20	10	NFP
Design 7	Service Design	< 5	2	Partnership
Design 8	Furniture, Interior Products	< 10	1	Sole Trader
Design 9	Jewellery	< 10	1	Sole Trader
Design 10	Gallery, workshops	15–20	70	Ltd
Design 11	Craft Association	< 15	4	Ltd & Reg. Charity
Design 12	Ceramic Art	< 15	1	Sole Trader
Design 13	Interior Products	20–30	1	Ltd
Design 14	Jewellery	< 10	1	Sole Trader
Design 15	Jewellery	< 15	1	Sole Trader
Design 16	Visual, Performance Art	< 10	1	Sole Trader
Design 17	Service Design	< 10	8	Ltd
Design 18	3-D Product Design	< 10	9	NFP Reg. Charity
Design 19	Jewellery, Visual Art	< 10	1	Sole Trader
Design 20	Book Design	15–20	1	Sole Trader
Design 21	Jewellery	< 15	1	Sole Trader
Design 22	Jewellery	< 15	1	Sole Trader
Design 23	Visual Arts	20–30	1	Sole Trader
Design 24	Tapestry, weaving	> 100	15	Ltd & Reg. Charity
Design 25	Jewellery	< 15	3	Ltd
Design 26	Interior Products	20–30	12	Partnership
F&T 27	Weaving	15–20	1	Sole Trader
F&T 28	Womenswear	< 10	1	Ltd
F&T 29	Textiles	< 15	1	Sole Trader
F&T 30	Knitwear	30–40	3	Ltd
F&T 31	Knitwear	< 10	1	Sole Trader
F&T 32	Textiles	< 15	1	Sole Trader
F&T 33	Knitwear	20–30	8	Ltd
F&T 34	Knitwear	30–40	10	Ltd
F&T 35	Textiles	15–20	1	Ltd
F&T 36	Fashion Accessories	< 10	2	Partnership
F&T 37	Fashion Accessories	20–30	1	Sole Trader

(continued)

Appendix

Interview Participants

Participant[a]	Creative Activity	Years' experience (organization)[b]	# Employed[c]	Organization Type[d]
F&T 38	Fashion design	< 10	1	Sole Trader
F&T 39	Womenswear	< 10	1	Sole Trader
F&T 40	Womenswear	< 10	1	Ltd
Games 41	Educational, Entertainment Games	< 10	1	Ltd
Games 42	Mobile, Handheld Games	< 10	32	Ltd
Games 43	Mobile, Online Games	< 5	4	Ltd Liability Partnership
Games 44	Mobile, Online Games	< 5	4	Ltd Liability Partnership
Games 45	Massively Multiplayer Online Games	< 10	29	Ltd
Games 46	Educational, Mobile Games	< 10	4	Ltd
Games 47	Interactive Games, Software	< 10	3	Ltd
Games 48	Branded, Original Games	< 10	25	Ltd
Games 49	Mobile, Online Games	< 5	7	Ltd
Games 50	Mobile, Online Games	< 10	1	Ltd
Games 51	Game Tool Development	< 10	25	Ltd
Games 52	Mobile, Online Games	< 10	1	Ltd
TV 53	Factual, Children's TV Production	20–30	9	Ltd
TV 54	Broadcasting and Production	50–60	200	Plc.
TV 55	Digital Media Production	15–20	2	Ltd
TV 56	TV and Digital Production	20–30	20	Ltd
TV 57	Corporate Video Production	20–30	1	Sole Trader
TV 58	Gaelic and Music Production	< 15	10	Ltd
TV 59	Comedy, Feature Production	20–30	2	Ltd
TV 60	Factual Production	< 15	6	Ltd
TV 61	Current Affairs, Factual Production	< 10	12	Ltd
TV 62	Music Video Production	< 15	2	Partnership
TV 63	Factual Production	15–20	1	Ltd
TV 64	Corporate Video Production	30–40	2	Ltd
Film 65	Film Sales, Distribution	< 15	8	Ltd
Film 66	Film (& TV) Production	40–50	1	Ltd
Film 67	Film (& TV) Production	< 15	4	Ltd
Film 68	Film (& TV, Radio) Production	15–20	6	Ltd
Film 69	Film Production	15–20	1	Ltd
Film 70	Film (& TV) Production	< 15	2	Ltd
Film 71	Film Distribution	< 5	4	Ltd
Film 72	Film (& TV) Production	< 15	1	Ltd
Publishing 73	Publishing, Writing	20–30	1	Ltd
Publishing 74	Publishing Association	40–50	5	Ltd & Reg. Charity
Publishing 75	Publishing Association	> 100	1	Ltd
Publishing 76	Fiction Publishing	< 10	1	Ltd
Publishing 77	Fiction Publishing	< 5	8	Ltd
Publishing 78	Fiction and Non-Fiction Publishing	< 15	3	Ltd
Publishing 79	Fiction and Non-Fiction Publishing	20–30	20	Ltd
Publishing 80	Writing, self-publishing	30–40	1	Sole Trader
Publishing 81	Writing	< 15	1	Sole Trader
Publishing 82	Fiction and Non-Fiction Publishing	30–40	12	Ltd

Publishing 83	Fiction and Non-Fiction Publishing	40–50	35	Ltd
Publishing 84	Fiction and Non-Fiction Publishing	15–20	4	Ltd
Music 85	Digital Music Production	< 10	4	Ltd
Music 86	Chamber Music Ensemble	20–30	5	Ltd
Music 87	Jazz Music Ensemble	20–30	2	Ltd & Reg. Charity
Music 88	Music Production, Publishing	15–20	9	Ltd
Music 89	Chamber Music Ensemble	40–50	5	Ltd & Reg. Charity
Music 90	Contemporary Music Ensemble	< 10	1	Ltd
Music 91	Music Archiving	40–50	10	Ltd & Reg. Charity
Music 92	Music Licensing	20–30	1	Ltd NFP
Music 93	Music Composition	20–30	1	Ltd
Music 94	Music Festival	< 15	1	Ltd
Music 95	Music Festival	20–30	3	Ltd & Reg. Charity
Music 96	Music Education	20–30	5	Ltd & Reg. Charity
Theatre 97	Theatre Production	20–30	3	Ltd
Theatre 98	Childrens Theatre	15–20	5	Ltd
Theatre 99	Theatre Productions	< 15	2	Ltd
Theatre 100	Theatre Production	20–30	3	Ltd
Theatre 101	Theatre Production	20–30	7	Ltd & Reg. Charity
Theatre 102	Theatre Production	50–60	70	Ltd
Theatre 103	Theatre Production	20–30	3	Ltd & Reg. Charity
Theatre 104	Theatre Production	< 15	2	Ltd
Theatre 105	Theatre Production	15–20	4	Ltd & Reg. Charity
Theatre 106	Theatre Production	20–30	2	Ltd
Theatre 107	Theatre Production	70	35	Ltd
Theatre 108	Theatre Production	< 15	2	Ltd
Theatre 109	Theatre Production	30–40	40	Ltd
Theatre 110	Theatre Production	< 15	1	Ltd
Theatre 111	Theatre Association	20–30	8	Ltd & Reg. Charity
Theatre 112	Theatre Production	40–50	50	Ltd
Theatre 113	Theatre Production	< 15	2	Ltd (NFP)
Theatre 114	Theatre Association	40–50	0 (volunteers)	Member Association
Dance 115	Contemporary Dance Production	< 15	2	Ltd
Dance 116	Contemporary Choreography, Production	< 15	1	Ltd & Reg. Charity
Dance 117	Contemporary Choreography, Production	15–20	1	Ltd & Reg. Charity
Dance 118	Contemporary Choreography, Production	< 10	1	Ltd & Reg. Charity
Dance 119	Ballet Production	< 10	2	Ltd & Reg. Charity
Dance 120	Contemporary Choreography, Production	< 15	1	Sole Trader
Dance 121	Contemporary Choreography, Production	< 10	1	Ltd
Dance 122	Contemporary Choreography, Production	20–30	21	Ltd

[a] Key: F&T = Fashion & Textiles
[b] Key: < = less than, > = more than
[c] Some organizations additionally employ sub-contractors and freelancers
[d] Key: Ltd = limited company, NFP = not for profit, PLC = public limited company, Reg = registered

References

Adams, J. 1995. *Risk*. London: UCL Press.

Adkins, L. 2005. 'The New Economy, Property and Personhood'. *Theory, Culture & Society* 22 (1): pp. 111–30.

Adorno, T., and M. Horkheimer. 1972. *Dialectic of Enlightenment*. London: Verso.

Akerlov, G. 1970. 'The Market for Lemons: Quality Uncertainty and Market Mechanisms'. *Quarterly Journal of Economics* 84: pp. 448–500.

Allen, J. 2002. 'Symbolic Economies: The "Culturization" of Economic Knowledge'. In *Cultural Economy: Cultural Analysis and Commercial Life*, edited by P. Du Gay and M. Pryke, pp. 39–58. London: Sage.

Anand, N., and G. Croidieu. 2015. 'Niches, Genres, and Classifications in the Creative Industries'. In *The Oxford Handbook of the Creative and Cultural Industries*, edited by C. Jones, M. Lorenzen, and J. Sapsed, pp. 327–50. Oxford: Oxford University Press.

Anand, N., and B. Jones. 2008. 'Tournament Rituals, Category Dynamics, and Field Configuration: The Case of the Booker Prize'. *Journal of Management Studies* 45: pp. 1036–60.

Anand, N., and M. Watson. 2004. 'Tournament Rituals in the Evolution of Fields: The Case of the Grammy Awards'. *Academy of Management Journal* 47: pp. 59–80.

Appadurai, A. 1986. 'Introduction: Commodities and the Politics of Value'. In The *Social Life of Things*, edited by A. Appadurai, pp. 3–63. Cambridge: Cambridge University Press.

Arthur, W. 2009. The *Nature of Technology: What It Is and How It Evolves*. New York: Free Press.

Ashton, D., and C. Noonan. 2013. *Cultural Work and Higher Education*. Basingstoke, UK: Palgrave Macmillan.

Aspers, P. 2005. *Markets in Fashion: A Phenomenological Approach*. London: Routledge.

Aspers, P. 2010. *Orderly Fashion: A Sociology of Markets*. Princeton, NJ: Princeton University Press.

Aspers, P., and J. Beckert. 2011. 'Value in Markets'. In *The Worth of Goods: Valuation and Pricing in the Economy*, edited by J. Beckert and P. Aspers, pp. 3–40. Oxford: Oxford University Press.

Austin, J. 1978. *How to Do Things with Words*. Oxford: Oxford University Press.

Australian Government Department of Communications and the Arts. 2018. 'Reviewing the Code of Conduct for Copyright Collecting Societies'. Consultation published 14 February. Accessed 27 April 2018 from: https://www.communications.gov.au/have-your-say/reviewing-code-conduct-copyright-collecting-societies.

Baines, S., and I. Robson. 2001. 'Being Self-Employed or Being Enterprising? The Case of Creative Work for the Media Industries'. *Journal of Small Business and Enterprise Development* 8 (4): pp. 349–62.

Bakhshi, H., S. Cunningham, and J. Mateos-Garcia. 2015. 'Public Policy for the Creative Industries'. In *The Oxford Handbook of the Creative and Cultural Industries*, edited by C. Jones, M. Lorenzen, and J. Sapsed, pp. 465–85. Oxford: Oxford University Press.

Bakker, G. 2015. 'Sunk Costs and the Dynamics of Creative Industries'. In *The Oxford Handbook of the Creative and Cultural Industries*, edited by C. Jones, M. Lorenzen, and J. Sapsed, pp. 351–86. Oxford: Oxford University Press.

Banks, M. 2007. *The Politics of Cultural Work*. Basingstoke, UK: Palgrave Macmillan.

Banks, M. 2010. 'Craft Labour and Creative Industries'. *International Journal of Cultural Policy* 16 (3): pp. 305–22.

Banks, M. 2014. 'Being in the Zone of Cultural Work'. *Culture Unbound* 6: pp. 241–62.

Banks, M. 2015. 'Valuing Cultural Industries'. In *The Routledge Companion to the Cultural Industries*, edited by K. Oakley and J. O'Connor, pp. 35–44. Abingdon, UK: Routledge.

Banks, M., and J. O'Connor. 2009. 'After the Creative Industries'. *International Journal of Cultural Policy* 1 (4): pp. 365–73.

Barnatt, C., and K. Starkey. 1994. 'The Emergence of Flexible Networks in the UK TV Industry'. *British Journal of Management* 5: pp. 251–60.

Barthes, R. 1977. 'The Death of the Author'. In *Image, Music, Text*. London: Fontana.

Bazalgette, P. 2017. *Independent Review of the Creative Industries*. Department for Digital, Culture, Media & Sport. London: UK Government.

Beck, A. 2003. 'Introduction: Cultural Work, Cultural Workplace—Looking at the Cultural Industries'. In *Cultural Work: Understanding the Cultural Industries*, edited by A. Beck, pp. 1–12. London: Routledge.

Beck, U. 1992. *Risk Society: Towards A New Modernity*. London: Sage.

Beck, U. 2000. *The Brave New World of Work*. Cambridge: Polity Press.

Becker, G. 1964. *Human Capital*. Chicago: University of Chicago Press.

Becker, H. 1974. 'Art as Collective Action'. *American Sociological Review* 39 (6): pp. 767–76.

Becker, H. 2008. *Art Worlds*. Berkeley: University of California Press.

Beckert, J. and Aspers, P. (eds). 2011. *The Worth of Goods*. Oxford: Oxford University Press.

Beckert, J., and C. Musselin. 2013. 'Introduction'. In *Constructing Quality: The Classification of Goods in Markets*, edited by J. Beckert and C. Musselin, pp. 1–30. Oxford: Oxford University Press.

Benjamin, W. 1968. 'The Work of Art in the Age of Mechanical Reproduction'. *Illuminations*, pp. 217–52. London: Fontana.

Bently, L. 1994. 'Copyright and the Death of the Author in Literature and Law'. *The Modern Law Review* 57: pp. 973–86.

Berkeley, D. 2003. 'Creativity and Economic Transactions in Television Drama Production'. In *Cultural Work: Understanding the Cultural Industries*, edited by A. Beck, pp. 103–20. London: Routledge.

Beverungen, A., S. Böhm, and C. Land. 2012. 'The Poverty of Journal Publishing'. *Organization* 19 (6): pp. 929–38.

Bielby, W., and D. Bielby. 1994. 'All Hits Are Flukes: Institutionalized Decision Making and the Rhetoric of Network Prime-Time Program Development.' *American Journal of Sociology* 99: pp. 1287–313.

Bielby, W., and D. Bielby. 1999. 'Organizational Mediation of Project-Based Labor Markets: Talent Agencies and the Careers of Screenwriters'. *American Sociological Review* 64: pp. 64–85.

Billboard. 2004. 'Labels Agree to $50 Million Payout'. Billboardbiz. 4 May. Accessed 2 August 2017 from: http://www.billboard.com/biz/articles/news/1438541/labels-agree-to-50-million-payout.

Blakley, J. 2010. 'Lessons from Fashion's Free Culture'. Video presentation to TedxUSC. Accessed 29 March 2018 from: https://www.ted.com/talks/johanna_blakley_lessons_from_fashion_s_free_culture.

Boltanski, L., and E. Chiapello. 2005. *The New Spirit of Capitalism*. London: Verso.

Boltanski, L., and L. Thévenot. 2006. *On Justification*. Princeton, NJ: Princeton University Press.

Bourdieu, P. 1979. 'Symbolic Power'. *Critique of Anthropology* 4: pp. 77–85.

Bourdieu, P. 1984. *Distinction*. London: Routledge.

Bourdieu, P. 1987. 'The Historical Genesis of a Pure Aesthetic'. *Journal of Aesthetics and Art Criticism* 46: pp. 201–10.

Bourdieu, P. 1989. Social Space and Symbolic Power. *Sociological Theory* 7 (June): pp. 18–26.

Bourdieu, P. 1993. *The Field of Cultural Production*. Cambridge: Polity Press.

Bourdieu, P. 1998. 'Job Insecurity Is Everywhere Now'. In *Acts of Resistance: Against the Tyranny of the Market*, translated by R. Nice. New York: New Books.

Bourdieu, P. 2005. *The Social Structures of the Economy*. Cambridge: Polity Press.

Bowker, G. and S. Leigh Starr. 1999. *Sorting Things Out*. Cambridge, MA: MIT Press.

Boyle, J. 1996. *Shamans, Software, and Spleens: Law and the Construction of the Information Society*. Cambridge, MA: Harvard University Press.

Braverman, H. 1974. *Labor and Monopoly Capital: The Degradation of Work in the Twentieth Century*. New York: Monthly Review Press.

Bröckling, U. 2016. *The Entrepreneurial Self: Fabricating a New Type of Subject*. Los Angeles: Sage.

Brown, A. 2018. 'Enforcement and Remedy: What Is Success? IP Litigation and the Creative Industries'. In *Research Handbook on Intellectual Property and Creative Industries*, edited by A. Brown and C. Waelde, pp. 143–58. Cheltenham, UK: Edward Elgar.

Buccafusco, C., and P. Heald. 2013. 'Do Bad Things Happen When Works Enter the Public Domain? Empirical Tests of Copyright Term Extension'. *Berkeley Technology Law Journal* 28 (1): pp. 1–44.

Butt, D. 2007. 'Craft, Context and Method: The Creative Industries and Alternative Models'. In *MyCreativity Reader: A Critique of Creative Industries*, edited by G. Lovink and N. Rossiter, pp. 207–18. Amsterdam: Institute of Network Cultures.

Çalışkan, K., and M. Callon. 2009. 'Economization, Part 1: Shifting Attention from the Economy towards Processes of Economization'. *Economy and Society* 38: pp. 369–98.

Çalışkan, K., and M. Callon. 2010. 'Economization, Part 2: A Research Programme for the Study of Markets'. *Economy and Society* 39 (1): pp. 1–32.

Callon, M. 1998. *The Laws of the Markets*. Oxford: Oxford University Press.

Callon, M. 1999. 'Actor-Network Theory: The Market Test'. In *Actor Network Theory and After*, edited by J. Law and J. Hassard, pp. 191–5. Oxford, UK: Blackwell.

Callon, M. 2007. 'An Essay on the Growing Contribution of Economic Markets to the Proliferation of the Social'. *Theory, Culture & Society* 24 (7/8): pp. 139–63.

Callon, M., and Muniesa, F. 2005. 'Economic Markets as Calculative Collective Devices'. *Organization Studies* 26 (8): pp. 1229–50.

Callon, M., C. Meadel, and V. Rabeharisoa. 2002. 'The Economy of Qualities'. *Economy and Society* 31: pp. 194–217.

Callon, M., F. Muniesa, and Y. Millo. 2007. *Market Devices*. Oxford: Blackwell Publishers.

Caves, R. 2000. *Creative Industries: Contracts between Art and Commerce*. Boston: Harvard University Press.

Cesareo, L., and A. Pastore. 2014. 'Consumers' Attitude and Behavior towards Online Music Piracy and Subscription-based Services'. *Journal of Consumer Marketing* 31 (6/7): pp. 515–25.

Chen, Y.-H., and P. Roscoe. 2018. 'Practices and Meanings of Non-Professional Stock-Trading in Taiwan: A Case of Relational Work'. *Economy and Society* 46 (3–4): pp. 576–600.

Chiapello, E. 2004. 'Evolution and Co-Optation. The Artist Critique of Management and Capitalism'. *Third Text* 18 (6): pp. 585–94.

Chiou, J., C. Huang, and H. Lee. 2005. 'The Antecedents of Music Piracy Attitudes and Intentions'. *Journal of Business Ethics* 57 (2): pp. 161–74.

Cho, S., X. Fang, and S. Tayur. 2015. 'Combating Strategic Counterfeiters in Licit and Illicit Supply Chains'. *Manufacturing & Service Operations Management* 17 (3): pp. 273–89.

Christopherson, S. 2006. 'Behind the Scenes: How Transnational Firms Are Constructing a New International Division of Labor in Media Work'. *Geoforum* 37 (5): pp. 739–51.

Christopherson, S. 2008. 'Beyond the Self-Expressive Creative Worker: An Industry Perspective on Entertainment Media'. *Theory, Culture & Society* 25: pp. 73–95.

Christopherson, S., and M. Storper. 1986. 'The City as Studio; The World as Back Lot: The Impact of Vertical Disintegration on the Location of the Motion Picture Industry'. *Environment and Planning D: Society and Space* 4: pp. 305–20.

Cochoy, F. 2014. 'A Theory of "Agencing": on Michel Callon's Contribution to Organizational Knowledge and Practice'. In *The Oxford Handbook of Sociology, Social Theory, and Organization Studies*, edited by P. Adler, P. Du Gay, G. Morgan, and M. Reed, pp. 106–24. Oxford: Oxford University Press.

Coe, N. 2015. 'Global Production Networks in the Creative Industries'. In *The Oxford Handbook of the Creative and Cultural Industries*, edited by C. Jones, M. Lorenzen, and J. Sapsed, pp. 486–501. Oxford: Oxford University Press.

Coe, N., and J. Johns. 2004. 'Beyond Production Clusters: Towards a Critical Political Economy of Networks in the Film and Television Industries'. In *The Cultural Industries and the Production of Culture*, edited by D. Power and A. Scott, pp. 188–204. London: Routledge.

Cohen, A. 1992. 'The Personal Right to Identity: A Polemic on the Self in the Enterprise Culture'. In *The Values of the Enterprise Culture: The Moral Debate*, edited by P. Heelas and P. Morris, pp. 179–93. London: Routledge.

Cohen, J. 2012. *Configuring the Networked Self: Law, Code, and the Play of Everyday Practice*. New Haven, CT: Yale University Press.

Cohen, W., R. Nelson, and J. Walsh. 2000. *'Protecting their Intellectual Assets: Appropriability Conditions and Why US Manufacturing Firms Patent or Not'*, Working Paper No. 7552. Cambridge, MA: National Bureau of Economic Research.

Cornwell, J. 2018. 'Intellectual Property Enforcement: Empirical Consideration of Enforcement Action'. In *Research Handbook on Intellectual Property and Creative Industries*, edited by A. Brown and C. Waelde, pp. 135–42. Cheltenham, UK: Edward Elgar.

Coslor, E. 2016. 'Transparency in an Opaque Market: Evaluative Frictions Between "Thick" Valuation and "Thin" Price Data in the Art Market'. *Accounting, Organizations and Society* 50: pp. 13–26.

Coslor, E., and C. Spaenjers. 2016. 'Organizational and Epistemic Change: The Growth of the Art Investment Field'. *Accounting, Organizations and Society* 55: pp. 48–62.

Cox, B. 2004. *Free for All? Public Service Television in the Digital Age*. London: DEMOS.

Currid, E. 2007. *The Warhol Economy*. Princeton, NJ: Princeton University Press.

Danaher, B., and J. Waldfogel. 2012. 'Reel Piracy: The Effect of Online Film Piracy on International Box Office Sales'. Social Science Research Network. Accessed 30 April 2018 from: https://ssrn.com/abstract=1986299.

De Clercq, D., and M. Voronov. 2009. 'Toward a Practice Perspective of Entrepreneurship'. *International Small Business Journal* 27 (4): pp. 395–419.

DeFillippi, R. 2015. 'Managing Project-Based Organization in Creative Industries'. In *The Oxford Handbook of the Creative and Cultural Industries,* edited by C. Jones, M. Lorenzen, and J. Sapsed, pp. 268–83. Oxford: Oxford University Press.

Department for Culture, Media and Sport (DCMS). 1998. *Creative Industries Mapping Document.* London: UK Government.

Department for Digital, Culture, Media and Sport (DCMS). 2017. *DCMS Sectors Economic Estimates 2016: Gross Value Added.* London: UK Government.

Deuze, M., and N. Lewis. 2013. 'Professional Identity and Media Work'. In *Theorizing Cultural Work: Labour, Continuity and Change in the Cultural and Creative Industries,* edited by M. Banks, R. Gill, and S. Taylor, pp. 161–74. London: Routledge.

Di Stefano, G., A. King, and G. Verona. 2013. 'Kitchen Confidential? Norms for the Use of Transferred Knowledge in Gourmet Cuisine'. *Strategic Management Journal* 35 (11): pp. 1645–70.

DiMaggio, P. 1977. 'Market Structure, the Creative Process and Popular Culture: Towards an Organizational Reinterpretation of Mass-Culture Theory'. *Journal of Popular Culture* 11: pp. 436–52.

Dotan, O., and C. Sprigman. 2008. 'There's No Free Laugh Anymore: The Emergence of Intellectual Property Norms and the Transformation of Stand-Up Comedy'. 94 *Virginia Law Review*: pp. 1787–867.

Drahos, P., and J. Braithwaite. 2003. *Information Feudalism: Who Owns the Knowledge Economy?* New York: New Press.

Du Gay, P. 1997. *Production of Culture/Cultures of Production*. London: Sage in association with the Open University.

Du Gay, P., and M. Pryke. 2002. 'Cultural Economy: An Introduction'. In *Cultural Economy: Cultural Analysis and Commercial Life*, edited by P. Du Gay and M. Pryke, pp. 1–20. London: Sage.

Dussauge, I., C.-F. Helgesson, F. Lee, and S. Woolgar (eds). 2015. *Value Practices in the Life Sciences*. Oxford: Oxford University Press.

Dyer-Witheford, N., and G. De Peuter. 2009. *Games of Empire: Global Capitalism and Video Games*. Minneapolis, MN: University of Minnesota Press.

Ekinsmyth, C. 2002. 'Project Organization, Embeddedness and Risk in Magazine Publishing'. *Regional Studies* 36 (3): pp. 229–43.

Ellmeier, A. 2003. 'Cultural Entrepreneurialism: on the Changing Relationship Between the Arts, Culture and Employment'. *International Journal of Cultural Policy* 9 (1): pp. 3–16.

Entwistle, J. 2009. *The Aesthetic Economy of Fashion: Markets and Value in Clothing and Modelling*. Oxford: Berg.

Entwistle, J., and D. Slater. 2014. 'Reassembling the Cultural: Fashion Models, Brands and the Meaning of "Culture" After ANT'. *Journal of Cultural Economy* 7 (2): pp. 161–77.

Erickson, K., P. Heald, F. Homberg, M. Kretschmer, and D. Mendis. 2015. *Copyright and the Value of the Public Domain: An Empirical Assessment.* Intellectual Property Office, UK Government. Accessed 29 March 2018, from: http://www.create.ac.uk/publications/copyright-and-the-value-of-the-public-domain/.

Espeland, W. 2013. 'Vigorous Verbs: Conveying the Action of People Producing Qualities'. In *Constructing Quality: The Classification of Goods in Markets*, edited by J. Beckert and C. Musselin, pp. 319–32. Oxford: Oxford University Press.

Espeland, W., and M. Stevens. 1998. 'Commensuration as Social Process'. *Annual Review of Sociology* 24 (1): pp. 313–43.

Espeland, W., and M. Stevens. 2008. 'A Sociology of Quantification'. *European Journal of Sociology* 49 (3): pp. 401–36.

European Commission. 2001. *Employment Trends and Sectors of Growth in the Cultural Economy*. Brussels: European Commission DG Employment and Social Affairs.

European Commission. 2012. 'Copyright: Commission proposes easier music licensing in the Single Market'. Press Release, 11 July. Accessed 27 April 2018 from: http://europa.eu/rapid/press-release_IP-12-772_en.htm.

Faulkner, S., A. Leaver, F. Vis, and K. Williams. 2008. 'Art for Art's Sake or Selling Up?' *European Journal of Communication* 23 (3): pp. 295–317.

Feher, M. 2009. 'Self-Appreciation: Or, the Aspirations of Human Capital'. *Public Culture* 21 (1): pp. 21–43.

Ferraro, F., J. Pfeffer, and R. Sutton. 2005. 'Economic Language and Assumptions: How Theories Can Become Self-Fulfilling'. *Academy of Management Review* 30: pp. 8–24.

Fitzgerald, S. 2015. 'The Structure of the Cultural Industries: Global Corporations to SMEs'. In *The Routledge Companion to the Cultural Industries*, edited by K. Oakley and J. O'Connor, pp. 70–85. Abingdon, UK: Routledge.

Fleming, P., S. Watson, E. Patouris, K. Bartholomew, and D. Zizzo. 2017. 'Why Do People File Share Unlawfully? A Systematic Review, Meta-Analysis and Panel Study'. *Computers in Human Behavior* 72: pp. 535–48.

Florida, R. 2002. The *Rise of the Creative Class*. New York: Basic Books.

Foster, P., and R. Ocejo. 2015. 'Brokerage, Mediation, and Social Networks in the Creative Industries'. In *The Oxford Handbook of the Creative and Cultural Industries,* edited by C. Jones, M. Lorenzen, and J. Sapsed, pp. 405–20. Oxford: Oxford University Press.

Foucault, M. 1984. 'What Is an Author?'. In *The Foucault Reader,* edited by P. Rabinow, pp. 101–20. New York: Penguin.

Foucault, M. 2008. *The Birth of Biopolitics. Lectures at the College De France, 1978–1979.* New York: Palgrave Macmillan.

Fourcade, M. 2011. 'Price and Prejudice: On Economics and the Enchantment and Disenchantment of Nature'. In *The Worth of Goods: Valuation and Pricing in the Economy,* edited by J. Beckert and P. Aspers, pp. 41–62. Oxford: Oxford University Press.

Fourcade, M., and K. Healy. 2013. 'Classification Situations: Life-Chances in the Neoliberal Era'. *Accounting, Organizations and Society* 38 (8): pp. 559–72.

Fourcade-Gourinchas, M. 2005. 'Politics, Institutional Structures, and the Rise of Economics: A Comparative Study'. *Theory and Society* 30: pp. 397–447.

Frank, R., and P. Cook. 1995. *The Winner-Take-All Society*. New York: Free Press.

Freemal, B. 1995. 'Theatre, Stage Directions and Copyright Law'. *Chicago-Kent Law Review* 71: pp. 1017–40.

French, S., L. Crewe, A. Leyshon, P. Webb, and N. Thrift. 2004. 'Putting E-Commerce in its Place: Reflections on the Impact of the Internet on the Cultural Industries'. In *Cultural Industries and the Production of Culture,* edited by D. Power and A. Scott, pp. 54–72. New York: Routledge.

Frey, B. 2000. *Arts and Economics*. New York: Springer.

Gans, H. 1974. *Popular Culture and High Culture: An Analysis and Evaluation of Taste.* New York: Basic Books.

Gantchev, D. 2004. 'The WIPO Guide on Surveying the Economic Contribution of the Copyright Industries'. *Review of Economic Research on Copyright Issues* 1 (1): pp. 5–15.

Garnham, N. 1987. 'Concepts of Culture: Public Policy and the Cultural Industries'. *Cultural Studies* 1 (1): pp. 23–37.

Garnham, N. 1990. *Capitalism and Communication: Global Culture and the Economics of Information*. London: Sage.

Garnham, N. 2000. *Emancipation, the Media, and Modernity: Arguments about the Media and Social Theory*. Oxford: Oxford University Press.

Garnham, N. 2005. 'From Cultural to Creative Industries: An Analysis of the Implications of the "Creative Industries" Approach to Arts and Media Policy Making in the United Kingdom'. *International Journal of Cultural Policy* 11 (1): pp. 15–29.

George, A. 2012. *Constructing Intellectual Property*. Cambridge: Cambridge University Press.

Gershon, I. 2017. *Down and Out in the New Economy*. Chicago: University of Chicago Press.

Gill, R. 2010. '"Life Is A Pitch": Managing the Self in New Media Work'. In *Managing Media Work,* edited by M. Deuze, pp. 249–62. London: Sage.

Gill, R. and A. Pratt. 2008. 'In the Social Factory? Immaterial Labour, Precariousness and Cultural Work'. *Theory, Culture & Society* 25 (7–8): pp. 1–30.

Glynn, M. 2000. 'When Cymbals Become Symbols: Conflict over Organizational Identity Within a Symphony Orchestra'. *Organization Science* 11 (3): pp. 285–98.

Goldman, W. 1983. *Adventures in the Screen Trade: A Personal View of Hollywood and Screenwriting*. New York: Warner Books.

Görling, S., and A. Rehn. 2008. 'Accidental Ventures: A Materialist Reading of Opportunity and Entrepreneurial Potential'. *Scandinavian Journal of Management* 24 (2): pp. 94–102.

Grabher, G. (2002a). 'Fragile Sector, Robust Practice: Project Ecologies in New Media'. *Environment and Planning A* 34: pp. 1911–32.

Grabher, G. (2002b). 'The Project Ecology of Advertising: Tasks, Talents and Teams'. *Regional Studies* 36: pp. 245–62.

Granovetter, M. 1973. 'The Strength of Weak Ties'. *American Journal of Sociology* 78 (6): pp. 1360–80.

Granovetter, M. 1985. 'Economic Action and Social Structure: The Problem of Embeddedness'. *American Journal of Sociology* 91 (3): pp. 481–510.

Granstrand, O. 2006. 'Intellectual Property Rights for Governance in and of Innovation Systems'. In *Intellectual Property Rights: Innovation, Governance and the Institutional Environment*, edited by B. Andersen, pp. 311–44. Cheltenham, UK: Edward Elgar.

Greenberg, C. 1961. *Art and Culture: Critical Essays*. Boston: Beacon Press.

Greenhalgh, C., J. Philips, R. Pitkethly, M. Rogers, and J. Tomalin. 2010. *Intellectual Property Enforcement in Smaller UK Firms*. Strategy Advisory Board for Intellectual Property Policy (SABIP), UK Government. Accessed 8 May 2018 at Social Science Research Network: https://ssrn.com/abstract=2707175.

Grewar, M., B. Townley, and E. Young. 2015. *Tales from the Drawing Board: IP Wisdom and Woes from Scotland's Creative Industries*. Institute for Capitalising on Creativity, University of St Andrews. Accessed 10 August 2018 from: https://www.st-andrews.ac.uk/media/icc/newwebsite/images/Tales%20from%20the%20Drawing%20Board%202015v2.pdf.

Grugulis, I. and D. Stoyanova. 2012. 'Social Capital and Networks in Film and TV: Jobs for the Boys?' *Organization Studies* 33 (10): pp. 1311–31.

Gulledge, E., P. Roscoe, and B. Townley. 2015. 'Economizing Habitus: Material Calculation and "the Rules of the Game" in the Publishing Industry'. *Journal of Cultural Economy* 8 (6): pp. 637–54.

Handke, C., and R. Towse. 2007. 'Economics of Copyright Collecting Societies'. *International Review of Intellectual Property and Competition Law* 38 (8): pp. 937–57.

Hardie, I. and D. MacKenzie. 2007. 'Assembling an Economic Actor: The *Agencement* of a Hedge Fund'. *The Sociological Review* 55: pp. 57–80.

Hardt, M. and A. Negri. 2000. *Empire*. Cambridge, MA: Harvard University Press.

Hargreaves, I. 2011. *Digital Opportunity: Review of Intellectual Property and Growth*. London: Department for Business, Innovation & Skills, UK Government.

Harvie, D., G. Lightfoot, S. Lilley, and K. Weir. 2012. 'What Are We to Do with Feral Publishers? *Organization* 19 (6): pp. 905–14.

Haskel, J. and S. Westlake. 2017. *Capitalism without Capital: The Rise of the Intangible Economy*. Princeton, NJ: Princeton University Press.

Hegel, G. 1991. *Elements of the Philosophy of Right*. Cambridge: Cambridge University Press.

Helgesson, C.-F., and H. Kjellberg. 2013. 'Introduction: Values and Valuations in Market Practice'. *Journal of Cultural Economy* 6: pp. 361–9.

Helmers, C., Y. Lefouili, and L. McDonagh. 2015. *Evaluation of the Reforms of the Intellectual Property Enterprise Court 2010–2013*. London: Intellectual Property Office, UK Government.

Hesmondhalgh, D. 2002. *The Cultural Industries*. London: Sage.

Hesmondhalgh, D. 2010. 'Normativity and Social Justice in the Analysis of Creative Labour'. *Journal for Cultural Research* 14 (3): pp. 231–49.

Hesmondhalgh, D., and S. Baker. 2011. *Creative Labour: Media Work in Three Cultural Industries*. London: Routledge.

Hesmondhalgh, D., and A. Pratt. 2005. 'Cultural Industries and Cultural Policy'. *International Journal of Cultural Policy* 11 (1): pp. 1–13.

Hirsch, P. 1972. 'Processing Fads and Fashions: An Organization-Set Analysis of Cultural Industry Systems'. *American Journal of Sociology* 77: pp. 639–59.

Hirsch, P. 2000. 'Cultural Industries Revisited'. *Organization Science* 11 (3): pp. 356–61.

Holden, J. 2004. *Capturing Cultural Value: How Culture Has Become a Tool of Government Policy*. London: Demos.

Howard, L. 2008. 'An Uningenious Paradox: Intellectual Property Protections for Fashion Designs'. *Columbia Journal of Law & The Arts* 32 (3): pp. 333–69.

Hutter, M. 2011. 'Infinite Surprises: On the Stabilization of Value in the Creative Industries'. In *The Worth of Goods: Valuation and Pricing in the Economy*, edited by J. Beckert and P. Aspers, pp. 201–22. Oxford: Oxford University Press.

Hutter, M. and G. Teubner. 1994. 'Der Gesellschaft fette Beute: homo juridicus und homo oeconomicus als kommunikationserhaltende Fiktionen'. In *Der Mensch—das Medium der Gesellschaft*, edited by P. Fuchs and A. Göbel, pp. 110–45. Frankfurt: Suhrkamp.

Hynynen, J. 2013. 'Supporting Invention and Innovation in Central Finland: Inspiring IP Awareness'. *World Patent Information* 35 (2): pp. 105–9.

Iljadica, M. 2016. *Copyright Beyond Law: Regulating Creativity in the Graffiti Subculture*. Oxford: Hart Publishing.

Intellectual Property Office. 2012. 'Collecting Societies Codes of Conduct'. Independent report commissioned by the Intellectual Property Office, UK Government. Accessed 27 April 2018 from: https://assets.publishing.service.gov.uk/government/uploads/system/uploads/attachment_data/file/310172/ipresearch-collecting-071212.pdf.

Jeffcutt, P., J. Pick, and R. Protherough. 2000. 'Culture and Industry'. *Organizations and Society* 6: pp. 129–43.

Jones, C., N. Anand, and J. Alvarez. 2005. 'Manufactured Authenticity and Creative Voice in Cultural Industries'. *Journal of Management Studies* 42 (5): pp. 893–9.

Jones, C., M. Lorenzen, and J. Sapsed. 2015. 'Creative Industries: A Typology of Change'. In *The Oxford Handbook of the Creative and Cultural Industries,* edited by C. Jones, M. Lorenzen, and J. Sapsed, pp. 3–32. Oxford: Oxford University Press.

Jones, M. 2003. 'The Music Industry as Workplace: An Approach to Analysis'. In *Cultural Work: Understanding the Cultural Industries*, edited by A. Beck, pp. 147–56. London: Routledge.

Karpik, L. 2010. *Valuing the Unique: The Economics of Singularities*. Princeton, NJ: Princeton University Press.

Karpik, L. 2011. 'What Is the Price of a Scientific Paper?'. In *The Worth of Goods: Valuation and Pricing in the Economy*, edited by J. Beckert and P. Aspers, pp. 63–85. Oxford: Oxford University Press.

KEA European Affairs. 2007. *The Economy of Culture in Europe*. Brussels: European Commission.

Keat, R. 2009. 'Anti-Perfectionism, Market Economies and the Right to Meaningful Work'. *Analyse Und Kritik* 31 (1): pp. 121–38.

Khaire, M. 2017. *Culture and Commerce: The Value of Entrepreneurship in Creative Industries*. Stanford, CA: Stanford University Press.

Knight, F. 1921. *Risk, Uncertainty and Profit*. Boston: Houghton Mifflin.

Knight, F. 1942. 'Profit and Entrepreneurial Functions'. *Journal of Economic History* 2: pp. 126–32.

Kopytoff, I. 1986. 'The Cultural Biography of Things: Commoditization as Process'. In *The Social Life of Things*, edited by A. Appadurai, pp. 64–94. Cambridge: Cambridge University Press.

Kornberger, M., L. Justesen, A. Madsen, and J. Mouritsen. 2015. 'Introduction: Making Things Valuable. In *Making Things Valuable,* edited by M. Kornberger, L. Justesen, A. Madsen and J. Mouritsen, pp. 1–17. Oxford: Oxford University Press.

Kretschmer, M. 2015. 'Copyright and its Discontents'. In *The Oxford Handbook of the Creative and Cultural Industries,* edited by C. Jones, M. Lorenzen, and J. Sapsed, pp. 456–64. Oxford: Oxford University Press.

Kretschmer, M., E. Derclaye, M. Favale, and R. Watt. 2010. *The Relationship Between Copyright and Contract Law*. London: UK Strategic Advisory Board for Intellectual Property Policy (SABIP), UK Government. Accessed 29 March 2018 from: https://papers.ssrn.com/sol3/papers.cfm?abstract_id=2624945.

Kretschmer, M., S. Singh, and J. Wardle. 2009. *Exploitation of Television Formats*. Poole, UK: ESRC Digital Resource, Bournemouth University. Accessed 30 April 2018 from: http://tvformats.bournemouth.ac.uk.

Krippner, G. 2001. 'The Elusive Market: Embeddedness and the Paradigm of Economic Sociology'. *Theory and Society* 30 (6): pp. 775–810.

Kuipers, G. 2014. 'Ethnographic Research and Cultural Intermediaries'. In *The Cultural Intermediaries Reader*, edited by J. Smith Maguire and J. Matthews, pp. 52–64. London: Sage.

Lampel, J., T. Lant, and J. Shamsie. 2000. 'Balancing Act: Learning from Organizing Practices in Cultural Industries'. *Organization Science* 11 (3): pp. 263–9.

Lampel, J., J. Shamsie, and T. Lant. 2006. 'Towards a Deeper Understanding of Cultural Industries'. In *The Business of Culture: Strategic Perspectives on Entertainment and Media,* edited by J. Lampel, J. Shamsie, and T. Lant, pp. 3–14. Mahwah, NJ: Lawrence Erlbaum.

Landes, W., and R. Posner. 1989. 'An Economic Analysis of Copyright Law'. *Journal of Legal Studies* 18 (2): pp. 325–63.

Landes, W., and R. Posner. 2003. *The Economic Structure of Intellectual Property Law*. Cambridge, MA: Belknap/Harvard University Press.

Lash, S. and J. Urry. 1994. *Economies of Signs and Space*. London: Sage.

Latour, B. 1988. *The Pasteurization of France,* translated by A. Sheridan and J. Law. Cambridge, MA: Harvard University Press.

Latour, B. 2007. *Reassembling the Social: An Introduction to Actor-Network-Theory*. Oxford: Oxford University Press.

Law, J. 2002. 'Economics as Interference'. In *Cultural Economy: Cultural Analysis and Commercial Life,* edited by P. Du Gay and M. Pryke, pp. 21–38. London: Sage.

Lazzarato, M. 1996. 'Immaterial Labor'. In *Radical Thought in Italy: A Potential Politics,* edited by P. Virno and M. Hardt, pp. 142–57. Minneapolis, MN: University of Minnesota Press.

Lazzarato, M. 2007. 'The Misfortunes of the "Artistic Critique" and of Cultural Employment', translated by Mary O'Neill. European Institute for Progressive Cultural Policies. Accessed 30 April 2018 from: http://eipcp.net/transversal/0207/lazzarato/en.

Leadbeater, C., and K. Oakley. 1999. *The Independents: Britain's New Cultural Entrepreneur.* London: Demos.

Lehtonen, T.-K., and I. Van Hoyweghen. 2014. 'Editorial'. *Journal of Cultural Economy* 7 (4): pp. 532–40.

Lemke, T. 2001. '"The Birth of Bio–Politics": Michel Foucault's Lecture at the College De France on Neo-Liberal Governmentality'. *Economy and Society* 30: pp. 190–207.

Lessig, L. 2002. *The Future of Ideas*. New York: Vintage.

Lindgren, M., and J. Packendorff. 2003. 'A Project-Based View of Entrepreneurship: Towards Action-Orientation, Seriality and Collectivity'. In C. Steyaert and D. Hjorth (eds), *Entrepreneurship: New Movements,* pp. 86–102. Cheltenham, UK: Edward Elgar.

Locke, J. 1966. *The Second Treatise of Government, and a Letter Concerning Toleration.* Oxford: Blackwell.

Loshin, J. 2007. 'Secrets Revealed: How Magicians Protect Intellectual Property without Law'. Social Science Research Network. Accessed 30 April 2018 from: https://ssrn.com/abstract=1005564.

Lovink, G., and N. Rossiter. 2007. 'Proposals for Creative Research: Introduction to the *MyCreativity Reader*'. In *MyCreativity Reader: A Critique of Creative Industries,* edited by G. Lovink and N. Rossiter, pp. 9–16. Amsterdam: Institute of Network Cultures.

Luckman, S. 2013. 'Precarious Labour Then and Now: The British Arts and Crafts Movement and Cultural Work Revisited'. In *Theorizing Cultural Work: Labour, Continuity and Change in the Cultural and Creative Industries,* edited by M. Banks, R. Gill, and S. Taylor, pp. 19–29. London: Routledge.

Lysonski, S. and S. Durvasula. 2008. 'Digital Piracy of MP3s: Consumer and Ethical Predispositions'. *Journal of Consumer Marketing* 25 (3): pp. 167–78.

MacIntyre, A. 1981. *After Virtue: A Study in Moral Theory.* London: Duckworth.

MacKenzie, D. 2006. *An Engine, Not A Camera: How Financial Models Shape Markets* Cambridge, MA: MIT Press.

MacMillan, F. 2015. 'Copyright, the Creative Industries, and the Public Domain'. In *The Oxford Handbook of the Creative and Cultural Industries,* edited by C. Jones, M. Lorenzen, and J. Sapsed, pp. 439–55. Oxford: Oxford University Press.

Marshall, A. 2013. 'Free Fashion'. *Marquette Intellectual Property Law Review* 17 (1): pp. 124–41.

Marx, K. 1976. *Capital, Vol. 1.* New York: Modern Library.

Matthews, J., and J. Smith Maguire. 2014. 'Introduction: Thinking with Cultural Intermediaries'. In *The Cultural Intermediaries Reader*, edited by J. Smith Maguire and J. Matthews, pp. 1–12. London: Sage.

Maxwell, R., and T. Miller. 2013. 'Learning from Luddites: Media Labour, Technology, and Life Below the Line'. In *Theorizing Cultural Work: Labour, Continuity and Change in the Cultural and Creative Industries*, edited by M. Banks, R. Gill, and S. Taylor, pp. 113–21. London: Routledge.

McFall, L. 2011. 'A "Good, Average Man": Calculation and the Limits of Statistics in Enrolling Insurance Customers'. *The Sociological Review* 59 (4): pp. 661–84.

McFall, L. 2014. 'The Problem of Cultural Intermediaries in the Economy of Qualities'. In *The Cultural Intermediaries Reader*, edited by J. Smith Maguire and J. Matthews, pp. 42–51. London: Sage.

McFall, L. 2015. 'What's Changing Cultural Economy?' *Journal of Cultural Economy* 8: pp. 1–15.

McFall, L., and J. Ossandón. 2014. 'What's New in the "New, New Economic Sociology" and Should Organization Studies Care?'. In *The Oxford Handbook of Sociology, Social Theory, and Organization Studies*, edited by P. Adler, P. Du Gay, G. Morgan, and M. Reed, pp. 10–533. Oxford: Oxford University Press.

McGuigan, J. 2010. 'Creative Labour, Cultural Work and Individualisation'. *International Journal of Cultural Policy* 16 (3): pp. 23–35.

McKinlay, A., and C. Smith (eds). 2009. *Creative Labour: Working in the Creative Industries*. Basingstoke, UK: Palgrave Macmillan.

McRobbie, A. 2002. 'Clubs to Companies: Notes on the Decline of Political Culture in Speeded-up Creative Worlds'. *Cultural Studies* 16: pp. 516–31.

McRobbie, A. 2004. 'Making a Living in London's Small-Scale Creative Sector'. In *Cultural Industries and the Production of Culture*, edited by D. Power and A. Scott, pp. 130–44. New York: Routledge.

McRobbie, A. 2010. 'Rethinking Creative Economy as Radical Social Enterprise'. Paper Presented at Art and Labour Conference, Glasgow, November 2010. Accessed 23 September 2016 from: http://www.variant.org.uk/41texts/amcrobbie41.html.

McRobbie, A. 2016. *Be Creative: Making a Living in the New Culture Industries*. London: John Wiley & Sons.

Mears, A. 2011. 'Pricing Looks: Circuits of Value in Fashion Modeling Markets'. In *The Worth of Goods: Valuation and Pricing in the Economy*, edited by J. Beckert and P. Aspers, pp. 155–77. Oxford: Oxford University Press.

Menger, P.-M. 1999. 'Artistic Labour Markets and Careers'. *Annual Review of Sociology* 25: pp. 541–74.

Menger, P.-M. 2014. *The Economics of Creativity: Art and Achievement under Uncertainty*. Cambridge, MA: Harvard University Press.

Menger, P.-M. 2015. 'The Market for Creative Labour: Talent and Inequalities'. In *The Oxford Handbook of the Creative and Cultural Industries*, edited by C. Jones, M. Lorenzen, and J. Sapsed, pp. 148–70. Oxford: Oxford University Press.

Mezias, J., and S. Mezias. 2000. 'Resource Partitioning, the Founding of Specialist Firms, and Innovation: The American Feature Film Industry, 1912–1929'. *Organization Science* 11 (3): pp. 306–22.

Miège, B. 1979. 'The Cultural Commodity'. *Media, Culture & Society* 1 (3): pp. 297–311.

Miège, B. 1989. *The Capitalization of Cultural Production*. New York: International General.

Miller, D. 2002. 'The Unintended Political Economy'. In *Cultural Economy: Cultural Analysis and Commercial Life*, edited by P. Du Gay and M. Pryke, pp. 166–84. London: Sage.

Miller, P. and T. O'Leary. 2007. 'Mediating Instruments and Making Markets: Capital Budgeting, Science and the Economy'. *Accounting, Organizations and Society* 32: pp. 701–34.

Moeran, B., and J. Strandgaard Pedersen (eds). 2011. *Negotiating Values in the Creative Industries: Fairs, Festivals and Competitive Events*. Cambridge: Cambridge University Press.

Moor, L. 2008. 'Branding Consultants as Cultural Intermediaries'. *The Sociological Review* 56 (3): pp. 408–28.

Muniesa, F. 2011. 'A Flank Movement in the Understanding of Valuation'. *The Sociological Review* 59: pp. 24–38.

Muniesa, F., L. Doganova, H. Ortiz, A. Pina-Stranger, F. Paterson, A. Bourgoin, V. Ehrenstein, P. Juven, D. Pontille, B. Sarac-Lesavre, and G. Yon. 2017. *Capitalization: A Cultural Guide*. Paris: Presses des Mines.

Murdock, G. 2003. 'Back to Work: Cultural Labor in Altered Times'. In *Cultural Work: Understanding the Cultural Industries*, edited by A. Beck, pp. 15–36. London: Routledge.

Na, N. 2006. 'Testing the Boundaries of Copyright Protection: The Google Books Library Project and the Fair Use Doctrine'. *Cornell Journal of Law and Public Policy* 16: pp. 417–48.

Neff, G. 2012. *Venture Labour: Work and the Burden of Risk in Innovation Industries*. Cambridge, MA: MIT Press.

Negus, K. 2002. 'Identities and Industries: The Cultural Formation of Aesthetic Economies'. In *Cultural Economy: Cultural Analysis and Commercial Life*, edited by P. du Gay and M. Pryke, pp. 115–31. London: Sage.

Negus, K., J. Street, and A. Behr. 2017. 'Copying, Copyright and Originality: Imitation Transformation and Popular Musicians'. *European Journal of Cultural Studies* 20 (4): pp. 363–80.

Negus, K., J. Street, and A. Behr. 2018. 'Copyrights: The Politics of Copying and Creativity. *Political Studies* 66 (1): pp. 63–80.

NESTA. 2006. *Creating Growth: How the UK Can Develop World-Class Creative Businesses*. London: NESTA.

O'Brien, D. 2014. *Cultural Policy: Management, Value and Modernity in the Creative Industries*. Abingdon, UK: Routledge.

O'Brien, D. 2015. 'Business as Usual: Creative Industries and the Specificity of the British State'. In *The Routledge Companion to the Cultural Industries*, edited by K. Oakley and J. O'Connor, pp. 452–63. Abingdon, UK: Routledge.

O'Connor, J. 2000. 'The Definition of the Cultural Industries'. *European Journal of Arts Education* 2 (3): pp. 15–27.

O'Connor, J. 2004. 'Cities, Culture and "Transitional" Economies: Developing Cultural Industries in St Petersburg'. In *The Cultural Industries and the Production of Culture*, edited by D. Power and A. Scott, pp. 37–53. London: Routledge.

O'Connor, J. 2010. *The Cultural and Creative Industries: A Review of the Literature*. London: Arts Council England.

O'Mahony, S. 2003. 'Guarding the Commons: How Community Managed Software Projects Protect their Work'. *Research Policy* 32: pp. 1179–98.

Oakley, K. 2009. *Art Works*. London: Creativity Culture & Education.

Oakley, K. 2013. 'Absentee Workers: Representation and Participation in the Cultural Industries'. In *Theorizing Cultural Work: Labour, Continuity and Change in the Cultural and Creative Industries*, edited by M. Banks, R. Gill, and S. Taylor, pp. 56–68. London: Routledge.

Organisation for Economic Co-Operation and Development (OECD). 2006. *International Measurement of the Economic and Social Importance of Culture*. Paris: OECD.

Osborne, T. 2003. 'Against "Creativity": A Philistine Rant'. *Economy and Society* 32 (4): pp. 507–25.

Pang, L. 2015. 'Art and Cultural Industries: Autonomy and Community'. In *The Routledge Companion to the Cultural Industries*, edited by K. Oakley and J. O'Connor, pp. 45–55. Abingdon, UK: Routledge.

Pasquinelli, M. 2007. 'ICW – Immaterial Civil War: Prototypes of Conflict within Cognitive Capitalism'. In *MyCreativity Reader: A Critique of Creative Industries*, edited by G. Lovink and N. Rossiter, pp. 69–80. Amsterdam: Institute of Network Cultures.

Pavis, M. 2016. 'Is there Anybody on Stage? A Legal (Mis)Understanding of Performances'. *Journal of World Intellectual Property* 19 (3–4): pp. 99–114.

Peterson, R., and D. Berger. 1971. 'Entrepreneurship in Organizations: Evidence from the Popular Music Industry'. *Administrative Science Quarterly* 16: pp. 97–106.

Peterson, R., and D. Berger. 1975. 'Cycles in Symbol Production: The Case of Popular Music'. *American Sociological Review* 40: pp. 158–73.

Phillips, T., and J. Street. 2015. 'Copyright and Musicians at the Digital Margins'. *Media, Culture & Society* 37 (3): pp. 342–58.

Polyani, K. 2001. *The Great Transformation: The Political and Economic Origins of Our Time*. Boston: Beacon Press.

Power, D., and D. Hallencreutz. 2004. 'Profiting from Creativity? The Music Industry in Stockholm, Sweden and Kingston, Jamaica'. In *The Cultural Industries and the Production of Culture*, edited by D. Power and A. Scott, pp. 224–42. London: Routledge.

Power, D., and A. Scott. 2004. 'A Prelude to Cultural Industries and the Production of Culture'. In *The Cultural Industries and the Production of Culture*, edited by D. Power and A. Scott, pp. 3–16. London: Routledge.

Pratt, A. 1997. 'The Cultural Industries Production System: A Case Study of Employment Change in Britain, 1984–91'. *Environment and Planning A* 29: pp. 1953–74.

Pratt, A. 2005. 'Cultural Industries and Public Policy: An Oxymoron?' *International Journal of Cultural Policy* 11 (1): pp. 31–44.

Pratt, A. 2007. 'The State of the Cultural Economy: The Rise of the Cultural Economy and the Challenges to Cultural Policy Making'. In *The Urgency of Theory*, edited by A. Ribiero, pp. 166–90. Manchester: Carcanet Press/Gulbenkian Foundation.

Qian, Y. 2008. 'Impacts of Entry by Counterfeiters'. *Quarterly Journal of Economics* 123 (4): pp. 1577–609.

Raffo, C., J. O'Connor, A. Lovatt, and M. Banks. 2000a. 'Attitudes to Formal Business Training and Learning Amongst Entrepreneurs in The Cultural Industries: Situated Learning Through "Doing With Others"'. *Journal of Education and Work* 12 (2): pp. 147–66.

Raffo, C., J. O'Connor, A. Lovatt, and M. Banks. 2000b. 'Risk and Trust in the Cultural Industries'. *Geoforum* 31 (4): pp. 453–64.

Rankin, J. 2018. 'Online streaming services face "30% made in Europe" law'. *The Guardian*, 26 April. Accessed 7 May 2018 from: https://www.theguardian.com/technology/2018/apr/26/eu-third-party-trader-amazon-google-ebay.

Rantisi, N. 2004. 'The Designer in the City and the City in the Designer'. In *Cultural Industries and the Production of Culture*, edited by D. Power and A. Scott, pp. 91–104. London: Routledge.

Raustiala, K., and C. Sprigman. 2006. 'The Piracy Paradox: Innovation and Intellectual Property in Fashion Design'. *Virginia Law Review* 92: pp. 1687–777.

Raustiala, K., and C. Sprigman. 2009. 'The Piracy Paradox Revisited'. *Stanford Law Review* 61 (5): pp. 1201–25.

Ravasi, D., V. Rindova, and I. Stigliani. 2011. 'Valuing Products as Cultural Symbols: A Conceptual Framework and Empirical Consideration'. In *The Worth of Goods: Valuation and Pricing in the Economy*, edited by J. Beckert and P. Aspers, pp. 297–318. Oxford: Oxford University Press.

Read, J. 2009. 'A Genealogy of Homo-Economicus: Neoliberalism and the Production of Subjectivity'. *Foucault Studies* 6: pp. 25–36.

Roscoe, P. 2014. *I Spend Therefore I Am*. London: Penguin Viking.

Roscoe, P. 2015. 'A Moral Economy of Transplantation: Competing Regimes of Value in the Allocation of Transplant Organs'. In *Value Practices in Life Sciences*, edited by C. Helgesson, F. Lee, and I. Dussauge, pp. 99–118. Oxford: Oxford University Press.

Roscoe, P., and S. Chillas. 2014. 'The State of Affairs: Critical Performativity and the Online Dating Industry'. *Organization* 21: pp. 797–820.

Rösell, J., and J. Beckert. 2013. 'Quality Classifications in Competition: Price Formation in the German Wine Market'. In *Constructing Quality: The Classification of Goods in Markets*, edited by J. Beckert and C. Musselin, pp. 288–318. Oxford: Oxford University Press.

Ross, A. 2000. 'The Mental Labour Problem'. *Social Text* 18: pp. 1–32.

Ross, A. 2003. *No Collar: The Humane Workplace and its Hidden Costs*. Philadelphia, PA: Temple University Press.

Ross, A. 2008. 'The New Geography of Work: Power to the Precarious?' *Theory, Culture & Society* 25: pp. 31–49.

Ross, A. 2013. 'Theorizing Cultural Work: An Interview with the Editors'. In *Theorizing Cultural Work: Labour, Continuity and Change in the Cultural and Creative Industries*, edited by M. Banks, R. Gill, and S. Taylor, pp. 175–82. London: Routledge.

Ryan, B. 1992. *Making Capital from Culture*. Berlin/New York: Walter De Gruyter.

Sandel, M. 2012. *What Money Can't Buy*. London: Allen Lane.

Santagata, W. 2004. 'Creativity, Fashion and Market Behavior'. In *Cultural Industries and the Production of Culture*, edited by D. Power and A. Scott, pp. 75–90. New York: Routledge.

Sarasvathy, S. 2002. 'Entrepreneurship as Economics with Imagination'. *Ethics and Entrepreneurship* 3: pp. 95–112.

Saundry, R., V. Antcliff, and M. Stuart. 2006. '"It's More Than Who You Know": Networks and Trade Unions in the Audio-visual Industries'. *Human Resource Management Journal* 16 (4): pp. 376–92.

Saundry, R., M. Stuart, and V. Antcliff. 2007. 'Broadcasting Discontent: Freelancers, Trade Unions and the Internet'. *New Technology, Work & Employment* 22: pp. 178–91.

Schlesinger, P. 2009. 'Creativity and the Experts: New Labour, Think Tanks and the Policy Process'. *International Journal of Press/Politics* 14 (3): pp. 3–20.

Schlesinger, P. 2016. 'The Creative Economy: Invention of a Global Orthodoxy'. *Innovation: The European Journal of Social Science Research* 30 (1): pp. 73–90.

Schlesinger, P., and C. Waelde. 2012. 'Copyright and Cultural Work: An Exploration'. *European Journal of Social Science Research* 25 (1): pp. 11–28.

Scholtz, T. 2013. *Digital Labor: The Internet as Playground and Factory*. New York: Routledge.

Schumpeter, J. 1934. *The Theory of Economic Development*. Oxford: Oxford University Press.

Searle, N. 2011. *Changing Business Models in the Creative Industries: The Cases of Television, Computer Games and Music*. London: Intellectual Property Office, UK Government.

Searle, N., and M. Brassell. 2016. *Economic Approaches to IP*. Oxford: Oxford University Press.

Sisario, B. 2015. 'Spotify in Dispute over Royalty Payments'. *New York Times*, 21 October. Accessed 2 August 2017 from: https://www.nytimes.com/2015/10/22/business/media/spotify-in-dispute-over-royalty-payments.html?_r=0s.

Siwek, S. 2016. 'U.S. Economy: The 2016 Report'. International Intellectual Property Alliance (IIPA). Accessed 15 April 2018 from: https://iipa.org/reports/copyright-industries-us-economy/.

Skidelsky, R. and E. Skidelsky. 2012. *How Much Is Enough? The Love of Money, and the Case for the Good Life*. London: Penguin.

Slater, D. 2002a. 'Capturing Markets from the Economists'. In *Cultural Economy: Cultural Analysis and Commercial Life*, edited by P. du Gay and M. Pryke, pp. 59–77. London: Sage.

Slater, D. 2002b. 'From Calculation to Alienation: Disentangling Economic Abstractions'. *Economy and Society* 31 (2): pp. 234–49.

Slater, D., and F. Tonkiss. 2001. *Market Society: Markets and Modern Social Theory*. Oxford: Polity Press.

Smiers, J. 2007. 'What If We Would Not Have Copyright? New Business Models for Cultural Entrepreneurs'. In *MyCreativity Reader: A Critique of Creative Industries*, edited by G. Lovink and N. Rossiter, pp. 191–206. Amsterdam: Institute of Network Cultures.

Smith, C. 2011. 'Coping with Contingencies in Equity Option Markets: The Rationality of Pricing'. In *The Worth of Goods: Valuation and Pricing in the Economy*, edited by J. Beckert and P. Aspers, pp. 272–94. Oxford: Oxford University Press.

Smith Maguire, J. 2014. 'Bourdieu on Cultural Intermediaries'. In *The Cultural Intermediaries Reader*, edited by J. Smith Maguire and J. Matthews, pp. 15–24. London: Sage.

Stahl, M. 2013. 'Specificity, Ambivalence, and the Commodity Form in Creative Work'. In *Theorizing Cultural Work: Labour, Continuity and Change in the Cultural and Creative Industries*, edited by M. Banks, R. Gill, and S. Taylor, pp. 71–84. London: Routledge.

Stark, D. 2009. *The Sense of Dissonance: Accounts of Worth in Economic Life*. Princeton, NJ: Princeton University Press.

Stark, D. 2011. 'What's Valuable?' In *The Worth of Goods: Valuation and Pricing in the Economy*, edited by J. Beckert and P. Aspers, pp. 319–38. Oxford: Oxford University Press.

Street, J., and T. Phillips. 2017. 'What Do Musicians Talk about When They Talk about Copyright?' *Popular Music and Society* 40 (4): pp. 422–33.

Street, J., D. Laing, and S. Schroff. 2016. 'Regulating for Creativity and Cultural Diversity: The Case of CMOs and the Music Industry'. *International Journal of Cultural Policy* 24 (3): pp. 368–86.

Sukarmijan, S., and O. Sapong. 2014. 'The Importance of Intellectual Property for SMEs: Challenges and Moving Forward'. *UMK Procedia* 1: pp. 74–81.

Swedberg, R. 2006. 'The Cultural Entrepreneur and the Creative Industries: Beginning in Vienna'. *Journal of Cultural Economy* 30: pp. 243–61.

Swedberg, R. 2010. 'The Economic Sociologies of Pierre Bourdieu'. *Cultural Sociology* 5 (1): pp. 1–18.

Taylor, S. 2003. '"I Am What I Play": The Radio DJ as Cultural Arbiter and Negotiator'. In *Cultural Work: Understanding the Cultural Industries*, edited by A. Beck, pp. 73–100. London: Routledge.

Taylor, S., and Littleton, K. 2008. 'Art Work or Money: Conflicts in the Construction of a Creative Identity'. *The Sociological Review* 56 (2): pp. 275–92.

Teece, D. 2010. 'Business Models, Business Strategy and Innovation'. *Long Range Planning* 43 (2): pp. 172–94.

Tellmann, U. 2016. 'Historical Ontologies of Uncertainty and Money: Rethinking the Current Critique of Finance'. *Jousrnal of Cultural Economy* 9 (1): pp. 63–85.

Thrift, N. 2002. 'Performing Cultures in the New Economy'. In *Cultural Economy: Cultural Analysis and Commercial Life*, edited by P. Du Gay and M. Pryke, pp. 201–34. London: Sage.

Throsby, D. 2001. *Economics and Culture*. Cambridge: Cambridge University Press.

Titmuss, R. 1970. *The Gift Relationship: from Human Blood to Social Policy*. London: Allen & Unwin.

Townley, B. 2008. *Reason's Neglect. Rationality and Organizing*. Oxford: Oxford University Press.

Townley, B. 2014. 'Bourdieu and Organisational Theory: A Ghostly Apparition?' In *The Oxford Handbook of Sociology, Social Theory, and Organization Studies*, edited by P. Adler, P. Du Gay, G. Morgan, and M. Reed, pp. 39–63. Oxford: Oxford University Press.

Townley, B. 2015. 'Exploring Different Forms of Capitals: Researching Capitals in the Field of Cultural and Creative Industries'. In *Pierre Bourdieu, Organisation and Management*, edited by A. Tatli, M. Özbilgin, and M. Karatas-Özkan, pp. 187–206. London: Routledge.

Towse, R. 1999. 'Copyright and Economic Incentives: An Application to Performers' Rights in the Music Industry'. *Kyklos International Review for Social Sciences* 52 (3): pp. 369–90.

Towse, R. 2002. *Copyright in the Cultural Industries*. Cheltenham: Edward Elgar.

Towse, R. 2003. 'Copyright and Cultural Policy for the Creative Industries'. In *Economics, Law and Intellectual Property*, edited by O. Granstrand, pp. 419–38. London: Kluwer Academic Publishers.

Towse, R. 2006a. 'Copyright and Artists: A View from Cultural Economics'. *Journal of Economic Surveys* 20: pp. 567–85.

Towse, R. 2006b. 'Copyright and Creativity: An Application of Cultural Economics'. *Review of Economic Research on Copyright Issues* 3: pp. 83–91.

Towse, R. 2007. 'The Singer or the Song? Developments in Performers' Rights from the Perspective of a Cultural Economist'. *Review of Law and Economics* 3: pp. 745–66.

Towse, R. 2010. 'Creativity, Copyright and the Creative Industries Paradigm'. *Kyklos International Review for Social Sciences* 63 (3): pp. 461–78.

Towse, R. 2012. 'Economics of Copyright Collecting Societies and Digital Rights: Is There a Case for a Centralised Digital Copyright Exchange?' *Review of Economic Research in Copyright Issues* 9 (2): pp. 3–30.

Towse, R. 2013. 'The Economic Effects of Digitization on the Administration of Musical Copyrights'. *Review of Economic Research on Copyright Issues* 10 (2): pp. 55–67.

Toynbee, J. 2001. 'Creating Problems: Social Authorship, Copyright and the Production of Culture'. *Pavis Papers in Social and Cultural Research 3*. Milton Keynes, UK: Open University Press.

Toynbee, J. 2003. 'Fingers to the Bone or Spaced Out on Creativity? Labor Process and Ideology in the Production of Pop'. In *Cultural Work: Understanding the Cultural Industries*, edited by A. Beck, pp. 39–55. London: Routledge.

Toynbee, J. 2013. 'How Special? Cultural Work, Copyright, Politics'. In *Theorizing Cultural Work: Labour, Continuity and Change in the Cultural and Creative Industries*, edited by M. Banks, R. Gill, and S. Taylor, pp. 85–98. London: Routledge.

United Nations Conference on Trade and Development (UNCTAD) and United Nations Development Programme. 2008. 'Creative Economy: Report 2008'. New York: United Nations.

Ursell, G. 1998. 'Labour Flexibility in the UK Commercial Television Sector'. *Media, Culture & Society* 20 (1): pp. 129–53.

Ursell, G. 2000. 'Television Production: Issues of Exploitation, Commodification and Subjectivity in UK Television Labour Markets'. *Media, Culture & Society* 22 (6): pp. 805–25.

Ursell, G. 2003. 'Creating Value and Value Creation in Contemporary UK Television: Or "Dumbing Down" the Workforce'. *Journalism Studies* 4 (1): pp. 31–46.

Ursell, G. 2006. 'Working in the Media'. In *Media Production*, edited by D. Hesmondhalgh, pp. 133–71. Maidenhead, UK: Open University Press.

Uzzi, B. 1997. 'Social Structure and Competition in Interfirm Networks: The Paradox of Embeddedness'. *Administrative Science Quarterly* 42: pp. 35–67.

Van Hoyweghen, I. 2014. 'On the Politics of Calculative Devices'. *Journal of Cultural Economy* 7 (3): pp. 334–52.

Van Zanten, A. 2013. 'A Good Match: Appraising Worth and Estimating Quality in School Choice'. In *Constructing Quality: The Classification of Goods in Markets*, edited by J. Beckert and C. Musselin, pp. 77–102. Oxford: Oxford University Press.

Velthuis, O. 2005. *Talking Prices: Symbolic Meanings of Prices on the Market for Contemporary Art*. Princeton, NJ: Princeton University Press.

Velthuis, O. 2011. 'Damien's Dangerous Idea: Valuing Contemporary Art at Auction'. In *The Worth of Goods: Valuation and Pricing in the Economy*, edited by J. Beckert and P. Aspers, pp. 178–200. Oxford: Oxford University Press.

Vinodrai, T., and S. Keddy. 2015. 'Projects and Project Ecologies in Creative Industries'. In *The Oxford Handbook of the Creative and Cultural Industries*, edited by C. Jones, M. Lorenzen, and J. Sapsed, pp. 251–67. Oxford: Oxford University Press.

Voss, G., Cable, D., and Voss, Z. 2000. 'Linking Organizational Values to Relationships with External Constituents: A Study of Nonprofit Professional Theatres'. *Organization Science* 11 (3): pp. 330–47.

Waelde, C., and P. Schlesinger. 2011. 'Music and Dance: Beyond Copyright Text?' *Script-Ed* 8 (3): pp. 257–91.

Warde, A. 2002. 'Production, Consumption, and "Cultural Economy"'. In *Cultural Economy: Cultural Analysis and Commercial Life*, edited by P. Du Gay and M. Pryke, pp. 185–200. London: Sage.

Watson, S., D. Zizzo, and P. Fleming. 2015. 'Determinants of Unlawful File Sharing: A Scoping Review'. *PloS One* 10 (6): E0127921.

Watson, S., D. Zizzo, and P. Fleming. 2016. 'Risk, Benefit, and Moderators of the Affect Heuristic in a Widespread Unlawful Activity: Evidence from a Survey of Unlawful File-Sharing Behavior'. *Risk Analysis* 37: pp. 1146–56.

Weber, M. 1978. *Economy and Society*. Berkeley, CA: University of California Press.

Wijnberg, N. and G. Gemser. 2000. 'Adding Value to Innovation: Impressionism and the Transformation of the Selection System in Visual Arts'. *Organization Science* 11 (3): pp. 323–9.

Williams, R. 1958. *Culture and Society*. London: Chatto and Windus.

Williamson, O. 1985. *The Economic Institutions of Capitalism*. New York: Free Press.

Wittel, A. 2001. 'Toward A Network Sociality'. *Theory, Culture & Society* 18 (6): pp. 51–76.

Work Foundation. 2007. *Staying Ahead: The Economic Performance of the UK's Creative Industries*. London: Work Foundation.

World Intellectual Property Organization (WIPO). 2004. *Intellectual Property Handbook: Policy, Law and Use*. WIPO. Accessed 3 April 2018 from: www.wipo.int/about-ip/en/iprm/.

World Intellectual Property Organization (WIPO). 2017. 'Intellectual Property for Business'. Accessed 11 July 2017 from: http://www.wipo.int/sme/en/ip_business/.

Wright, D. 2005. 'Mediating Production and Consumption: Cultural Capital and "Cultural Workers"'. *British Journal of Sociology* 56 (1): pp. 105–21.

Yar, M. 2005. 'The Global "Epidemic" of Movie "Piracy": Crime-Wave or Social Construction?' *Media, Culture & Society* 27 (5): pp. 677–96.

Zelizer, V. 1994. *The Social Meaning of Money: Pin Money, Paychecks, Poor Relief, and Other Currencies*. New York: Basic Books.

Zelizer, V. 2005. *The Purchase of Intimacy*. Princeton, NJ: Princeton University Press.

Zelizer, V. 2012. 'How I Became a Relational Economic Sociologist and What Does that Mean?' *Politics & Society* 40: pp. 145–74.

Zoellner, A. 2009. 'Professional Ideology and Programme Conventions: Documentary Development in Independent British Television Production'. *Mass Communication & Society* 12 (4): pp. 503–36.

Index